The Essential

MEDITERRANEAN

Diet Cookbook

for Beginners 2024

2000+ Days of Wholesome Mediterranean Recipes for a Healthier Lifestyle | Stress-Free 30-Day Meal Plans

Kimberly N. Bains

TABLE OF CONTENTS

INTRODUCTION

My journey with Mediterranean food began with a childhood steeped in the flavors of sun-ripened fruits, fragrant herbs, and hearty grains. Growing up, I was fortunate to have parents who instilled in me a love for fresh, wholesome ingredients and the art of simple, flavorful cooking.

As I embarked on my own culinary adventures, I found myself drawn to the vibrant tapestry of Mediterranean cuisine—a cuisine shaped by centuries of history, trade, and cultural exchange. I delved into cookbooks, traveled to Mediterranean countries, and immersed myself in local markets and kitchens, eager to learn the secrets of this storied culinary tradition.

What captivated me most was the Mediterranean diet's holistic approach to health and wellness. It wasn't just about what you ate, but also how you ate—slow, leisurely meals shared with loved ones, savoring each bite and celebrating the joys of good food and good company.

But my connection to Mediterranean cuisine goes beyond the kitchen. It's a reflection of my values—a commitment to sustainability, seasonality, and supporting local farmers and artisans. Whether it's sourcing fresh produce from a nearby market or incorporating traditional cooking techniques passed down through generations, I strive to honor the spirit of Mediterranean cooking in all that I do.

As I write my recipes, I draw inspiration from the diverse culinary traditions that converge along the shores of the Mediterranean—from the vibrant mezze of the Middle East to the rustic simplicity of Italian cucina povera. Each dish is a reflection of this rich tapestry, infused with the flavors, aromas, and stories of the region.

But perhaps most importantly, my connection to Mediterranean cuisine is a deeply personal one. It's a way for me to pay homage to my heritage, to connect with my roots, and to share the flavors of my upbringing with others. It's a journey of discovery, creativity, and passion—a journey that I am grateful to embark on every time I step into the kitchen.Why Choose The Mediterranean Diet?

Chapter
1

The Basics of Mediterranean Diet

Chapter 1 The Basics of Mediterranean Diet

Why Choose The Mediterranean Diet?

Choose the Mediterranean diet for its rich heritage of wholesome, flavorful foods that promote heart health and longevity. Embrace its emphasis on fresh fruits, vegetables, whole grains, and olive oil for a delicious and sustainable approach to eating. Experience the joy of gathering with loved ones to share meals, celebrating not just nourishment, but also community and connection.

1. Learn about Mediterranean culture through food: Exploring the Mediterranean diet offers a fascinating journey into the rich tapestry of Mediterranean culture through its diverse and vibrant dishes. It's like embarking on a culinary adventure, uncovering the ancient roots of this diet that stretch back to civilizations like Greece and Rome. By embracing the Mediterranean way of eating, we not only savor delicious meals but also gain insight into the traditions and values of these ancient societies, who cherished the simplicity and freshness of locally sourced ingredients.

2. Environmental Sustainability of the diet: The Mediterranean diet isn't just about nourishing our bodies—it's also about nurturing the planet. Its emphasis on plant-based foods, such as fruits, vegetables, whole grains, and legumes, aligns closely with principles of environmental sustainability. By consuming a predominantly plant-based diet, we reduce our ecological footprint by decreasing the demand for resource-intensive animal agriculture.

Furthermore, the Mediterranean diet promotes the use of local and seasonal ingredients, which supports small-scale farmers and reduces the carbon emissions associated with transportation. By sourcing fresh produce from nearby markets, we minimize the environmental impact of long-distance food distribution networks.

3. The delicious and Savory nature of the diet: Indulge in the tantalizing flavors of Mediterranean cuisine, where herbs and spices reign supreme, elevating dishes with their aromatic and savory essence. From the earthy richness of basil and oregano to the vibrant zest of garlic and mint, each ingredient adds depth and complexity to every bite.

Experience the joy of sharing small plates, known as "mezze" and "tapas," with friends and family—a tradition that encourages exploration of diverse flavors and textures. Dive into a world of seafood, legumes, whole grains, fruits, and vegetables, where every dish tells a story of culinary innovation and cultural fusion.

4. Social Bonding: The convivial spirit of Mediterranean dining invites moments of genuine connection and camaraderie. With each bite savored slowly, the intricate blend of spices and flavors sets the stage for engaging conversations and heartfelt interactions, fostering a sense of relaxation and togetherness.

In Mediterranean cultures, the act of sharing meals transcends mere sustenance—it's a cherished tradition that strengthens bonds and nurtures friendships. Whether gathering around the family table or meeting friends at a local café, these shared moments of dining create opportunities for laughter, storytelling, and the forging of lasting connections.

5. Mindful Eating: Portion control and awareness of hunger are central to the Mediterranean diet. By emphasising moderation and listening to your body's signals, this approach can help you maintain a healthy relationship with food, whether you're on a weight loss journey or simply seeking balance in your eating habits.

The cornerstone of Mediterranean cuisine is the selection of fresh, seasonal and locally sourced ingredients. As you savour each bite, your senses will take full advantage of the fresh flavours and textures, transforming mealtimes into a sensory experience to be savoured and enjoyed.

6. Skin Health: Unlock the secret to radiant skin with the Mediterranean diet, abundant in antioxidant-rich foods like colorful fruits, vibrant vegetables, and nourishing nuts. These antioxidants work tirelessly to shield your skin from the harmful effects of environmental stressors, such as UV rays and pollution, while combating signs of aging.

Elevate your skin's health with vitamin E, found abundantly in nuts and seeds—a key nutrient known for its ability to maintain skin elasticity and ward off oxidative damage. And don't forget to stay hydrated with plenty of water, a fundamental pillar of the

Mediterranean lifestyle that helps maintain skin moisture and overall vitality.

Health Benefits Of The Mediterranean Diet

Discover the myriad health benefits of the Mediterranean diet, a culinary treasure trove brimming with wholesome ingredients and time-honored traditions. From promoting heart health and reducing the risk of chronic diseases to fostering longevity and enhancing overall well-being, this ancient eating pattern offers a holistic approach to nourishment and vitality. Join me on a journey to explore the science-backed benefits of the Mediterranean diet and unlock the secrets to a healthier, happier life.

1. Reduced Risk of Heart Diseases And Improvement Of Cardiovascular Health:

The Mediterranean diet offers significant protection against heart disease and promotes cardiovascular well-being through various mechanisms. Olive oil, a cornerstone of the diet, provides beneficial monounsaturated fats that lower LDL cholesterol and reduce the risk of atherosclerosis. Fatty fish, a frequent feature, supplies omega-3 fatty acids, renowned for their anti-inflammatory effects and ability to lower triglycerides, crucial for maintaining healthy arteries.

Furthermore, the diet's abundance of fiber-rich foods like fruits, vegetables, and whole grains helps regulate blood pressure and enhances vascular function. Red wine, enjoyed in moderation, contributes to heart health with its antioxidant content, particularly resveratrol, which supports optimal blood vessel function.

2. Balancing Blood Sugar and Enhancing Emotional Mental Health:

The Mediterranean diet is increasingly recognized for its potential to positively impact mental health and mood regulation. By incorporating omega-3-rich fish, antioxidants, and whole foods, it nourishes the brain and supports optimal cognitive function. Antioxidants found abundantly in fruits, vegetables, and olive oil combat oxidative stress and inflammation, known contributors to mood disorders and cognitive decline.

Moreover, the inclusion of whole grains like whole wheat and oats helps maintain stable blood sugar levels, crucial for sustaining a balanced mood and consistent energy levels throughout the day. Olive oil, with its wealth of monounsaturated fats and polyphenols, further promotes brain health and may mitigate the risk of neurodegenerative conditions.

3. Longevity

The Mediterranean diet offers more than just delicious meals—it provides a roadmap to a longer, healthier life. Research indicates that adhering to this dietary pattern is linked to increased longevity, thanks to its focus on nutrient-rich foods and healthy fats that support overall well-being.

Unlike restrictive diets, the Mediterranean way of eating is sustainable and adaptable, making it a lifelong companion on the journey to better health. By consistently embracing this lifestyle, individuals can enjoy a host of health benefits that extend well into their later years.

4. Improves digestive function:

The Mediterranean diet is high in fibre-rich foods, including fruits, vegetables, whole grains and legumes, which promote optimal digestive health by supporting regular bowel movements and preventing constipation. In addition, these fibre-rich foods help the gut microbiome to thrive, which is essential for efficient digestion and reducing the risk of gastrointestinal problems. By prioritising whole, unprocessed foods and avoiding high-fat and heavily processed foods, this dietary pattern helps to reduce the likelihood of irritable bowel syndrome (IBS) symptoms appearing or worsening.

In addition, foods such as berries and leafy greens in the Mediterranean diet are rich in antioxidants, which can inhibit inflammation in the digestive tract, thereby alleviating symptoms associated with inflammatory bowel disease. In essence, the Mediterranean diet offers a holistic approach to digestive health that promotes comfort and vitality from within.

5. Weight Management:

Beyond its renowned health benefits, the Mediterranean diet offers an effective approach to weight management. By emphasizing whole, minimally processed foods and practicing portion control, individuals can achieve and maintain a healthy weight more easily.

The diet's abundance of fiber from fruits, vegetables, legumes, and whole grains contributes to feelings of fullness and helps regulate hunger, leading to reduced calorie intake. Additionally, Mediterranean foods are packed with nutrients, providing essential vitamins, minerals, and antioxidants per calorie consumed, supporting overall health while facilitating weight loss.

6. Anti-Inflammatory Effects:

The Mediterranean diet's emphasis on antioxidants and healthy fats serves as a powerful defense against inflammation, a common underlying factor in many chronic diseases. By discouraging highly processed and refined foods that are pro-inflammatory, this dietary pattern reduces exposure to substances that can trigger inflammation.

Fatty fish varieties like salmon, sardines, and mackerel are prized components of the Mediterranean diet due to their rich omega-3 fatty acid content, particularly EPA and DHA. These omega-3s exert potent anti-inflammatory effects, mitigating chronic inflammation within the body.Furthermore, whole grains such as whole wheat, oats, and barley feature prominently in the Mediterranean diet, providing complex carbohydrates and fiber. Fiber not only aids in regulating blood sugar levels but also possesses anti-inflammatory properties, helping to alleviate inflammation associated with conditions like insulin resistance. In essence, the Mediterranean diet offers a natural and holistic approach to combating inflammation and promoting overall health and well-being.

The Mediterranean Diet Food Pyramid

Embark on a journey through the Mediterranean Diet Food Pyramid—a visual representation of the dietary patterns and lifestyle habits that have sustained generations of Mediterranean communities. At its foundation lies an abundance of plant-based foods, followed by healthy fats, lean proteins, and moderate portions of dairy, seafood, and poultry. This pyramid not only guides dietary choices but also encapsulates the holistic approach to health and well-being that defines the Mediterranean way of life.

1. Foundation of Plant-Based Foods: Found at the base of the pyramid are plant-based foods like fruits, vegetables, whole grains, nuts, seeds, and legumes. These nutrient-dense foods form the cornerstone of the diet, providing essential vitamins, minerals, fiber, and antioxidants.

2. Healthy Fats: Healthy fats sourced from olive oil, avocados, and nuts are prominently featured in the Mediterranean diet. Rich in monounsaturated and polyunsaturated fats, these fats support heart health and help reduce the risk of chronic diseases.

3. Lean Proteins: The Mediterranean diet emphasizes lean protein sources such as fish, poultry, eggs, and dairy products. Fatty fish varieties like salmon and mackerel, rich in omega-3 fatty acids, are particularly beneficial for their anti-inflammatory properties and overall health benefits.

4. Moderate Consumption of Red Meat and Sweets: Red meat and sweets are positioned near the top of the pyramid, indicating that they should be consumed in moderation. While not completely excluded, these foods are enjoyed sparingly in the Mediterranean diet to promote overall health and well-being.

Foods To Eat And Foods To Avoid

To follow the Mediterranean diet, we'd need to know the right foods to eat and the ones to avoid. An easy way to do this would be to follow the pattern of the pyramid. Here are the tiers and the foods to eat and avoid.

Here's an expanded list of foods to include in the Mediterranean diet:

1. Fruits: Incorporate a variety of fruits like apples, oranges, berries (strawberries, blueberries, raspberries), grapes, and melons into your daily meals and snacks for a burst of vitamins, minerals, and antioxidants.

2. Vegetables: Opt for a colorful array of vegetables such as tomatoes, cucumbers, bell peppers, spinach, kale, broccoli, zucchini, and carrots to provide ample fiber, vitamins, and phytonutrients.

3. Whole grains: Choose whole grains like brown rice, quinoa, oats, barley, bulgur, farro, and whole wheat bread to fuel your body with complex carbohydrates, fiber, and essential nutrients.

4. Nuts and seeds: Snack on almonds, walnuts, pistachios, pumpkin seeds, flaxseeds, and chia seeds for a dose of healthy fats, protein, and micronutrients.

5. Legumes: Include lentils, chickpeas, black beans, kidney beans, and peas in soups, salads, stews, and main dishes to boost your intake of plant-based protein, fiber, and minerals.

6. Fish and seafood: Enjoy fatty fish like salmon, mackerel, trout, sardines, and tuna regularly for omega-3 fatty acids, which are beneficial for heart health and inflammation reduction.

7. Poultry: Incorporate lean sources of poultry such as chicken and turkey into your meals for high-quality protein and essential nutrients like iron and zinc.

8. Dairy: Include dairy products like yogurt and cheese, with an emphasis on Greek yogurt for probiotics, calcium, and protein.

9. Healthy fats: Cook with olive oil, drizzle avocado oil over salads, and snack on olives f or monounsaturated fats, which are linked to heart health and inflammation reduction.

10. Herbs and spices: Flavor your dishes with an assortment of herbs and spices such as basil, oregano, rosemary, thyme, garlic, turmeric, and cinnamon to enhance taste and provide additional health benefits.

These Mediterranean diet foods offer a diverse and delicious way to nourish your body while promoting longevity, heart health, and overall vitality.

Here are some foods to avoid in the Mediterranean diet:

1. Processed meats: Such as bacon, sausage, hot dogs, and deli meats, which are high in saturated fats, sodium, and preservatives.

2. Refined grains: Like white bread, white rice, and pasta made from refined flour, which lack fiber and nutrients compared to whole grains.

3. Added sugars: Found in sugary beverages like soda, energy drinks, and sweetened teas, as well as candies, pastries, and desserts, which contribute to inflammation and weight gain.

4. Trans fats: Present in partially hydrogenated oils and margarine, often found in processed snacks, fried foods, and baked goods, which increase the risk of heart disease.

5. Processed and fried foods: Such as fast food, frozen meals, and deep-fried snacks, which are high in unhealthy fats, calories, and sodium.

6. Excess salt: Avoid adding excessive salt to meals and limit consumption of salty foods like chips, crackers, and canned soups, as high sodium intake can raise blood pressure and increase the risk of heart disease.

7. Sweetened beverages: Including sugary soft drinks, fruit juices with added sugars, and sweetened alcoholic beverages, which provide empty calories and contribute to weight gain and metabolic issues.

By avoiding these foods and focusing on whole, nutrient-rich options, you can better adhere to the principles of the Mediterranean diet and promote optimal health and well-being.

The fundamental elements of the Mediterranean diet

1. Emphasis on plant-based foods: The diet prioritizes fruits, vegetables, whole grains, nuts, seeds, legumes, and olive oil as primary sources of nutrition. These plant-based foods provide a rich array of vitamins, minerals, antioxidants, and fiber essential for overall health.

2. Moderate consumption of dairy and lean proteins: Dairy products such as yogurt and cheese, as well as lean protein sources like fish, poultry, eggs, and occasional red meat, are included in moderate amounts. These foods supply essential nutrients like calcium, protein, and omega-3 fatty acids while promoting satiety and supporting muscle health.

3. Healthy fats: Olive oil is a cornerstone of the Mediterranean diet, providing monounsaturated fats that support heart health and reduce inflammation. Additionally, nuts, seeds, and fatty fish contribute healthy fats like omega-3s, which play a crucial role in brain function and cardiovascular health.

4. Limited intake of processed foods and added sugars: Highly processed foods, sugary snacks, and beverages are minimized in the Mediterranean diet. Instead, the focus is on whole, unprocessed foods to minimize the intake of refined sugars, unhealthy fats, and artificial additives.

5. Dining culture and social interaction: The Mediterranean diet emphasizes relaxation and socializing during meals, often enjoyed with family or friends. This culture fosters connections and communication among people, aiding in stress relief and promoting mental well-being.

6. Seasonal and local ingredients: The Mediterranean diet encourages the selection of locally sourced and seasonal ingredients, such as fresh fruits, vegetables, and seafood. This helps reduce the transportation distance of food, minimizing environmental impact, and ensuring the freshness and nutritional value of ingredients.

7. Moderate alcohol consumption: Moderate alcohol consumption in the Mediterranean diet is typically red wine, often enjoyed with meals. Moderate drinking may be associated with heart health and antioxidant intake, but alcohol intake should be limited based on individual circumstances and health status.

8. Exercise and physical activity: The Mediterranean diet not only focuses on dietary habits but also emphasizes moderate physical activity. Regular exercise combined with the Mediterranean diet may help maintain a healthy weight, promote cardiovascular health, and enhance overall quality of life.

By following these fundamental principles, the Mediterranean diet promotes longevity, reduces the risk of chronic diseases such as heart disease and diabetes, and supports overall well-being

30-Day Meal Plan

DAYS	BREAKFAST	LUNCH	DINNER	SNACK/DESSERT
1	Spiced Potatoes with Chickpeas 12	Simple Herbed Rice 21	Salmon Poached in Red Wine 31	Sweet Potato Fries 54
2	Greek Eggs and Potatoes 12	Old Delhi Butter Chicken 37	Garlicky Sautéed Zucchini with Mint 63	Crispy Spiced Chickpeas 57
3	Berry Warming Smoothie 12	Farro and Mushroom Risotto 22	Shrimp Salad 27	Black Bean Corn Dip 54
4	South of the Coast Sweet Potato Toast 14	Mediterranean Pork with Olives 45	Stuffed Pepper Stew 69	Ricotta-Lemon Cheesecake 83
5	Peachy Green Smoothie 18	Insalata Caprese 75	Fava Beans with Ground Meat 23	Pea and Arugula Crostini with Pecorino Romano 56
6	Mini Shrimp Frittata 14	Chicken and Mushroom Marsala 36	Prassorizo (Leeks and Rice) 23	Fig-Pecan Energy Bites 56
7	Spanish Tortilla with Potatoes and Peppers 18	Steamed Shrimp and Asparagus 27	Roasted Acorn Squash 60	Roasted Plums with Nut Crumble 83
8	Golden Egg Skillet 16	Zucchini Lasagna 70	Pepper Steak 51	Savory Lentil Dip 57
9	Nuts and Fruit Oatmeal 13	Lentil Bowl 24	Fish Gratin 30	Classic Hummus with Tahini 58
10	Egg in a "Pepper Hole" with Avocado 14	Quinoa, Broccoli, and Baby Potatoes 23	Garlic-Marinated Flank Steak 45	Mascarpone and Fig Crostini 81
11	Mashed Chickpea, Feta, and Avocado Toast 14	Grain-Free Kale Tabbouleh 76	Gigantes (Greek Roasted Butter Beans) 23	Spanish-Style Pan-Roasted Cod 54
12	Greek Yogurt Parfait with Granola 13	Mussels with Fennel and Leeks 29	Citrus Asparagus with Pistachios 60	Classic Hummus with Tahini 58
13	Savory Zucchini Muffins 13	One-Pan Greek Pork and Vegetables 47	Herb Vinaigrette Potato Salad 65	Red Grapefruit Granita 81
14	Spanish Tuna Tortilla with Roasted Peppers 15	Marinated Swordfish Skewers 30	Three-Cheese Zucchini Boats 72	Pesto Cucumber Boats 55
15	Sunshine Overnight Oats 15	Braised Duck with Fennel Root 42	Brown Rice with Dried Fruit 21	Black-Eyed Pea "Caviar" 55
16	Tortilla Española (Spanish Omelet) 17	Root Vegetable Soup with Garlic Aioli 68	Herb Vinaigrette Potato Salad 65	Nutty Apple Salad 57

DAYS	BREAKFAST	LUNCH	DINNER	SNACK/DESSERT
17	Mediterranean Omelet 18	Pork Loin in Dried Fig Sauce 50	Herb Vinaigrette Potato Salad 65	Blueberry Compote 82
18	Breakfast Quinoa with Figs and Walnuts 12	Classic Margherita Pizza 86	Revithosoupa (Chickpea Soup) 24	Bravas-Style Potatoes 56
19	Harissa Shakshuka with Bell Peppers and Tomatoes 13	Salmon Croquettes 33	Mediterranean Lentil Casserole 25	Sardine and Herb Bruschetta 58
20	Gluten-Free Granola Cereal 16	Herbed Lamb Steaks 47	Glazed Carrots 62	Apricot and Mint No-Bake Parfait 82
21	Creamy Cinnamon Porridge 17	Baked Spanish Salmon 28	Raw Zucchini Salad 77	Mini Lettuce Wraps 55
22	Broccoli-Mushroom Frittata 17	Garlic Balsamic London Broil 48	Dill Salmon Salad Wraps 87	Pea and Arugula Crostini with Pecorino Romano 56
23	Oatmeal with Apple and Cardamom 15	Chicken Artichoke Rice Bake 21	Citrus Swordfish 30	Lightened-Up Baklava Rolls 81
24	Savory Feta, Spinach, and Red Pepper Muffins 16	Parmesan Mushrooms 64	Tortellini in Red Pepper Sauce 71	Bite-Size Stuffed Peppers 54
25	Grilled Halloumi with Whole-Wheat Pita Bread 19	Taco Chicken 41	Barley and Vegetable Casserole 21	Red-Wine Poached Pears 82
26	Mediterranean Frittata 19	Lemon-Oregano Grilled Shrimp 32	Hearty Minestrone Soup 64	Roasted Stuffed Figs 55
27	Quick Low-Carb Avocado Toasts 15	Pesto Spinach Flatbread 71	Beef, Mushroom, and Green Bean Soup 45	Lemon Coconut Cake 82
28	Feta and Herb Frittata 18	White Bean Cassoulet 22	Quick Seafood Paella 29	Manchego Crackers 56
29	Garlic Scrambled Eggs with Basil 17	Greek Fasolakia (Green Beans) 66	Cheesy Low-Carb Lasagna 46	Ranch Oyster Snack Crackers 57
30	Tomato and Asparagus Frittata 16	Pesto Spinach Flatbread 71	Beef Burger 48	Grilled Pineapple and Melon 83

Chapter
2

Breakfasts

Chapter 2 Breakfasts

Spiced Potatoes with Chickpeas

Prep time: 10 minutes | Cook time: 10 minutes | Serves 4

- ¼ cup olive oil
- 3 medium potatoes, peeled and shredded
- 2 cups finely chopped baby spinach
- 1 medium onion, finely diced
- 1 tablespoon minced fresh ginger
- 1 teaspoon ground cumin
- 1 teaspoon ground coriander
- ½ teaspoon ground turmeric
- ½ teaspoon salt
- 1 (15-ounce / 425-g) can chickpeas, drained and rinsed
- 1 medium zucchini, diced
- ¼ cup chopped cilantro
- 1 cup plain yogurt

1. Heat the olive oil in a large skillet over medium heat. Add the potatoes, spinach, onions, ginger, cumin, coriander, turmeric, and salt and stir to mix well. Spread the mixture out into an even layer and let cook, without stirring, for about 5 minutes until the potatoes are crisp and browned on the bottom. 2. Add the chickpeas and zucchini and mix to combine, breaking up the layer of potatoes. Spread the mixture out again into an even layer and continue to cook, without stirring, for another 5 minutes or so, until the potatoes are crisp on the bottom. 3. To serve, garnish with cilantro and yogurt.

Per Serving:
calories: 679 | fat: 20g | protein: 28g | carbs: 100g | fiber: 24g | sodium: 388mg

Greek Eggs and Potatoes

Prep time: 5 minutes | Cook time: 30 minutes | Serves 4

- 3 medium tomatoes, seeded and coarsely chopped
- 2 tablespoons fresh chopped basil
- 1 garlic clove, minced
- 2 tablespoons plus ½ cup olive oil, divided
- Sea salt and freshly ground pepper, to taste
- 3 large russet potatoes
- 4 large eggs
- 1 teaspoon fresh oregano, chopped

1. Put tomatoes in a food processor and purée them, skins and all. 2. Add the basil, garlic, 2 tablespoons olive oil, sea salt, and freshly ground pepper, and pulse to combine. 3. Put the mixture in a large skillet over low heat and cook, covered, for 20–25 minutes, or until the sauce has thickened and is bubbly. 4. Meanwhile, dice the potatoes into small cubes. Put ½ cup olive oil in a nonstick skillet over medium-low heat. 5. Fry the potatoes for 5 minutes until crisp and browned on the outside, then cover and reduce heat to low. Steam potatoes until done. 6. Carefully crack the eggs into the tomato sauce. Cook over low heat until the eggs are set in the sauce, about 6 minutes. 7. Remove the potatoes from the pan and drain them on paper towels, then place them in a bowl. 8. Sprinkle with sea salt and freshly ground pepper to taste and top with the oregano. 9. Carefully remove the eggs with a slotted spoon and place them on a plate with the potatoes. Spoon sauce over the top and serve.

Per Serving:
calories: 548 | fat: 32g | protein: 13g | carbs: 54g | fiber: 5g | sodium: 90mg

Berry Warming Smoothie

Prep time: 5 minutes | Cook time: 0 minutes | Serves 1

- ⅔ cup plain kefir or plain yogurt
- ½ cup frozen mixed berries
- ½ cup baby spinach
- ½ cup cucumber, chopped
- 2 tablespoons unsweetened shredded coconut
- ¼ teaspoon grated ginger
- ¼ teaspoon ground cinnamon
- ¼ teaspoon ground nutmeg
- ⅛ teaspoon ground cardamom
- ¼ teaspoon vanilla extract (optional)

1. In a blender or Vitamix, add all the ingredients. Blend to combine.

Per Serving:
calories: 165 | fat: 7g | protein: 7g | carbs: 20g | fiber: 4g | sodium: 100mg

Breakfast Quinoa with Figs and Walnuts

Prep time: 10 minutes | Cook time: 12 minutes | Serves 4

- 1½ cups quinoa, rinsed and drained
- 2½ cups water
- 1 cup almond milk
- 2 tablespoons honey
- 1 teaspoon vanilla extract
- ½ teaspoon ground
- cinnamon
- ¼ teaspoon salt
- ½ cup low-fat plain Greek yogurt
- 8 fresh figs, quartered
- 1 cup chopped toasted walnuts

1. Place quinoa, water, almond milk, honey, vanilla, cinnamon, and salt in the Instant Pot®. Stir to combine. Close lid, set steam release to Sealing, press the Rice button, and set time to 12 minutes. When the timer beeps, let pressure release naturally, about 20 minutes. 2. Press the Cancel button, open lid, and fluff quinoa with a fork. Serve warm with yogurt, figs, and walnuts.

Per Serving:
calories: 413 | fat: 25g | protein: 10g | carbs: 52g | fiber: 7g | sodium: 275mg

Greek Yogurt Parfait with Granola

Prep time: 10 minutes | Cook time: 30 minutes | Serves 4

For the Granola:
- ¼ cup honey or maple syrup
- 2 tablespoons vegetable oil
- 2 teaspoons vanilla extract
- ½ teaspoon kosher salt
- 3 cups gluten-free rolled oats
- 1 cup mixed raw and unsalted nuts, chopped
- ¼ cup sunflower seeds
- 1 cup unsweetened dried cherries

For the Parfait:
- 2 cups plain Greek yogurt
- 1 cup fresh fruit, chopped (optional)

Make the Granola: 1. Preheat the oven to 325ºF (163ºC). Line a baking sheet with parchment paper or foil. 2. Heat the honey, oil, vanilla, and salt in a small saucepan over medium heat. Simmer for 2 minutes and stir together well. 3. In a large bowl, combine the oats, nuts, and seeds. Pour the warm oil mixture over the top and toss well. Spread in a single layer on the prepared baking sheet. Bake for 30 minutes, stirring halfway through. 4. Remove from the oven and add in the dried cherries. Cool completely and store in an airtight container at room temperature for up to 3 months. Make the Parfait: 5. For one serving: In a bowl or lowball drinking glass, spoon in ½ cup yogurt, ½ cup granola, and ¼ cup fruit (if desired). Layer in whatever pattern you like.

Per Serving:
calories: 370 | fat: 144g | protein: 19g | carbs: 44g | fiber: 6g | sodium: 100mg

Savory Zucchini Muffins

Prep time: 10 minutes | Cook time: 35 minutes | Serves 13

- 1 tablespoon extra virgin olive oil plus extra for brushing
- 2 medium zucchini, grated
- ⅛ teaspoon fine sea salt
- 1 large egg, lightly beaten
- 1½ ounces (43 g) crumbled feta
- ¼ medium onion (any variety), finely chopped
- 1 tablespoon chopped fresh parsley
- 1 tablespoon chopped fresh dill
- 1 tablespoon chopped fresh mint
- ¼ teaspoon freshly ground black pepper
- 3 tablespoons unseasoned breadcrumbs
- 1 tablespoon grated Parmesan cheese

1. Preheat the oven to 400°F (205ºC), and line a medium muffin pan with 6 muffin liners. Lightly brush the bottoms of the liners with olive oil. 2. Place the grated zucchini in a colander and sprinkle with the sea salt. Set aside for 10 minutes to allow the salt to penetrate. 3. Remove the zucchini from the colander, and place it on a tea towel. Pull the edges of the towel in and then twist and squeeze the towel to remove as much of the water from the zucchini as possible. (This will prevent the muffins from becoming soggy.) 4. In a large bowl, combine the egg, feta, onions, parsley, dill, mint, pepper, and the remaining tablespoon of olive oil. Mix well, and add the zucchini to the bowl. Mix again, and add the breadcrumbs. Use a fork to mash the ingredients until well combined. 5. Divide

the mixture among the prepared muffins liners and then sprinkle ½ teaspoon grated Parmesan over each muffin. Transfer to the oven, and bake for 35 minutes or until the muffins turn golden brown. 6. When the baking time is complete, remove the muffins from the oven and set aside to cool for 5 minutes before removing from the pan. Store in an airtight container in the refrigerator for 3 days, or tightly wrap individual muffins in plastic wrap and freeze for up to 3 months.

Per Serving:
calories: 39 | fat: 2g | protein: 2g | carbs: 3g | fiber: 1g | sodium: 80mg

Harissa Shakshuka with Bell Peppers and Tomatoes

Prep time: 10 minutes | Cook time: 20 minutes | Serves 4

- 1½ tablespoons extra-virgin olive oil
- 2 tablespoons harissa
- 1 tablespoon tomato paste
- ½ onion, diced
- 1 bell pepper, seeded and diced
- 3 garlic cloves, minced
- 1 (28-ounce / 794-g) can no-salt-added diced tomatoes
- ½ teaspoon kosher salt
- 4 large eggs
- 2 to 3 tablespoons fresh basil, chopped or cut into ribbons

1. Preheat the oven to 375ºF (190ºC). 2. Heat the olive oil in a 12-inch cast-iron pan or ovenproof skillet over medium heat. Add the harissa, tomato paste, onion, and bell pepper; sauté for 3 to 4 minutes. Add the garlic and cook until fragrant, about 30 seconds. Add the diced tomatoes and salt and simmer for about 10 minutes. 3. Make 4 wells in the sauce and gently break 1 egg into each. Transfer to the oven and bake until the whites are cooked and the yolks are set, 10 to 12 minutes. 4. Allow to cool for 3 to 5 minutes, garnish with the basil, and carefully spoon onto plates.

Per Serving:
calories: 190 | fat: 10g | protein: 9g | carbs: 15g | fiber: 4g | sodium: 255mg

Nuts and Fruit Oatmeal

Prep time: 10 minutes | Cook time: 7 minutes | Serves 2

- 1 cup rolled oats
- 1¼ cups water
- ¼ cup orange juice
- 1 medium pear, peeled, cored, and cubed
- ¼ cup dried cherries
- ¼ cup chopped walnuts
- 1 tablespoon honey
- ¼ teaspoon ground ginger
- ¼ teaspoon ground cinnamon
- ⅛ teaspoon salt

1. Place oats, water, orange juice, pear, cherries, walnuts, honey, ginger, cinnamon, and salt in the Instant Pot®. Stir to combine. 2. Close lid, set steam release to Sealing, press the Manual button, and set time to 7 minutes. When the timer beeps, let pressure release naturally, about 20 minutes. Press the Cancel button, open lid, and stir well. Serve warm.

Per Serving:
calories: 362 | fat: 8g | protein: 7g | carbs: 69g | fiber: 8g | sodium: 164mg

South of the Coast Sweet Potato Toast

Prep time: 5 minutes | Cook time: 15 minutes | Serves 4

- 2 plum tomatoes, halved
- 6 tablespoons extra-virgin olive oil, divided
- Salt
- Freshly ground black pepper
- 2 large sweet potatoes, sliced lengthwise
- 1 cup fresh spinach
- 8 medium asparagus,
- trimmed
- 4 large cooked eggs or egg substitute (poached, scrambled, or fried)
- 1 cup arugula
- 4 tablespoons pesto
- 4 tablespoons shredded Asiago cheese

1. Preheat the oven to 450°F(235°C). 2. On a baking sheet, brush the plum tomato halves with 2 tablespoons of olive oil and season with salt and pepper. Roast the tomatoes in the oven for approximately 15 minutes, then remove from the oven and allow to rest. 3. Put the sweet potato slices on a separate baking sheet and brush about 2 tablespoons of oil on each side and season with salt and pepper. Bake the sweet potato slices for about 15 minutes, flipping once after 5 to 7 minutes, until just tender. Remove from the oven and set aside. 4. In a sauté pan or skillet, heat the remaining 2 tablespoons of olive oil over medium heat and sauté the fresh spinach until just wilted. Remove from the pan and rest on a paper-towel-lined dish. In the same pan, add the asparagus and sauté, turning throughout. Transfer to a paper towel-lined dish. 5. Place the slices of grilled sweet potato on serving plates and divide the spinach and asparagus evenly among the slices. Place a prepared egg on top of the spinach and asparagus. Top this with ¼ cup of arugula. 6. Finish by drizzling with 1 tablespoon of pesto and sprinkle with 1 tablespoon of cheese. Serve with 1 roasted plum tomato.

Per Serving:
calories: 441 | fat: 35g | protein: 13g | carbs: 23g | fiber: 4g | sodium: 481mg

Mini Shrimp Frittata

Prep time: 15 minutes | Cook time: 20 minutes | Serves 4

- 1 teaspoon olive oil, plus more for spraying
- ½ small red bell pepper, finely diced
- 1 teaspoon minced garlic
- 1 (4-ounce / 113-g) can of
- tiny shrimp, drained
- Salt and freshly ground black pepper, to taste
- 4 eggs, beaten
- 4 teaspoons ricotta cheese

1. Spray four ramekins with olive oil. 2. In a medium skillet over medium-low heat, heat 1 teaspoon of olive oil. Add the bell pepper and garlic and sauté until the pepper is soft, about 5 minutes 3. Add the shrimp, season with salt and pepper, and cook until warm, 1 to 2 minutes. Remove from the heat. 4. Add the eggs and stir to combine. 5. Pour one quarter of the mixture into each ramekin. 6. Place 2 ramekins in the air fryer basket and bake at 350ºF (177ºC) for 6 minutes. 7. Remove the air fryer basket from the air fryer and stir the mixture in each ramekin. Top each fritatta with 1 teaspoon of ricotta cheese. Return the air fryer basket to the air fryer and cook until eggs are set and the top is lightly browned, 4 to 5

minutes. 8. Repeat with the remaining two ramekins.

Per Serving:
calories: 114 | fat: 6g | protein: 12g | carbs: 1g | fiber: 0g | sodium: 314mg

Mashed Chickpea, Feta, and Avocado Toast

Prep time: 10 minutes |Cook time: 0 minutes| Serves: 4

- 1 (15-ounce / 425-g) can chickpeas, drained and rinsed
- 1 avocado, pitted
- ½ cup diced feta cheese (about 2 ounces / 57 g)
- 2 teaspoons freshly
- squeezed lemon juice or 1 tablespoon orange juice
- ½ teaspoon freshly ground black pepper
- 4 pieces multigrain toast
- 2 teaspoons honey

1. Put the chickpeas in a large bowl. Scoop the avocado flesh into the bowl. 2. With a potato masher or large fork, mash the ingredients together until the mix has a spreadable consistency. It doesn't need to be totally smooth. 3. Add the feta, lemon juice, and pepper, and mix well. 4. Evenly divide the mash onto the four pieces of toast and spread with a knife. Drizzle with honey and serve.

Per Serving:
calories: 301 | fat: 14g | protein: 12g | carbs: 35g | fiber: 11g | sodium: 450mg

Egg in a "Pepper Hole" with Avocado

Prep time: 15 minutes | Cook time: 5 minutes | Serves 4

- 4 bell peppers, any color
- 1 tablespoon extra-virgin olive oil
- 8 large eggs
- ¾ teaspoon kosher salt, divided
- ¼ teaspoon freshly ground
- black pepper, divided
- 1 avocado, peeled, pitted, and diced
- ¼ cup red onion, diced
- ¼ cup fresh basil, chopped
- Juice of ½ lime

1. Stem and seed the bell peppers. Cut 2 (2-inch-thick) rings from each pepper. Chop the remaining bell pepper into small dice, and set aside. 2. Heat the olive oil in a large skillet over medium heat. Add 4 bell pepper rings, then crack 1 egg in the middle of each ring. Season with ¼ teaspoon of the salt and ⅛ teaspoon of the black pepper. Cook until the egg whites are mostly set but the yolks are still runny, 2 to 3 minutes. Gently flip and cook 1 additional minute for over easy. Move the egg-bell pepper rings to a platter or onto plates, and repeat with the remaining 4 bell pepper rings. 3. In a medium bowl, combine the avocado, onion, basil, lime juice, reserved diced bell pepper, the remaining ¼ teaspoon kosher salt, and the remaining ⅛ teaspoon black pepper. Divide among the 4 plates.

Per Serving:
2 egg-pepper rings: calories: 270 | fat: 19g | protein: 15g | carbs: 12g | fiber: 5g | sodium: 360mg

Spanish Tuna Tortilla with Roasted Peppers

Prep time: 15 minutes | Cook time: 15 minutes | Serves 4

- 6 large eggs
- ¼ cup olive oil
- 2 small russet potatoes, diced
- 1 small onion, chopped
- 1 roasted red bell pepper, sliced
- 1 (7-ounce / 198-g) can tuna packed in water, drained well and flaked
- 2 plum tomatoes, seeded and diced
- 1 teaspoon dried tarragon

1. Preheat the broiler on high. 2. Crack the eggs in a large bowl and whisk them together until just combined. Heat the olive oil in a large, oven-safe, nonstick or cast-iron skillet over medium-low heat. 3. Add the potatoes and cook until slightly soft, about 7 minutes. Add the onion and the peppers and cook until soft, 3–5 minutes. 4. Add the tuna, tomatoes, and tarragon to the skillet and stir to combine, then add the eggs. 5. Cook for 7–10 minutes until the eggs are bubbling from the bottom and the bottom is slightly brown. 6. Place the skillet into the oven on 1 of the first 2 racks, and cook until the middle is set and the top is slightly brown. 7. Slice into wedges and serve warm or at room temperature.

Per Serving:
calories: 247 | fat: 14g | protein: 12g | carbs: 19g | fiber: 2g | sodium: 130mg

Quick Low-Carb Avocado Toasts

Prep time: 10 minutes | Cook time: 10 minutes | Makes 4 toasts

Quick Bread Base:
- ¼ cup (28 g/1 ounce) flax meal
- 2 tablespoons (16 g/0.6 ounce) coconut flour
- 2 teaspoons (2 g) psyllium powder
- ⅛ teaspoon baking soda
- Optional: ½ teaspoon dried herbs, ¼ teaspoon paprika or ground turmeric

Avocado Topping:
- 1 large ripe avocado
- ¼ small red onion or 1 spring onion, minced
- 1 tablespoon extra-virgin olive oil
- 1 tablespoon fresh lemon juice
- Salt, black pepper, and/or

- Salt and black pepper, to taste
- ¼ teaspoon apple cider vinegar
- 1 teaspoon extra-virgin olive oil or ghee, plus more for greasing
- 1 large egg
- 2 tablespoons water

chile flakes, to taste
- 2 teaspoons chopped fresh herbs, such as parsley or chives
- Optional: 2 ounces (57 g) smoked salmon and/or poached egg

Make The Bread Base: 1. Combine all the dry ingredients in a bowl. Add the wet ingredients. Combine and set aside for 5 minutes. 2.Divide the mixture between two wide ramekins lightly greased with the olive oil and microwave on high for about 2 minutes, checking every 30 to 60 seconds to avoid overcooking. (If the bread ends up too dry, you can "rehydrate" it: Pour 1 tablespoon [15 ml] of water evenly over it, then return it to the microwave for 30 seconds.) 3.Let it cool slightly, then cut widthwise. Place on a dry nonstick pan and toast for 1 to 2 minutes per side. Set aside. Make The Topping: 4. In a bowl, mash the avocado with the onion, oil, lemon juice, salt, pepper, and chile flakes. To serve, spread the avocado mixture on top of the sliced bread and add fresh herbs. Optionally, top with smoked salmon. 5.Store the bread separately from the topping at room temperature in a sealed container for 1 day, in the fridge for up to 5 days, or freeze for up to 3 months. 6.Refrigerate the topping in a sealed jar for up to 3 days.

Per Serving:
calories: 112 | fat: 10g | protein: 3g | carbs: 4g | fiber: 3g | sodium: 71mg

Sunshine Overnight Oats

Prep time: 5 minutes | Cook time: 0 minutes | Serves 2

- ⅔ cup vanilla, unsweetened almond milk (not Silk brand)
- ⅓ cup rolled oats
- ¼ cup raspberries
Pinch ground cloves
- 1 teaspoon honey
- ¼ teaspoon turmeric
- ⅛ teaspoon ground cinnamon

1. In a mason jar, combine the almond milk, oats, raspberries, honey, turmeric, cinnamon, and cloves and shake well. Store in the refrigerator for 8 to 24 hours, then serve cold or heated.

Per Serving:
calories: 82 | fat: 2g | protein: 2g | carbs: 14g | fiber: 3g | sodium: 98mg

Oatmeal with Apple and Cardamom

Prep time: 10 minutes | Cook time: 7 minutes | Serves 4

- 1 tablespoon light olive oil
- 1 large Granny Smith, Honeycrisp, or Pink Lady apple, peeled, cored, and diced
- ½ teaspoon ground

cardamom
- 1 cup steel-cut oats
- 3 cups water
- ¼ cup maple syrup
- ½ teaspoon salt

1. Press the Sauté button on the Instant Pot® and heat oil. Add apple and cardamom and cook until apple is just softened, about 2 minutes. Press the Cancel button. 2. Add oats, water, maple syrup, and salt to pot, and stir well. Close lid, set steam release to Sealing, press the Manual button, and set time to 5 minutes. 3. When the timer beeps, let pressure release naturally for 10 minutes, then quick-release the remaining pressure until the float valve drops. Press the Cancel button, open lid, and stir well. Serve hot.

Per Serving:
calories: 249 | fat: 6g | protein: 6g | carbs: 48g | fiber: 5g | sodium: 298mg

Savory Feta, Spinach, and Red Pepper Muffins

Prep time: 10 minutes | Cook time: 22 minutes | Serves 12

- 2 cups all-purpose flour
- ¾ cup whole-wheat flour
- ¼ cup granulated sugar
- 2 teaspoons baking powder
- 1 teaspoon paprika
- ¾ teaspoonp salt
- ½ cup extra virgin olive oil
- 2 eggs
- ¾ cup low-fat 2% milk
- ¾ cup crumbled feta
- 1¼ cups fresh baby leaf spinach, thinly sliced
- ⅓ cup jarred red peppers, drained, patted dry, and chopped

1. Preheat the oven to 375°F (190°C) and line a large muffin pan with 12 muffin liners. 2. In a large bowl, combine the all-purpose flour, whole-wheat flour, sugar, baking powder, paprika, and salt. Mix well.3.In a medium bowl, whisk the olive oil, eggs, and milk. 4. Add the wet ingredients to the dry ingredients, and use a wooden spoon to stir until the ingredients are just blended and form a thick dough. 5. Add the feta, spinach, and peppers, and mix gently until all the ingredients are incorporated. Evenly divide the mixture among the muffin liners. 6. Transfer to the oven, and bake for 25 minutes or until a toothpick inserted into the middle of a muffin comes out clean. 7. Set the muffins aside to cool for 10 minutes, and remove them from the pan. Store in an airtight container in the refrigerator for up to 3 days. (Remove from the refrigerator 10 minutes before consuming.)

Per Serving:
calories: 243 | fat: 12g | protein: 6g | carbs: 27g | fiber: 2g | sodium: 306mg

Golden Egg Skillet

Prep time: 15 minutes | Cook time: 20 minutes | Serves 2

- 2 tablespoons extra-virgin avocado oil or ghee
- 2 medium spring onions, white and green parts separated, sliced
- 1 clove garlic, minced
- 3½ ounces (99 g) Swiss chard or collard greens, stalks and leaves separated, chopped
- 1 medium zucchini, sliced into coins
- 2 tablespoons water
- 1 teaspoon Dijon or yellow mustard
- ½ teaspoon ground turmeric
- ¼ teaspoon black pepper
- Salt, to taste
- 4 large eggs
- ¾ cup grated Manchego or Pecorino Romano cheese
- 2 tablespoons (30 ml) extra-virgin olive oil

1. Preheat the oven to 360°F (182°C) fan assisted or 400°F (205°C) conventional. 2. Grease a large, ovenproof skillet (with a lid) with the avocado oil. Cook the white parts of the spring onions and the garlic for about 1 minute, until just fragrant. Add the chard stalks, zucchini, and water. Stir, then cover with a lid. Cook over medium-low heat for about 10 minutes or until the zucchini is tender. Add the mustard, turmeric, pepper, and salt. Add the chard leaves and cook until just wilted. 3. Use a spatula to make 4 wells in the mixture. Crack an egg into each well and cook until the egg whites start to set while the yolks are still runny. Top with the cheese, transfer to the oven, and bake for 5 to 7 minutes. Remove from the oven and sprinkle with the reserved spring onions. Drizzle with the olive oil and serve warm.

Per Serving:
calories: 600 | fat: 49g | protein: 31g | carbs: 10g | fiber: 4g | sodium: 213mg

Gluten-Free Granola Cereal

Prep time: 7 minutes | Cook time: 30 minutes | Makes 3½ cups

- Oil, for spraying
- 1½ cups gluten-free rolled oats
- ½ cup chopped walnuts
- ½ cup chopped almonds
- ½ cup pumpkin seeds
- ¼ cup maple syrup or honey
- 1 tablespoon toasted sesame oil or vegetable oil
- 1 teaspoon ground cinnamon
- ½ teaspoon salt
- ½ cup dried cranberries

1. Preheat the air fryer to 250ºF (121ºC). Line the air fryer basket with parchment and spray lightly with oil. (Do not skip the step of lining the basket; the parchment will keep the granola from falling through the holes.) 2. In a large bowl, mix together the oats, walnuts, almonds, pumpkin seeds, maple syrup, sesame oil, cinnamon, and salt. 3. Spread the mixture in an even layer in the prepared basket. 4. Cook for 30 minutes, stirring every 10 minutes. 5. Transfer the granola to a bowl, add the dried cranberries, and toss to combine. 6. Let cool to room temperature before storing in an airtight container.

Per Serving:
calories: 322 | fat: 17g | protein: 11g | carbs: 35g | fiber: 6g | sodium: 170mg

Tomato and Asparagus Frittata

Prep time: 5 minutes | Cook time: 15 minutes | Serves 4

- 1 cup water
- 1 teaspoon olive oil
- 1 cup halved cherry tomatoes
- 1 cup cooked asparagus tips
- ¼ cup grated Parmesan cheese
- 6 large eggs
- ¼ cup low-fat plain Greek yogurt
- ½ teaspoon salt
- ½ teaspoon ground black pepper

1. Place the rack in the Instant Pot® and add water. Brush a 1.5-liter baking dish with olive oil. Add tomatoes, asparagus, and cheese to dish. 2. In a medium bowl, beat eggs, yogurt, salt, and pepper. Pour over vegetable and cheese mixture. Cover dish tightly with aluminum foil, then gently lower into machine. 3. Close lid, set steam release to Sealing, press the Manual button, and set time to 15 minutes. When the timer beeps, let pressure release naturally for 10 minutes, then quick-release any remaining pressure until the float valve drops. Press the Cancel button and open lid. Let stand for 10–15 minutes before carefully removing dish from pot. 4. Run a thin knife around the edge of the frittata and turn it out onto a serving platter. Serve warm.

Per Serving:
calories: 170 | fat: 11g | protein: 14g | carbs: 4g | fiber: 1g | sodium: 509mg

Broccoli-Mushroom Frittata

Prep time: 10 minutes | Cook time: 20 minutes | Serves 2

- 1 tablespoon olive oil
- 1½ cups broccoli florets, finely chopped
- ½ cup sliced brown mushrooms
- ¼ cup finely chopped onion
- ½ teaspoon salt
- ¼ teaspoon freshly ground black pepper
- 6 eggs
- ¼ cup Parmesan cheese

1. In a nonstick cake pan, combine the olive oil, broccoli, mushrooms, onion, salt, and pepper. Stir until the vegetables are thoroughly coated with oil. Place the cake pan in the air fryer basket and set the air fryer to 400ºF (204ºC). Air fry for 5 minutes until the vegetables soften. 2. Meanwhile, in a medium bowl, whisk the eggs and Parmesan until thoroughly combined. Pour the egg mixture into the pan and shake gently to distribute the vegetables. Air fry for another 15 minutes until the eggs are set. 3. Remove from the air fryer and let sit for 5 minutes to cool slightly. Use a silicone spatula to gently lift the frittata onto a plate before serving.

Per Serving:
calories: 329 | fat: 23g | protein: 24g | carbs: 6g | fiber: 0g | sodium: 793mg

Tortilla Española (Spanish Omelet)

Prep time: 10 minutes | Cook time: 40 minutes | Serves 4

- 1½ pounds (680 g) Yukon gold potatoes, scrubbed and thinly sliced
- 3 tablespoons olive oil, divided
- 1 teaspoon kosher salt, divided
- 1 sweet white onion, thinly sliced
- 3 cloves garlic, minced
- 8 eggs
- ½ teaspoon ground black pepper

1. Preheat the oven to 350°F(180°C). Line 2 baking sheets with parchment paper. 2. In a large bowl, toss the potatoes with 1 tablespoon of the oil and ½ teaspoon of the salt until well coated. Spread over the 2 baking sheets in a single layer. Roast the potatoes, rotating the baking sheets halfway through cooking, until tender but not browned, about 15 minutes. Using a spatula, remove the potatoes from the baking sheets and let cool until warm. 3. Meanwhile, in a medium skillet over medium-low heat, cook the onion in 1 tablespoon of the oil, stirring, until soft and golden, about 10 minutes. Add the garlic and cook until fragrant, about 2 minutes. Transfer the onion and garlic to a plate and let cool until warm. 4. In a large bowl, beat the eggs, pepper, and the remaining ½ teaspoon salt vigorously until the yolks and whites are completely combined and slightly frothy. Stir in the potatoes and onion and garlic and combine well, being careful not to break too many potatoes. 5. In the same skillet over medium-high heat, warm the remaining 1 tablespoon oil until shimmering, swirling to cover the whole surface. Pour in the egg mixture and spread the contents evenly. Cook for 1 minute and reduce the heat to medium-low. Cook until the edges of the egg are set and the center is slightly wet, about 8 minutes. Using a spatula, nudge the omelet to make sure it moves freely in the skillet. 6. Place a rimless plate, the size of the skillet, over the omelet. Place one hand over the plate and, in a swift motion, flip the omelet onto the plate. Slide the omelet back into the skillet, cooked side up. Cook until completely set, a toothpick inserted into the middle comes out clean, about 6 minutes. 7. Transfer to a serving plate and let cool for 5 minutes. Serve warm or room temperature.

Per Serving:
calories: 376 | fat: 19g | protein: 15g | carbs: 37g | fiber: 5g | sodium: 724mg

Creamy Cinnamon Porridge

Prep time: 10 minutes | Cook time: 10 minutes | Serves 2

- ¼ cup coconut milk
- ¾ cup unsweetened almond milk or water
- ¼ cup almond butter or hazelnut butter
- 1 tablespoon virgin coconut oil
- 2 tablespoons chia seeds
- 1 tablespoon flax meal
- 1 teaspoon cinnamon
- ¼ cup macadamia nuts
- ¼ cup hazelnuts
- 4 Brazil nuts
- Optional: low-carb sweetener, to taste
- ¼ cup unsweetened large coconut flakes
- 1 tablespoon cacao nibs

1. In a small saucepan, mix the coconut milk and almond milk and heat over medium heat. Once hot (not boiling), take off the heat. Add the almond butter and coconut oil. Stir until well combined. If needed, use an immersion blender and process until smooth. 2. Add the chia seeds, flax meal, and cinnamon, and leave to rest for 5 to 10 minutes. Roughly chop the macadamias, hazelnuts, and Brazil nuts and stir in. Add sweetener, if using, and stir. Transfer to serving bowls. In a small skillet, dry-roast the coconut flakes over medium-high heat for 1 to 2 minutes, until lightly toasted and fragrant. Top the porridge with the toasted coconut flakes and cacao nibs (or you can use chopped 100% chocolate). Serve immediately or store in the fridge for up to 3 days.

Per Serving:
calories: 646 | fat: 61g | protein: 13g | carbs: 23g | fiber: 10g | sodium: 40mg

Garlic Scrambled Eggs with Basil

Prep time: 5 minutes | Cook time: 5 minutes | Serves 2

- 4 large eggs
- 2 tablespoons finely chopped fresh basil
- 2 tablespoons grated Gruyère cheese
- 1 tablespoon cream
- 1 tablespoon olive oil
- 2 cloves garlic, minced
- Sea salt and freshly ground pepper, to taste

1. In a large bowl, beat together the eggs, basil, cheese, and cream with a whisk until just combined. 2. Heat the oil in a large, heavy nonstick skillet over medium-low heat. Add the garlic and cook until golden, about 1 minute. 3. Pour the egg mixture into the skillet over the garlic. Work the eggs continuously and cook until fluffy and soft. 4. Season with sea salt and freshly ground pepper to taste. Divide between 2 plates and serve immediately.

Per Serving:
calories: 267 | fat: 21g | protein: 16g | carbs: 3g | fiber: 0g | sodium: 394mg

Spanish Tortilla with Potatoes and Peppers

Prep time : 5 minutes | Cook time: 50 minutes | Serves 6

- ½ cup olive oil, plus 2 tablespoons, divided
- 2 pounds (907 g) baking potatoes, peeled and cut into ¼-inch slices
- 2 onions, thinly sliced
- 1 roasted red pepper, drained and cut into strips
- 6 eggs
- 2 teaspoons salt
- 1 teaspoon freshly ground black pepper

1. In a large skillet over medium heat, heat ½ cup of the olive oil. Add the potatoes and cook, stirring occasionally, until the potatoes are tender, about 20 minutes. Remove the potatoes from the pan with a slotted spoon and discard the remaining oil. 2. In a medium skillet over medium heat, heat the remaining 2 tablespoons of olive oil. Add the onions and cook, stirring frequently, until softened and golden brown, about 10 minutes. Remove the onions from the pan with a slotted spoon, leaving the oil in the pan, and add them to the potatoes. Add the pepper slices to the potatoes as well. 3. In a large bowl, whisk together the eggs, salt, and pepper. Add the cooked vegetables to the egg mixture and gently toss to combine. 4. Heat the medium skillet over low heat. Add the egg-vegetable mixture to the pan and cook for about 10 minutes, until the bottom is lightly browned. Use a spatula to loosen the tortilla and transfer the whole thing to a large plate, sliding it out of the pan so that the browned side is on the bottom. Invert the skillet over the tortilla and then lift the plate to flip it back into the skillet with the browned side on top. Return to the stove and continue to cook over low heat until the tortilla is fully set in the center, about 5 more minutes. 5. Serve the tortilla warm or at room temperature.

Per Serving:
calories: 370 | fat: 26g | protein: 9g | carbs: 29g | fiber: 5g | sodium: 876mg

Feta and Herb Frittata

Prep time : 10 minutes | Cook time: 30 minutes | Serves 6

- ¼ cup olive oil, divided
- 1 medium onion, halved and thinly sliced
- 1 clove garlic, minced
- 8 sheets phyllo dough
- 8 eggs
- ¼ cup chopped fresh basil, plus additional for garnish
- ¼ cup chopped flat-leaf parsley, plus additional for garnish
- 1 teaspoon salt
- ½ teaspoon freshly ground black pepper
- 4 ounces (113 g) crumbled feta cheese

1. Preheat the oven to 400°F(205°C). 2. Heat 2 tablespoons of the olive oil in a medium skillet over medium-high heat. Add the onions and cook, stirring frequently, until softened, about 5 minutes. Add the garlic and cook, stirring, for 1 minute more. Remove from the heat and set aside to cool. 3. While the onion mixture is cooling, make the crust. Place a damp towel on the counter and cover with a sheet of parchment paper. Lay the phyllo sheets in a stack on top of the parchment and cover with a second sheet of parchment and then a second damp towel. 4. Brush some of the remaining olive oil in a 9-by-9-inch baking dish or a 9-inch pie dish. Layer the softened phyllo sheets in the prepared dish, brushing each with some of the olive oil before adding the next phyllo sheet. 5. Next, make the filling. In a large bowl, whisk the eggs with the onion mixture, basil, parsley, salt, and pepper. Add the feta cheese and mix well. Pour the egg mixture into the prepared crust, folding any excess phyllo inside the baking dish. 6. Bake in the preheated oven for about 25 to 30 minutes, until the crust is golden brown and the egg filling is completely set in the center. Cut into rectangles or wedges and serve garnished with basil and parsley.

Per Serving:
calories: 298 | fat: 20g | protein: 12g | carbs: 17g | fiber: 1g | sodium: 769mg

Peachy Green Smoothie

Prep time: 10 minutes | Cook time: 0 minutes | Serves 2

- 1 cup almond milk
- 3 cups kale or spinach
- 1 banana, peeled
- 1 orange, peeled
- 1 small green apple
- 1 cup frozen peaches
- ¼ cup vanilla Greek yogurt

1. Put the ingredients in a blender in the order listed and blend on high until smooth. 2. Serve and enjoy.

Per Serving:
calories: 257 | fat: 5g | protein: 9g | carbs: 50g | fiber: 7g | sodium: 87mg

Mediterranean Omelet

Prep time: 10 minutes | Cook time: 12 minutes | Serves 2

- 2 teaspoons extra-virgin olive oil, divided
- 1 garlic clove, minced
- ½ red bell pepper, thinly sliced
- ½ yellow bell pepper, thinly sliced
- ¼ cup thinly sliced red onion
- 2 tablespoons chopped fresh basil
- 2 tablespoons chopped fresh parsley, plus extra for garnish
- ½ teaspoon salt
- ½ teaspoon freshly ground black pepper
- 4 large eggs, beaten

1. In a large, heavy skillet, heat 1 teaspoon of the olive oil over medium heat. Add the garlic, peppers, and onion to the pan and sauté, stirring frequently, for 5 minutes. 2. Add the basil, parsley, salt, and pepper, increase the heat to medium-high, and sauté for 2 minutes. Slide the vegetable mixture onto a plate and return the pan to the heat. 3. Heat the remaining 1 teaspoon olive oil in the same pan and pour in the beaten eggs, tilting the pan to coat evenly. Cook the eggs just until the edges are bubbly and all but the center is dry, 3 to 5 minutes. 4. Either flip the omelet or use a spatula to turn it over. 5. Spoon the vegetable mixture onto one-half of the omelet and use a spatula to fold the empty side over the top. Slide the omelet onto a platter or cutting board. 6. To serve, cut the omelet in half and garnish with fresh parsley.

Per Serving:
calories: 218 | fat: 14g | protein: 14g | carbs: 9g | fiber: 1g | sodium: 728mg

Grilled Halloumi with Whole-Wheat Pita Bread

Prep time: 5 minutes | Cook time: 10 minutes | Serves 4

- 2 teaspoons olive oil
- 8 (½-inch-thick) slices of halloumi cheese
- 4 whole-wheat pita rounds
- 1 Persian cucumber, thinly sliced
- 1 large tomato, sliced
- ½ cup pitted Kalamata olives

1. Brush a bit of olive oil on a grill pan and heat it over medium-high heat. 2. Brush the cheese slices all over with olive oil. Add the cheese slices in a single layer and cook until grill marks appear on the bottom, about 3 minutes. Flip the slices over and grill until grill marks appear on the second side, about 2 to 3 minutes more. 3. While the cheese is cooking, heat the pita bread, either in a skillet or in a toaster. 4. Serve the cheese inside of the pita pockets with the sliced cucumber, tomato, and olives.

Per Serving:
calories: 358 | fat: 24g | protein: 17g | carbs: 21g | fiber: 4g | sodium: 612mg

Mediterranean Frittata

Prep time: 10 minutes | Cook time: 15 minutes | Serves 2

- 4 large eggs
- 2 tablespoons fresh chopped herbs, such as rosemary, thyme, oregano, basil or 1 teaspoon dried herbs
- ¼ teaspoon salt
- Freshly ground black pepper
- 4 tablespoons extra-virgin olive oil, divided
- 1 cup fresh spinach, arugula, kale, or other leafy greens
- 4 ounces (113 g) quartered artichoke hearts, rinsed, drained, and thoroughly dried
- 8 cherry tomatoes, halved
- ½ cup crumbled soft goat cheese

1. Preheat the oven to broil on low. 2. In small bowl, combine the eggs, herbs, salt, and pepper and whisk well with a fork. Set aside. 3. In a 4- to 5-inch oven-safe skillet or omelet pan, heat 2 tablespoons olive oil over medium heat. Add the spinach, artichoke hearts, and cherry tomatoes and sauté until just wilted, 1 to 2 minutes. 4. Pour in the egg mixture and let it cook undisturbed over medium heat for 3 to 4 minutes, until the eggs begin to set on the bottom. 5. Sprinkle the goat cheese across the top of the egg mixture and transfer the skillet to the oven. 6. Broil for 4 to 5 minutes, or until the frittata is firm in the center and golden brown on top. 7. Remove from the oven and run a rubber spatula around the edge to loosen the sides. Invert onto a large plate or cutting board and slice in half. Serve warm and drizzled with the remaining 2 tablespoons olive oil.

Per Serving:
calories: 520 | fat: 44g | protein: 22g | carbs: 10g | fiber: 5g | sodium: 665mg

Chapter 3

Beans and Grains

Chapter 3 Beans and Grains

Simple Herbed Rice

Prep time: 10 minutes | Cook time: 32 minutes | Serves 8

- 2 tablespoons extra-virgin olive oil
- ½ medium yellow onion, peeled and chopped
- 4 cloves garlic, peeled and minced
- ¼ teaspoon salt
- ½ teaspoon ground black pepper
- 2¼ cups brown rice
- 2 cups water
- ¼ cup chopped fresh flat-leaf parsley
- ¼ cup chopped fresh basil
- 2 tablespoons chopped fresh oregano
- 2 teaspoons fresh thyme leaves

1. Press the Sauté button on the Instant Pot® and heat oil. Add onion and cook until soft, about 6 minutes. Add garlic, salt, and pepper and cook until fragrant, about 30 seconds. Add rice and cook, stirring constantly, until well-coated and starting to toast, about 3 minutes. Press the Cancel button. 2. Stir in water. Close lid, set steam release to Sealing, press the Manual button, and set time to 22 minutes. When the timer beeps, let pressure release naturally for 10 minutes, then quick-release the remaining pressure. Open lid and fold in parsley, basil, oregano, and thyme. Serve warm.

Per Serving:
calories: 102 | fat: 4g | protein: 2g | carbs: 15g | fiber: 1g | sodium: 96mg

Chicken Artichoke Rice Bake

Prep time: 10 minutes | Cook time: 3 to 5 hours | Serves 4

- Nonstick cooking spray
- 1 cup raw long-grain brown rice, rinsed
- 2½ cups low-sodium chicken broth
- 1 (14-ounce/ 397-g) can artichoke hearts, drained and rinsed
- ½ small onion, diced
- 2 garlic cloves, minced
- 10 ounces (283 g) fresh spinach, chopped
- 1 teaspoon dried thyme
- ½ teaspoon sea salt
- ½ teaspoon freshly ground black pepper
- 1 pound (454 g) boneless, skinless chicken breast

1. Generously coat a slow-cooker insert with cooking spray. Put the rice, chicken broth, artichoke hearts, onion, garlic, spinach, thyme, salt, and pepper in a slow cooker. Gently stir to mix well. 2. Place the chicken on top of the rice mixture. 3. Cover the cooker and cook for 3 to 5 hours on Low heat. 4. Remove the chicken from the cooker, shred it, and stir it back into the rice in the cooker.

Per Serving:
calories: 323 | fat: 4g | protein: 32g | carbs: 44g | fiber: 6g | sodium: 741mg

Brown Rice with Dried Fruit

Prep time: 15 minutes | Cook time: 20 minutes | Serves 6

- 2 tablespoons olive oil
- 2 stalks celery, thinly sliced
- 2 large carrots, peeled and diced
- 1 large sweet potato, peeled and diced
- 1½ cups brown rice
- ⅓ cup chopped prunes
- ⅓ cup chopped dried
- apricots
- ½ teaspoon ground cinnamon
- 2 teaspoons grated orange zest
- 3 cups water
- 1 bay leaf
- ½ teaspoon salt

1. Press the Sauté button on the Instant Pot® and heat oil. Add celery, carrots, sweet potato, and rice. Cook until vegetables are just tender, about 3 minutes. Stir in prunes, apricots, cinnamon, and orange zest. Cook until cinnamon is fragrant, about 30 seconds. Add water, bay leaf, and salt. 2. Press the Cancel button, close lid, set steam release to Sealing, press the Manual button, and set time to 16 minutes. When the timer beeps, let pressure release naturally for 10 minutes. Quick-release any remaining pressure until the float valve drops and open the lid. Fluff rice with a fork. 3. Remove and discard bay leaf. Transfer to a serving bowl. Serve hot.

Per Serving:
calories: 192 | fat: 5g | protein: 3g | carbs: 34g | fiber: 4g | sodium: 272mg

Barley and Vegetable Casserole

Prep time: 10 minutes | Cook time: 6 to 8 hours | Serves 6

- 1 cup raw barley (not the quick-cooking type)
- 3 cups low-sodium vegetable broth
- 3 garlic cloves, minced
- 2 bell peppers, any color, seeded and chopped
- 1 small onion, chopped
- 2 ounces (57 g) mushrooms,
- sliced
- 1 teaspoon extra-virgin olive oil
- 2 tablespoons Italian seasoning
- 1 teaspoon sea salt
- ¼ teaspoon freshly ground black pepper

1. In a slow cooker, combine the barley, vegetable broth, garlic, bell peppers, onion, mushrooms, olive oil, Italian seasoning, salt, and black pepper. Stir to mix well. 2. Cover the cooker and cook for 6 to 8 hours on Low heat.

Per Serving:
calories: 147 | fat: 2g | protein: 5g | carbs: 30g | fiber: 8g | sodium: 464mg

Garlic-Asparagus Israeli Couscous

**Prep time: 5 minutes |Cook time: 25 minutes|
Serves: 6**

- 1 cup garlic-and-herb goat cheese (about 4 ounces/ 113 g)
- 1½ pounds (680 g) asparagus spears, ends trimmed and stalks chopped into 1-inch pieces (about 2¾ to 3 cups chopped)
- 1 tablespoon extra-virgin olive oil
- 1 garlic clove, minced
- (about ½ teaspoon)
- ¼ teaspoon freshly ground black pepper
- 1¾ cups water
- 1 (8-ounce/ 227-g) box uncooked whole-wheat or regular Israeli couscous (about 1⅓ cups)
- ¼ teaspoon kosher or sea salt

1. Preheat the oven to 425°F (220ºC). Put the goat cheese on the counter to bring to room temperature. 2. In a large bowl, mix together the asparagus, oil, garlic, and pepper. Spread the asparagus on a large, rimmed baking sheet and roast for 10 minutes, stirring a few times. Remove the pan from the oven, and spoon the asparagus into a large serving bowl. 3. While the asparagus is roasting, in a medium saucepan, bring the water to a boil. Add the couscous and salt. Reduce the heat to medium-low, cover, and cook for 12 minutes, or until the water is absorbed. 4. Pour the hot couscous into the bowl with the asparagus. Add the goat cheese, mix thoroughly until completely melted, and serve.
Per Serving:
calories: 98 | fat: 1g | protein: 10g | carbs: 14g | fiber:4g | sodium: 262mg

White Bean Cassoulet

Prep time: 30 minutes | Cook time: 45 minutes | Serves 8

- 1 tablespoon olive oil
- 1 medium onion, peeled and diced
- 2 cups dried cannellini beans, soaked overnight and drained
- 1 medium parsnip, peeled and diced
- 2 medium carrots, peeled and diced
- 2 stalks celery, diced
- 1 medium zucchini,
- trimmed and chopped
- ½ teaspoon fennel seed
- ¼ teaspoon ground nutmeg
- ½ teaspoon garlic powder
- 1 teaspoon sea salt
- ½ teaspoon ground black pepper
- 2 cups vegetable broth
- 1 (14½-ounce / 411-g) can diced tomatoes, including juice
- 2 sprigs rosemary

1. Press the Sauté button on the Instant Pot® and heat oil. Add onion and cook until translucent, about 5 minutes. Add beans and toss. 2. Add a layer of parsnip, then a layer of carrots, and next a layer of celery. Finally, add a layer of zucchini. Sprinkle in fennel seed, nutmeg, garlic powder, salt, and pepper. Press the Cancel button. 3. Gently pour in broth and canned tomatoes. Top with rosemary. 4. Close lid, set steam release to Sealing, press the Bean button, and cook for the default time of 30 minutes. When the timer beeps, let pressure release naturally for 10 minutes. Quick-release any remaining pressure until the float valve drops and open lid. Press the Cancel button. 5. Press the Sauté button, then press the

Adjust button to change the temperature to Less, and simmer bean mixture uncovered for 10 minutes to thicken. Transfer to a serving bowl and carefully toss. Remove and discard rosemary and serve.
Per Serving:
calories: 128 | fat: 2g | protein: 6g | carbs: 21g | fiber: 5g | sodium: 387mg

Farro and Mushroom Risotto

Prep time: 10 minutes | Cook time: 20 minutes | Serves 6

- 2 tablespoons olive oil
- 1 medium yellow onion, peeled and diced
- 16 ounces (454 g) sliced button mushrooms
- ½ teaspoon salt
- ½ teaspoon ground black pepper
- ½ teaspoon dried thyme
- ½ teaspoon dried oregano
- 1 clove garlic, peeled and minced
- 1 cup farro, rinsed and drained
- 1½ cups vegetable broth
- ¼ cup grated Parmesan cheese
- 2 tablespoons minced fresh flat-leaf parsley

1. Press the Sauté button on the Instant Pot® and heat oil. Add onion and mushrooms and sauté 8 minutes. Add salt, pepper, thyme, and oregano and cook 30 seconds. Add garlic and cook for 30 seconds. Press the Cancel button. 2. Stir in farro and broth. Close lid, set steam release to Sealing, press the Manual button, and set time to 10 minutes. When timer beeps, let pressure release naturally for 10 minutes, then quick-release the remaining pressure until the float valve drops. 3. Top with cheese and parsley before serving.
Per Serving:
calories: 215 | fat: 8g | protein: 11g | carbs: 24g | fiber: 3g | sodium: 419mg

Bulgur Salad with Cucumbers, Olives, and Dill

Prep time: 10 minutes | Cook time: 12 minutes | Serves 4

- 1 cup bulgur wheat
- 2 cups water
- ¼ cup olive oil
- 2 tablespoons balsamic vinegar
- 1 clove garlic, peeled and minced
- ½ teaspoon ground black pepper
- ½ teaspoon salt
- 1 large English cucumber, chopped
- ½ medium red onion, peeled and diced
- ¼ cup chopped salt-cured olives
- ¼ cup chopped fresh dill

1. Add bulgur and water to the Instant Pot® and stir well. Close lid, set steam release to Sealing, press the Rice button, adjust pressure to Low, and set time to 12 minutes. When the timer beeps, quick-release the pressure until the float valve drops. Open lid and fluff bulgur with a fork. Transfer to a medium bowl and set aside to cool to room temperature, about 40 minutes. 2. Stir in oil, vinegar, garlic, pepper, salt, cucumber, onion, olives, and dill, and toss well. Refrigerate for 4 hours before serving.
Per Serving:
calories: 290 | fat: 27g | protein: 2g | carbs: 11g | fiber: 2g | sodium: 352mg

Prassorizo (Leeks and Rice)

Prep time: 10 minutes | Cook time: 12 minutes | Serves 6

- 6 large leeks
- 5 cups water
- 4 scallions, chopped
- ⅓ cup minced fresh dill
- ¼ cup minced fresh mint
- ½ tablespoon dried thyme
- ½ teaspoon salt
- ¼ teaspoon ground black pepper
- 1 cup Arborio rice
- ⅓ cup extra-virgin olive oil
- 3 tablespoons lemon juice

1. Cut white ends of leeks into thick slices. Discard green part of leeks. 2. Place leeks, water, scallions, dill, mint, thyme, salt, and pepper in the Instant Pot®. Stir well. Add rice and stir to combine. 3. Close lid, set steam release to Sealing, press the Rice button, and set time to 12 minutes. When the timer beeps, let pressure release naturally for 10 minutes, then quick-release the remaining pressure. 4. Open lid and stir well. Add olive oil and lemon juice. Serve hot.

Per Serving:
calories: 224 | fat: 12g | protein: 4g | carbs: 28g | fiber: 4g | sodium: 408mg

Gigantes (Greek Roasted Butter Beans)

Prep time: 10 minutes | Cook time: 1 hour 45 minutes | Serves 4

- 1 pound (454 g) uncooked gigantes or butter beans
- 2 bay leaves
- ¾ cup extra virgin olive oil, divided
- 2 medium red onions, chopped
- 4 garlic cloves, thinly sliced
- 1½ cups canned crushed tomatoes
- 2 tablespoons tomato paste mixed with 2 tablespoonsp
- water
- 1 teaspoon paprika
- 1 teaspoon dried oregano
- 3 tablespoons chopped fresh parsley
- 2 tablespoons chopped fresh dill
- 1 teaspoon fine sea salt, divided
- ¼ teaspoon freshly ground black pepper
- Pinch of kosher salt

1. Place the beans in a large bowl and cover with cold water. Soak for 10 hours or overnight, then drain and rinse. 2. When ready to cook, add the beans to a large pot and fill the pot with enough fresh water to cover the beans. Add the bay leaves and place the pot over high heat. Bring the beans to a boil, cover, and reduce the heat to low. Simmer for about 40 minutes to 1 hour or until the beans are soft but not mushy. 3. While the beans are cooking, begin preparing the sauce by adding ¼ cup olive oil to a medium pan placed over medium heat. When the oil begins to shimmer, add the onions and sauté for 5 minutes or until the onions are soft. Add the garlic and sauté for 1 more minute. 4. Add the crushed tomatoes, tomato paste mixture, paprika, oregano, parsley, dill, ½ teaspoon of the sea salt, black pepper, and another ¼ cup of the olive oil, then stir to combine. Let the sauce simmer for about 10 minutes or until it thickens. 5. Preheat the oven to 350° (180°C). When the beans are done cooking, remove them from the heat. Reserve 2 cups of the cooking water, drain the remaining water from the pot, and remove the bay leaves. 6. Add the sauce to the beans, then add the remaining ½ teaspoon of sea salt, and mix gently. Pour the mixture into a baking dish and spread it evenly. Add the reserved cooking water to one corner of the dish and tilt the dish to spread the water across the beans. Drizzle the remaining ¼ cup of olive oil over the beans. Transfer the beans to the oven and bake for 45 minutes or until the sauce is thick and the beans are tender. 7. Remove the beans from the oven and set aside to cool for 15 minutes. Sprinkle a pinch of kosher salt over the top before serving warm or at room temperature. Store covered in the refrigerator for up to 3 days.

Per Serving:
calories: 564 | fat: 42g | protein: 2g | carbs: 13g | fiber: 3g | sodium: 596mg

Quinoa, Broccoli, and Baby Potatoes

Prep time: 10 minutes | Cook time: 5 minutes | Serves 4

- 2 tablespoons olive oil
- 1 cup baby potatoes, cut in half
- 1 cup broccoli florets
- 2 cups cooked quinoa
- Zest of 1 lemon
- Sea salt and freshly ground pepper, to taste

1. Heat the olive oil in a large skillet. 2. Add the potatoes and cook until tender and golden brown. Add the broccoli and cook until soft, about 3 minutes. 3. Remove from heat and add the quinoa and lemon zest. Season and serve.

Per Serving:
calories: 204 | fat: 9g | protein: 5g | carbs: 27g | fiber: 4g | sodium: 12mg

Fava Beans with Ground Meat

Prep time: 15 minutes | Cook time: 6 to 8 hours | Serves 6

- 8 ounces (227 g) raw ground meat
- 1 pound (454 g) dried fava beans, rinsed well under cold water and picked over to remove debris, or 1 (15-ounce/ 425-g) can fava beans, drained and rinsed
- 10 cups water or 5 cups water and 5 cups low-sodium vegetable broth
- 1 small onion, diced
- 1 bell pepper, any color, seeded and diced
- 1 teaspoon sea salt
- 1 teaspoon garlic powder
- 1 teaspoon dried parsley
- 1 teaspoon dried oregano
- 1 teaspoon paprika
- 1 teaspoon cayenne pepper
- ½ teaspoon freshly ground black pepper
- ½ teaspoon dried thyme

1. In a large skillet over medium-high heat, cook the ground meat for 3 to 5 minutes, stirring and breaking it up with a spoon, until it has browned and is no longer pink. Drain any grease and put the meat in a slow cooker. 2. Add the fava beans, water, onion, bell pepper, salt, garlic powder, parsley, oregano, paprika, cayenne pepper, black pepper, and thyme to the meat. Stir to mix well. 3. Cover the cooker and cook for 6 to 8 hours on Low heat, or until the beans are tender.

Per Serving:
calories: 308 | fat: 4g | protein: 26g | carbs: 43g | fiber: 19g | sodium: 417mg

Earthy Lentil and Rice Pilaf

Prep time: 5 minutes | Cook time: 50 minutes | Serves 6

- ¼ cup extra-virgin olive oil
- 1 large onion, chopped
- 6 cups water
- 1 teaspoon ground cumin
- 1 teaspoon salt
- 2 cups brown lentils, picked over and rinsed
- 1 cup basmati rice

1. In a medium pot over medium heat, cook the olive oil and onions for 7 to 10 minutes until the edges are browned. 2. Turn the heat to high, add the water, cumin, and salt, and bring this mixture to a boil, boiling for about 3 minutes. 3. Add the lentils and turn the heat to medium-low. Cover the pot and cook for 20 minutes, stirring occasionally. 4. Stir in the rice and cover; cook for an additional 20 minutes. 5. Fluff the rice with a fork and serve warm.

Per Serving:
calories: 397 | fat: 11g | protein: 18g | carbs: 60g | fiber: 18g | sodium: 396mg

Lentil Bowl

Prep time: 10 minutes | Cook time: 6 to 8 hours | Serves 6

- 1 cup dried lentils, any color, rinsed well under cold water and picked over to remove debris
- 3 cups low-sodium vegetable broth
- 1 (15-ounce/ 425-g) can no-salt-added diced tomatoes
- 1 small onion, chopped
- 3 celery stalks, chopped
- 3 carrots, chopped
- 3 garlic cloves, minced
- 2 tablespoons Italian seasoning
- 1 teaspoon sea salt
- ½ teaspoon freshly ground black pepper
- 2 bay leaves
- 1 tablespoon freshly squeezed lemon juice

1. In a slow cooker, combine the lentils, vegetable broth, tomatoes, onion, celery, carrots, garlic, Italian seasoning, salt, pepper, and bay leaves. Stir to mix well. 2. Cover the cooker and cook for 6 to 8 hours on Low heat. 3. Stir in the lemon juice before serving.

Per Serving:
calories: 152 | fat: 1g | protein: 10g | carbs: 29g | fiber: 13g | sodium: 529mg

Revithosoupa (Chickpea Soup)

Prep time: 10 minutes | Cook time: 30 minutes | Serves 8

- 1 pound (454 g) dried chickpeas
- 4 cups water
- ¾ teaspoon salt
- ½ teaspoon ground black pepper
- 10 strands saffron
- 2 medium onions, peeled and diced
- 1 cup extra-virgin olive oil
- 1 teaspoon dried oregano
- 3 tablespoons lemon juice
- 2 tablespoons chopped fresh parsley

1. Add chickpeas, water, salt, pepper, saffron, onions, oil, and oregano to the Instant Pot® and stir well. Close lid, set steam release to Sealing, press the Bean button, and cook for the default time of 30 minutes. 2. When the timer beeps, let pressure release naturally, about 25 minutes. Open lid. Serve hot or cold, sprinkled with lemon juice. Garnish with chopped parsley.

Per Serving:
calories: 464 | fat: 30g | protein: 12g | carbs: 38g | fiber: 10g | sodium: 236mg

Lentil Pâté

Prep time: 10 minutes | Cook time: 34 minutes | Serves 12

- 2 tablespoons olive oil, divided
- 1 cup diced yellow onion
- 3 cloves garlic, peeled and minced
- 1 teaspoon red wine vinegar
- 2 cups dried green lentils, rinsed and drained
- 4 cups water
- 1 teaspoon salt
- ¼ teaspoon ground black pepper

1. Press the Sauté button on the Instant Pot® and heat 1 tablespoon oil. Add onion and cook until translucent, about 3 minutes. Add garlic and vinegar, and cook for 30 seconds. Add lentils, water, remaining 1 tablespoon oil, and salt to pot and stir to combine. Press the Cancel button. 2. Close lid, set steam release to Sealing, press the Bean button, and allow to cook for default time of 30 minutes. When the timer beeps, let pressure release naturally for 10 minutes. Quick-release any remaining pressure until the float valve drops, then open lid. 3. Transfer lentil mixture to a food processor or blender, and blend until smooth. Season with pepper and serve warm.

Per Serving:
calories: 138 | fat: 3g | protein: 8g | carbs: 20g | fiber: 10g | sodium: 196mg

Lentil and Spinach Curry

Prep time: 10 minutes | Cook time: 17 minutes | Serves 4

- 1 tablespoon olive oil
- ½ cup diced onion
- 1 clove garlic, peeled and minced
- 1 cup dried yellow lentils, rinsed and drained
- 4 cups water
- ½ teaspoon ground coriander
- ½ teaspoon ground turmeric
- ½ teaspoon curry powder
- ½ cup diced tomatoes
- 5 ounces (142 g) baby spinach leaves

1. Press the Sauté button on the Instant Pot® and heat oil. Add onion and cook until translucent, about 5 minutes. Add garlic and cook for 30 seconds. Add lentils and toss to combine. Press the Cancel button. 2. Pour in water. Close lid, set steam release to Sealing, press the Manual button, and set time to 6 minutes. When the timer beeps, quick-release the pressure until the float valve drops and open lid. Press the Cancel button. Drain any residual liquid. Stir in coriander, turmeric, curry powder, tomatoes, and spinach. 3. Press the Sauté button, press the Adjust button to change the heat to Less, and simmer uncovered until tomatoes are heated through and spinach has wilted, about 5 minutes. 4. Transfer to a dish and serve.

Per Serving:
calories: 195 | fat: 4g | protein: 13g | carbs: 26g | fiber: 8g | sodium: 111mg

Mediterranean Lentil Casserole

Prep time: 15 minutes | Cook time: 8 to 10 hours | Serves 6

- 1 pound (454 g) lentils, rinsed well under cold water and picked over to remove debris
- 4 cups low-sodium vegetable broth
- 3 carrots, diced
- 3 cups chopped kale
- 1 small onion, diced
- 2 garlic cloves, minced
- 1 teaspoon sea salt
- 1 teaspoon dried basil
- 1 teaspoon dried oregano
- ½ teaspoon dried parsley
- 1 lemon, thinly sliced

1. In a slow cooker, combine the lentils, vegetable broth, carrots, kale, onion, garlic, salt, basil, oregano, and parsley. Stir to mix well. 2. Cover the cooker and cook for 8 to 10 hours on Low heat, or until the lentils are tender. 3. Garnish with lemon slices for serving.

Per Serving:
calories: 302 | fat: 2g | protein: 22g | carbs: 54g | fiber: 26g | sodium: 527mg

No-Stir Polenta with Arugula, Figs, and Blue Cheese

Prep time: 15 minutes | Cook time: 40 minutes | Serves 4

- 1 cup coarse-ground cornmeal
- ½ cup oil-packed sun-dried tomatoes, chopped
- 1 teaspoon minced fresh thyme or ¼ teaspoon dried
- ½ teaspoon table salt
- ¼ teaspoon pepper
- 3 tablespoons extra-virgin olive oil, divided
- 2 ounces (57 g) baby arugula
- 4 figs, cut into ½-inch-thick wedges
- 1 tablespoon balsamic vinegar
- 2 ounces (57 g) blue cheese, crumbled (½ cup)
- 2 tablespoons pine nuts, toasted

1. Arrange trivet included with Instant Pot in base of insert and add 1 cup water. Fold sheet of aluminum foil into 16 by 6-inch sling, then rest 1½-quart round soufflé dish in center of sling. Whisk 4 cups water, cornmeal, tomatoes, thyme, salt, and pepper together in bowl, then transfer mixture to soufflé dish. Using sling, lower soufflé dish into pot and onto trivet; allow narrow edges of sling to rest along sides of insert. 2. Lock lid in place and close pressure release valve. Select high pressure cook function and cook for 40 minutes. Turn off Instant Pot and quick-release pressure. Carefully remove lid, allowing steam to escape away from you. 3. Using sling, transfer soufflé dish to wire rack. Whisk 1 tablespoon oil into polenta, smoothing out any lumps. Let sit until thickened slightly, about 10 minutes. Season with salt and pepper to taste. 4. Toss arugula and figs with vinegar and remaining 2 tablespoons oil in bowl, and season with salt and pepper to taste. Divide polenta among individual serving plates and top with arugula mixture, blue cheese, and pine nuts. Serve.

Per Serving:
calories: 360 | fat: 21g | protein: 7g | carbs: 38g | fiber: 8g | sodium: 510mg

Chapter
4

Fish and Seafood

Chapter 4 Fish and Seafood

Shrimp Salad

Prep time: 30 minutes | Cook time: 5 minutes | Serves 4

For the Vinaigrette:
- ⅛ cup red wine vinegar
- Juice of 1 lemon
- 1 small shallot, finely minced
- 1 tablespoon fresh mint, chopped
- ¼ teaspoon dried oregano
- ¼ cup olive oil
- Sea salt and freshly ground pepper, to taste

For the Salad:
- 1 pound (454 g) shrimp, deveined and shelled
- Juice and zest of 1 lemon
- 1 clove garlic, minced
- 2 cups baby spinach leaves
- 1 cup romaine lettuce, chopped
- ½ cup grape tomatoes
- 1 medium cucumber, peeled, seeded, and diced
- ½ cup low-salt olives, pitted
- ¼ cup low-fat feta cheese

Make the vinaigrette: 1. Combine the wine vinegar, lemon juice, shallot, chopped mint, and oregano in a bowl. 2. Add the olive oil, whisking constantly for up to 1 minute, or until you create a smooth emulsion, then season with sea salt and freshly ground pepper. 3. Refrigerate for 1 hour and whisk before serving if separated. Make the salad: 1. Combine the shrimp with the lemon juice and garlic in a shallow bowl or bag. Marinate for at least 2 hours. 2. Grill the shrimp in a grill basket or sauté in a frying pan 2–3 minutes until pink. 3. In a large bowl, toss the greens, tomatoes, cucumber, olives, and feta cheese together. 4. Toss the shrimp with the salad mixture, and drizzle with the vinaigrette. Serve immediately.

Per Serving:
calories: 284 | fat: 18g | protein: 26g | carbs: 6g | fiber: 2g | sodium: 339mg

Italian Tuna Roast

Prep time: 15 minutes | Cook time: 21 to 24 minutes | Serves 8

- Cooking spray
- 1 tablespoon Italian seasoning
- ⅛ teaspoon ground black pepper
- 1 tablespoon extra-light olive oil
- 1 teaspoon lemon juice
- 1 tuna loin (approximately 2 pounds / 907 g, 3 to 4 inches thick)

1. Spray baking dish with cooking spray and place in air fryer basket. Preheat the air fryer to 390°F (199°C). 2. Mix together the Italian seasoning, pepper, oil, and lemon juice. 3. Using a dull table knife or butter knife, pierce top of tuna about every half inch: Insert knife into top of tuna roast and pierce almost all the way to the bottom. 4. Spoon oil mixture into each of the holes and use the knife to push seasonings into the tuna as deeply as possible. 5. Spread any remaining oil mixture on all outer surfaces of tuna. 6.

Place tuna roast in baking dish and roast at 390°F (199°C) for 20 minutes. Check temperature with a meat thermometer. Cook for an additional 1 to 4 minutes or until temperature reaches 145°F (63°C). 7. Remove basket from the air fryer and let tuna sit in the basket for 10 minutes.

Per Serving:
calories: 178 | fat: 7g | protein: 26g | carbs: 0g | fiber: 0g | sodium: 44mg

Steamed Shrimp and Asparagus

Prep time: 15 minutes | Cook time: 1 minute | Serves 4

- 1 cup water
- 1 bunch asparagus, trimmed
- ½ teaspoon salt, divided
- 1 pound (454 g) shrimp, peeled and deveined
- 1½ tablespoons lemon juice
- 2 tablespoons olive oil

1. Pour water into the Instant Pot®. Insert rack and place steamer basket onto rack. 2. Spread asparagus on the bottom of the steamer basket. Sprinkle with ¼ teaspoon salt. Add shrimp. Drizzle with lemon juice and sprinkle with remaining ¼ teaspoon salt. Drizzle olive oil over shrimp. 3. Close lid, set steam release to Sealing, press the Manual button, and set time to 1 minute. When the timer beeps, quick-release the pressure until the float valve drops and open lid. 4. Transfer shrimp and asparagus to a platter and serve.

Per Serving:
calories: 145 | fat: 8g | protein: 19g | carbs: 1g | fiber: 0g | sodium: 295mg

Balsamic-Glazed Black Pepper Salmon

Prep time: 5 minutes | Cook time: 8 minutes | Serves 4

- ½ cup balsamic vinegar
- 1 tablespoon honey
- 4 (8-ounce / 227-g) salmon fillets
- Sea salt and freshly ground pepper, to taste
- 1 tablespoon olive oil

1. Heat a cast-iron skillet over medium-high heat. Mix the vinegar and honey in a small bowl. 2. Season the salmon fillets with the sea salt and freshly ground pepper; brush with the honey-balsamic glaze. 3. Add olive oil to the skillet, and sear the salmon fillets, cooking for 3–4 minutes on each side until lightly browned and medium rare in the center. 4. Let sit for 5 minutes before serving.

Per Serving:
calories: 478 | fat: 17g | protein: 65g | carbs: 10g | fiber: 0g | sodium: 246mg

Sicilian Baked Cod with Herbed Breadcrumbs

Prep time: 5 minutes | Cook time: 25 minutes | Serves 4

- 2 tablespoons olive oil, divided
- 1 medium red onion, halved and cut into half circles
- 1 tablespoon red wine vinegar
- ¾ teaspoon salt, divided, plus more for seasoning
- ¼ teaspoon freshly ground black pepper, plus more for seasoning
- ½ teaspoon anchovy paste
- 3 tablespoons dried breadcrumbs
- 2 tablespoons chopped flat-leaf parsley
- 2 tablespoons chopped fresh mint leaves
- 2 tablespoons chopped fresh basil leaves
- 4 (6-ounce / 170-g) cod fillets
- ½ cup dry white wine

1. Preheat the oven to 400ºF (205ºC). 2. Heat 1 tablespoon of olive oil in a medium skillet over medium-high heat. Add the onion and cook, stirring frequently, until softened, about 5 minutes. Add the vinegar and season with the salt and pepper. Cook for about 30 seconds more. Spread the onions into an even layer in a baking dish large enough to hold the fish in a single layer. 3. Heat the remaining 1 tablespoon of olive oil in the same skillet over low heat. Add the anchovy paste and cook, stirring, for about 1 minute. Add the breadcrumbs and toss to coat them in oil. Remove the breadcrumbs to a bowl and let them cool a bit. Add the parsley, mint, and basil, ¼ teaspoon of salt, and a pinch of pepper. 4. Arrange the fish fillets on top of the onions and season with the remaining ½ teaspoon of salt and ¼ teaspoon of pepper. Sprinkle the breadcrumbs equally over the fillets. Pour the wine into the dish. 5. Bake, adding a little more wine or water if necessary until cooked through, about 10 to 15 minutes, depending on the thickness of the fish fillets. Serve hot.

Per Serving:
calories: 299 | fat: 10g | protein: 40g | carbs: 8g | fiber: 1g | sodium: 652mg

Linguine with Clams and White Wine

Prep time: 20 minutes | Cook time: 12 minutes | Serves 4

- 2 tablespoons olive oil
- 4 cups sliced mushrooms
- 1 medium yellow onion, peeled and diced
- 2 tablespoons chopped fresh oregano
- 3 cloves garlic, peeled and minced
- ¼ teaspoon salt
- ¼ teaspoon ground black pepper
- ½ cup white wine
- 1½ cups water
- 8 ounces (227 g) linguine, broken in half
- 1 pound (454 g) fresh clams, rinsed and purged
- 3 tablespoons lemon juice
- ¼ cup grated Parmesan cheese
- 2 tablespoons chopped fresh parsley

1. Press the Sauté button on the Instant Pot® and heat oil. Add mushrooms and onion. Cook until tender, about 5 minutes. Add oregano, garlic, salt, and pepper, and cook until very fragrant, about 30 seconds. Add wine, water, and pasta, pushing pasta down until submerged in liquid. Press the Cancel button. 2. Top pasta with clams and sprinkle lemon juice on top. Close lid, set steam release to Sealing, press the Manual button, and set time to 5 minutes. When the timer beeps, quick-release the pressure until the float valve drops and open lid. Transfer to a serving bowl and top with cheese and parsley. Serve immediately.

Per Serving:
calories: 486 | fat: 11g | protein: 39g | carbs: 52g | fiber: 5g | sodium: 301mg

Baked Spanish Salmon

Prep time: 10 minutes | Cook time: 20 minutes | Serves 4

- 2 small red onions, thinly sliced
- 1 cup shaved fennel bulbs
- 1 cup cherry tomatoes
- 15 green pimiento-stuffed olives
- Salt
- Freshly ground black pepper
- 1 teaspoon cumin seeds
- ½ teaspoon smoked paprika
- 4 (8-ounce / 227-g) salmon fillets
- ½ cup low-sodium chicken broth
- 2 to 4 tablespoons extra-virgin olive oil
- 2 cups cooked couscous

1. Put the oven racks in the middle of the oven and preheat the oven to 375ºF. 2. On 2 baking sheets, spread out the onions, fennel, tomatoes, and olives. Season them with salt, pepper, cumin, and paprika. 3. Place the fish over the vegetables, season with salt, and gently pour the broth over the 2 baking sheets. Drizzle a light stream of olive oil over baking sheets before popping them in the oven. 4. Bake the vegetables and fish for 20 minutes, checking halfway to ensure nothing is burning. Serve over couscous.

Per Serving:
calories: 476 | fat: 18g | protein: 50g | carbs: 26g | fiber: 3g | sodium: 299mg

Pan-Roasted Wild Cod with Tomatoes, Olives, and Artichokes

Prep time: 10 minutes | Cook time: 20 minutes | Serves 2

- 1 tablespoon olive oil
- ½ medium onion, minced
- 2 garlic cloves, minced
- 1 teaspoon oregano
- 1 (15-ounce / 425-g) can diced tomatoes with basil
- 1 (15-ounce / 425-g) can artichoke hearts in water,
- drained and halved
- ¼ cup pitted Greek olives, drained
- 10 ounces (283 g) wild cod (2 smaller pieces may fit better in the pan)
- Salt
- Freshly ground black pepper

1. Heat olive oil in a sauté pan over medium-high heat. Add the onion and sauté for about 10 minutes, or until golden. Add the garlic and oregano and cook for another 30 seconds. 2. Mix in the tomatoes, artichoke hearts, and olives. 3. Place the cod on top of the vegetables. Cover the pan and cook for 10 minutes, or until the fish is opaque and flakes apart easily. Season with salt and pepper.

Per Serving:
calories: 346 | fat: 10g | protein: 34g | carbs: 35g | fiber: 17g | sodium: 423mg

South Indian Fried Fish

Prep time: 20 minutes | Cook time: 8 minutes | Serves 4

- 2 tablespoons olive oil
- 2 tablespoons fresh lime or lemon juice
- 1 teaspoon minced fresh ginger
- 1 clove garlic, minced
- 1 teaspoon ground turmeric
- ½ teaspoon kosher salt
- ¼ to ½ teaspoon cayenne pepper
- 1 pound (454 g) tilapia fillets (2 to 3 fillets)
- Olive oil spray
- Lime or lemon wedges (optional)

1. In a large bowl, combine the oil, lime juice, ginger, garlic, turmeric, salt, and cayenne. Stir until well combined; set aside. 2. Cut each tilapia fillet into three or four equal-size pieces. Add the fish to the bowl and gently mix until all of the fish is coated in the marinade. Marinate for 10 to 15 minutes at room temperature. (Don't marinate any longer or the acid in the lime juice will "cook" the fish.) 3. Spray the air fryer basket with olive oil spray. Place the fish in the basket and spray the fish. Set the air fryer to 325°F (163°C) for 3 minutes to partially cook the fish. Set the air fryer to 400°F (204°C) for 5 minutes to finish cooking and crisp up the fish. (Thinner pieces of fish will cook faster so you may want to check at the 3-minute mark of the second cooking time and remove those that are cooked through, and then add them back toward the end of the second cooking time to crisp.) 4. Carefully remove the fish from the basket. Serve hot, with lemon wedges if desired.

Per Serving:
calories: 175 | fat: 9g | protein: 23g | carbs: 2g | fiber: 0g | sodium: 350mg

Quick Seafood Paella

Prep time: 20 minutes | Cook time: 20 minutes | Serves 4

- ¼ cup plus 1 tablespoon extra-virgin olive oil
- 1 large onion, finely chopped
- 2 tomatoes, peeled and chopped
- 1½ tablespoons garlic powder
- 1½ cups medium-grain Spanish paella rice or arborio rice
- 2 carrots, finely diced
- Salt
- 1 tablespoon sweet paprika
- 8 ounces (227 g) lobster meat or canned crab
- ½ cup frozen peas
- 3 cups chicken stock, plus more if needed
- 1 cup dry white wine
- 6 jumbo shrimp, unpeeled
- ⅓ pound calamari rings
- 1 lemon, halved

1. In a large sauté pan or skillet (16-inch is ideal), heat the oil over medium heat until small bubbles start to escape from oil. Add the onion and cook for about 3 minutes, until fragrant, then add tomatoes and garlic powder. Cook for 5 to 10 minutes, until the tomatoes are reduced by half and the consistency is sticky. 2. Stir in the rice, carrots, salt, paprika, lobster, and peas and mix well. In a pot or microwave-safe bowl, heat the chicken stock to almost boiling, then add it to the rice mixture. Bring to a simmer, then add the wine. 3. Smooth out the rice in the bottom of the pan. Cover and cook on low for 10 minutes, mixing occasionally, to prevent burning. 4. Top the rice with the shrimp, cover, and cook for 5 more minutes. Add additional broth to the pan if the rice looks dried out. 5. Right before removing the skillet from the heat, add the calamari

rings. Toss the ingredients frequently. In about 2 minutes, the rings will look opaque. Remove the pan from the heat immediately—you don't want the paella to overcook). Squeeze fresh lemon juice over the dish.

Per Serving:
calories: 613 | fat: 15g | protein: 26g | carbs: 86g | fiber: 7g | sodium: 667mg

Baked Monkfish

Prep time: 20 minutes | Cook time: 12 minutes | Serves 2

- 2 teaspoons olive oil
- 1 cup celery, sliced
- 2 bell peppers, sliced
- 1 teaspoon dried thyme
- ½ teaspoon dried marjoram
- ½ teaspoon dried rosemary
- 2 monkfish fillets
- 1 tablespoon coconut
- aminos
- 2 tablespoons lime juice
- Coarse salt and ground black pepper, to taste
- 1 teaspoon cayenne pepper
- ½ cup Kalamata olives, pitted and sliced

1. In a nonstick skillet, heat the olive oil for 1 minute. Once hot, sauté the celery and peppers until tender, about 4 minutes. Sprinkle with thyme, marjoram, and rosemary and set aside. 2. Toss the fish fillets with the coconut aminos, lime juice, salt, black pepper, and cayenne pepper. Place the fish fillets in the lightly greased air fryer basket and bake at 390°F (199°C) for 8 minutes. 3. Turn them over, add the olives, and cook an additional 4 minutes. Serve with the sautéed vegetables on the side. Bon appétit!

Per Serving:
calories: 263 | fat: 11g | protein: 27g | carbs: 13g | fiber: 5g | sodium: 332mg

Mussels with Fennel and Leeks

Prep time: 20 minutes | Cook time: 6 minutes | Serves 4

- 1 tablespoon extra-virgin olive oil, plus extra for drizzling
- 1 fennel bulb, 1 tablespoon fronds minced, stalks discarded, bulb halved, cored, and sliced thin
- 1 leek, ends trimmed, leek halved lengthwise, sliced
- 1 inch thick, and washed thoroughly
- 4 garlic cloves, minced
- 3 sprigs fresh thyme
- ¼ teaspoon red pepper flakes
- ½ cup dry white wine
- 3 pounds (1.4 kg) mussels, scrubbed and debearded

1. Using highest sauté function, heat oil in Instant Pot until shimmering. Add fennel and leek and cook until softened, about 5 minutes. Stir in garlic, thyme sprigs, and pepper flakes and cook until fragrant, about 30 seconds. Stir in wine, then add mussels. 2. Lock lid in place and close pressure release valve. Select high pressure cook function and set cook time for 0 minutes. Once Instant Pot has reached pressure, immediately turn off pot and quick-release pressure. Carefully remove lid, allowing steam to escape away from you. 3. Discard thyme sprigs and any mussels that have not opened. Transfer mussels to individual serving bowls, sprinkle with fennel fronds, and drizzle with extra oil. Serve.

Per Serving:
calories: 384 | fat: 11g | protein: 42g | carbs: 23g | fiber: 2g | sodium: 778mg

Citrus Swordfish

Prep time: 10 minutes | Cook time: 1½ hours | Serves 2

- Nonstick cooking oil spray
- 1½ pounds (680 g) swordfish fillets
- Sea salt
- Black pepper
- 1 yellow onion, chopped
- 5 tablespoons chopped fresh flat-leaf parsley
- 1 tablespoon olive oil
- 2 teaspoons lemon zest
- 2 teaspoons orange zest
- Orange and lemon slices, for garnish
- Fresh parsley sprigs, for garnish

1. Coat the interior of the slow cooker crock with nonstick cooking oil spray. 2. Season the fish fillets with salt and pepper. Place the fish in the slow cooker. 3. Distribute the onion, parsley, olive oil, lemon zest, and orange zest over fish. 4. Cover and cook on low for 1½ hours. 5. Serve hot, garnished with orange and lemon slices and sprigs of fresh parsley.

Per Serving:
calories: 578 | fat: 30g | protein: 68g | carbs: 7g | fiber: 2g | sodium: 283mg

Grilled Herbed Tuna

Prep time: 10 minutes | Cook time: 12 minutes | Serves 4

- 2 tablespoons olive oil
- 2 tablespoons fresh basil, chopped
- Juice and zest of 1 lemon
- 2 teaspoons fresh cilantro, chopped
- 1 clove garlic, minced
- Sea salt and freshly ground pepper, to taste
- 4 fresh tuna steaks
- 2 tablespoons flat-leaf parsley, chopped

1. Preheat the grill to medium-high. 2. Combine all the ingredients except the fish and parsley in a bowl. Brush each side of the tuna with the herb mixture, and let marinate for at least 30 minutes in the refrigerator. 3. Grill 8–12 minutes depending on thickness, turning halfway through the cooking time. 4. Garnish with chopped parsley, season to taste, and serve immediately.

Per Serving:
calories: 472 | fat: 11g | protein: 87g | carbs: 1g | fiber: 0g | sodium: 148mg

Marinated Swordfish Skewers

Prep time: 30 minutes | Cook time: 6 to 8 minutes | Serves 4

- 1 pound (454 g) filleted swordfish
- ¼ cup avocado oil
- 2 tablespoons freshly squeezed lemon juice
- 1 tablespoon minced fresh
- parsley
- 2 teaspoons Dijon mustard
- Sea salt and freshly ground black pepper, to taste
- 3 ounces (85 g) cherry tomatoes

1. Cut the fish into 1½-inch chunks, picking out any remaining bones. 2. In a large bowl, whisk together the oil, lemon juice, parsley, and Dijon mustard. Season to taste with salt and pepper. Add the fish and toss to coat the pieces. Cover and marinate the fish

chunks in the refrigerator for 30 minutes. 3. Remove the fish from the marinade. Thread the fish and cherry tomatoes on 4 skewers, alternating as you go. 4. Set the air fryer to 400°F (204°C). Place the skewers in the air fryer basket and air fry for 3 minutes. Flip the skewers and cook for 3 to 5 minutes longer, until the fish is cooked through and an instant-read thermometer reads 140°F (60°C).

Per Serving:
calories: 291 | fat: 21g | protein: 23g | carbs: 2g | fiber: 0g | sodium: 121mg

Fish Gratin

Prep time: 30 minutes | Cook time: 17 minutes | Serves 4

- 1 tablespoon avocado oil
- 1 pound (454 g) hake fillets
- 1 teaspoon garlic powder
- Sea salt and ground white pepper, to taste
- 2 tablespoons shallots, chopped
- 1 bell pepper, seeded and
- chopped
- ½ cup Cottage cheese
- ½ cup sour cream
- 1 egg, well whisked
- 1 teaspoon yellow mustard
- 1 tablespoon lime juice
- ½ cup Swiss cheese, shredded

1. Brush the bottom and sides of a casserole dish with avocado oil. Add the hake fillets to the casserole dish and sprinkle with garlic powder, salt, and pepper. 2. Add the chopped shallots and bell peppers. 3. In a mixing bowl, thoroughly combine the Cottage cheese, sour cream, egg, mustard, and lime juice. Pour the mixture over fish and spread evenly. 4. Cook in the preheated air fryer at 370°F (188°C) for 10 minutes. 5. Top with the Swiss cheese and cook an additional 7 minutes. Let it rest for 10 minutes before slicing and serving. Bon appétit!

Per Serving:
calories: 256 | fat: 12g | protein: 28g | carbs: 8g | fiber: 1g | sodium: 523mg

Shrimp with Marinara Sauce

Prep time: 15 minutes | Cook time: 6 to 7 hours | Serves 4

- 1 (15-ounce / 425-g) can diced tomatoes, with the juice
- 1 (6-ounce / 170-g) can tomato paste
- 1 clove garlic, minced
- 2 tablespoons minced fresh flat-leaf parsley
- ½ teaspoon dried basil
- 1 teaspoon dried oregano
- 1 teaspoon garlic powder
- 1½ teaspoons sea salt
- ¼ teaspoon black pepper
- 1 pound (454 g) cooked shrimp, peeled and deveined
- 2 cups hot cooked spaghetti or linguine, for serving
- ½ cup grated parmesan cheese, for serving

1. Combine the tomatoes, tomato paste, and minced garlic in the slow cooker. Sprinkle with the parsley, basil, oregano, garlic powder, salt, and pepper. 2. Cover and cook on low for 6 to 7 hours. 3. Turn up the heat to high, stir in the cooked shrimp, and cover and cook on high for about 15 minutes longer. 4. Serve hot over the cooked pasta. Top with Parmesan cheese.

Per Serving:
calories: 313 | fat: 5g | protein: 39g | carbs: 32g | fiber: 7g | sodium: 876mg

Salmon Poached in Red Wine

Prep time: 15 minutes | Cook time: 16 minutes | Serves 6

- 1 medium onion, peeled and quartered
- 2 cloves garlic, peeled and smashed
- 1 stalk celery, diced
- 1 bay leaf
- ½ teaspoon dried thyme
- 3½ cups water
- 2 cups dry red wine
- 2 tablespoons red wine vinegar
- ½ teaspoon salt
- ½ teaspoon black peppercorns
- 1 (2½-pound / 1.1-kg) center-cut salmon roast
- 1 medium lemon, cut into wedges

1. Add all ingredients except salmon and lemon to the Instant Pot®. Close lid, set steam release to Sealing, press the Manual button, and set time to 10 minutes. When the timer beeps, quick-release the pressure until the float valve drops and open lid. Press the Cancel button. 2. Set the rack in the pot and put steamer basket on rack. Wrap salmon in cheesecloth, leaving ends long enough to extend about 3". Use two sets of tongs to hold on to the 3" cheesecloth extensions and place the salmon on the rack. Close lid, set steam release to Sealing, press the Manual button, and set time to 6 minutes. When the timer beeps, let pressure release naturally for 20 minutes. 3. Quick-release any remaining pressure until the float valve drops and open lid. Use tongs to hold on to the 3" cheesecloth extensions to lift salmon out of the Instant Pot®. Set in a metal colander to allow extra moisture to drain away. When salmon is cool enough to handle, unwrap the cheesecloth. Peel away and discard any skin. 4. Transfer salmon to a serving platter. Garnish with lemon wedges.

Per Serving:
calories: 435 | fat: 24g | protein: 43g | carbs: 4g | fiber: 0g | sodium: 213mg

Cod and Cauliflower Chowder

Prep time: 15 minutes | Cook time: 40 minutes | Serves 4

- 2 tablespoons extra-virgin olive oil
- 1 leek, white and light green parts only, cut in half lengthwise and sliced thinly
- 4 garlic cloves, sliced
- 1 medium head cauliflower, coarsely chopped
- 1 teaspoon kosher salt
- ¼ teaspoon freshly ground
- black pepper
- 2 pints cherry tomatoes
- 2 cups no-salt-added vegetable stock
- ¼ cup green olives, pitted and chopped
- 1 to 1½ pounds (454 to 680 g) cod
- ¼ cup fresh parsley, minced

1. Heat the olive oil in a Dutch oven or large pot over medium heat. Add the leek and sauté until lightly golden brown, about 5 minutes. Add the garlic and sauté for 30 seconds. Add the cauliflower, salt, and black pepper and sauté 2 to 3 minutes. 2. Add the tomatoes and vegetable stock, increase the heat to high and bring to a boil, then turn the heat to low and simmer for 10 minutes. 3. Add the olives and mix together. Add the fish, cover, and simmer 20 minutes, or until fish is opaque and flakes easily. Gently mix in the parsley.

Per Serving:
calories: 270 | fat: 9g | protein: 30g | carbs: 19g | fiber: 5g | sodium: 545mg

Shrimp and Fish Chowder

Prep time: 20 minutes | Cook time: 4 to 6 hours | Serves 4

- 3 cups low-sodium vegetable broth
- 1 (28-ounce / 794-g) can no-salt-added crushed tomatoes
- 1 large bell pepper, any color, seeded and diced
- 1 large onion, diced
- 2 zucchini, chopped
- 3 garlic cloves, minced
- 1 teaspoon dried thyme
- 1 teaspoon dried basil
- ½ teaspoon sea salt
- ¼ teaspoon freshly ground black pepper
- ¼ teaspoon red pepper flakes
- 8 ounces (227 g) whole raw medium shrimp, peeled and deveined
- 8 ounces (227 g) fresh cod fillets, cut into 1-inch pieces

1. In a slow cooker, combine the vegetable broth, tomatoes, bell pepper, onion, zucchini, garlic, thyme, basil, salt, black pepper, and red pepper flakes. Stir to mix well. 2. Cover the cooker and cook for 4 to 6 hours on Low heat. 3. Stir in the shrimp and cod. Replace the cover on the cooker and cook for 15 to 30 minutes on Low heat, or until the shrimp have turned pink and the cod is firm and flaky.
Per Serving:
calories: 201 | fat: 1g | protein: 26g | carbs: 24g | fiber: 7g | sodium: 598mg

Sicilian Kale and Tuna Bowl

Prep time: 5 minutes |Cook time: 15 minutes| Serves: 6

- 1 pound (454 g) kale, chopped, center ribs removed (about 12 cups)
- 3 tablespoons extra-virgin olive oil
- 1 cup chopped onion (about ½ medium onion)
- 3 garlic cloves, minced (about 1½ teaspoons)
- 1 (2¼-ounce / 35-g) can sliced olives, drained (about ½ cup)
- ¼ cup capers
- ¼ teaspoon crushed red pepper
- 2 teaspoons sugar
- 2 (6-ounce / 170-g) cans tuna in olive oil, undrained
- 1 (15-ounce / 425-g) can cannellini beans or great northern beans, drained and rinsed
- ¼ teaspoon freshly ground black pepper
- ¼ teaspoon kosher or sea salt

1. Fill a large stockpot three-quarters full of water, and bring to a boil. Add the kale and cook for 2 minutes. (This is to make the kale less bitter.) Drain the kale in a colander and set aside. 2. Set the empty pot back on the stove over medium heat, and pour in the oil. Add the onion and cook for 4 minutes, stirring often. Add the garlic and cook for 1 minute, stirring often. Add the olives, capers, and crushed red pepper, and cook for 1 minute, stirring often. Add the partially cooked kale and sugar, stirring until the kale is completely coated with oil. Cover the pot and cook for 8 minutes. 3. Remove the kale from the heat, mix in the tuna, beans, pepper, and salt, and serve.

Per Serving:
calories: 323 | fat: 14g | protein: 26g | carbs: 26g | fiber: 7g | sodium: 653mg

Citrus Mediterranean Salmon with Lemon Caper Sauce

Prep time: 15 minutes | Cook time: 22 minutes | Serves 2

- 2 tablespoons fresh lemon juice
- ⅓ cup orange juice
- 1 tablespoon extra virgin olive oil
- ⅛ teaspoon freshly ground black pepper
- 2 (6-ounce / 170-g) salmon fillets
- Lemon Caper Sauce:
- 2 tablespoons extra virgin

- olive oil
- 1 tablespoon finely chopped red onion
- 1 garlic clove, minced
- 2 tablespoons fresh lemon juice
- 5 ounces (142) dry white wine
- 2 tablespoons capers, rinsed
- ⅛ teaspoon freshly ground black pepper

1. Preheat the oven to 350°F (180°C). 2. In a small bowl, combine the lemon juice, orange juice, olive oil, and black pepper. Whisk until blended, then pour the mixture into a zipper-lock bag. Place the fillets in the bag, shake gently, and transfer the salmon to the refrigerator to marinate for 10 minutes. 3. When the salmon is done marinating, transfer the fillets and marinade to a medium baking dish. Bake for 10–15 minutes or until the salmon is cooked through and the internal temperature reaches 165ºF (74ºC). Remove the salmon from the oven and cover loosely with foil. Set aside to rest. 4. While the salmon is resting, make the lemon caper sauce by heating the olive oil in a medium pan over medium heat. When the olive oil begins to shimmer, add the onions and sauté for 3 minutes, stirring frequently, then add the garlic and sauté for another 30 seconds. 5. Add the lemon juice and wine. Bring the mixture to a boil and cook until the sauce becomes thick, about 2–3 minutes, then remove the pan from the heat. Add the capers and black pepper, and stir. 6. Transfer the fillets to 2 plates, and spoon 1½ tablespoons of the sauce over each fillet. Store covered in the refrigerator for up to 3 days.

Per Serving:
calories: 485 | fat: 28g | protein: 36g | carbs: 11g | fiber: 1g | sodium: 331mg

Lemon-Oregano Grilled Shrimp

Prep time: 10 minutes | Cook time: 6 minutes | Serves 6

- ½ cup oregano leaves
- 1 clove garlic, minced
- 1 teaspoon finely grated lemon zest
- 3 tablespoons lemon juice
- ¾ teaspoon salt, plus more for seasoning shrimp

- ½ teaspoon freshly ground black pepper, plus more for seasoning shrimp
- ½ cup olive oil, plus 2 tablespoons, divided
- 2½ pounds (1.1 kg) large shrimp, peeled and deveined

1. In a small bowl, stir together the oregano, garlic, lemon zest, lemon juice, salt, and pepper. Whisk in ½ cup of olive oil until well combined. 2. Preheat the grill to high heat. 3. Place the shrimp in a large bowl and toss with the remaining 2 tablespoons of olive oil and a pinch or two of salt and pepper. Thread the shrimp onto skewers, 3 to 5 at a time depending on the size of the shrimp. Place the skewers on the grill and cook for 2 to 3 minutes per side, just until the shrimp are cooked through and just beginning to char. As the shrimp are cooked, transfer the skewers to a serving platter. Spoon the sauce over the skewers and serve immediately.

Per Serving:
calories: 389 | fat: 26g | protein: 36g | carbs: 8g | fiber: 3g | sodium: 530mg

Tuna Steaks with Olive Tapenade

Prep time: 10 minutes | Cook time: 10 minutes | Serves 4

- 4 (6-ounce / 170-g) ahi tuna steaks
- 1 tablespoon olive oil
- Salt and freshly ground black pepper, to taste
- ½ lemon, sliced into 4 wedges
- Olive Tapenade:

- ½ cup pitted kalamata olives
- 1 tablespoon olive oil
- 1 tablespoon chopped fresh parsley
- 1 clove garlic
- 2 teaspoons red wine vinegar
- 1 teaspoon capers, drained

1. Preheat the air fryer to 400ºF (204ºC). 2. Drizzle the tuna steaks with the olive oil and sprinkle with salt and black pepper. Arrange the tuna steaks in a single layer in the air fryer basket. Pausing to turn the steaks halfway through the cooking time, air fry for 10 minutes until the fish is firm. 3. To make the tapenade: In a food processor fitted with a metal blade, combine the olives, olive oil, parsley, garlic, vinegar, and capers. Pulse until the mixture is finely chopped, pausing to scrape down the sides of the bowl if necessary. Spoon the tapenade over the top of the tuna steaks and serve with lemon wedges.

Per Serving:
calories: 269 | fat: 9g | protein: 42g | carbs: 2g | fiber: 1g | sodium: 252mg

Lemon Pesto Salmon

Prep time: 5 minutes | Cook time: 10 minutes | Serves 2

- 10 ounces (283 g) salmon fillet (1 large piece or 2 smaller ones)
- Salt

- Freshly ground black pepper
- 2 tablespoons prepared pesto sauce
- 1 large fresh lemon, sliced

1. Oil the grill grate and heat the grill to medium-high heat. Alternatively, you can roast the salmon in a 350°F (180°C) oven. 2. Prepare the salmon by seasoning with salt and freshly ground black pepper, and then spread the pesto sauce on top. 3. Make a bed of fresh lemon slices about the same size as your fillet on the hot grill (or on a baking sheet if roasting), and rest the salmon on top of the lemon slices. Place any additional lemon slices on top of the salmon. 4. Grill the salmon for 6 to 10 minutes, or until it's opaque and flakes apart easily. If roasting, it will take about 20 minutes. There is no need to flip the fish over.

Per Serving:
calories: 315 | fat: 21g | protein: 29g | carbs: 1g | fiber: 0g | sodium: 176mg

Baked Red Snapper with Potatoes and Tomatoes

Prep time: 10 minutes | Cook time: 45 minutes | Serves 4

- 5 sprigs fresh thyme, divided
- 2 sprigs fresh oregano, divided
- 1½ pounds (680 g) new potatoes, halved (or quartered if large)
- 4 Roma tomatoes, quartered lengthwise
- 1 tablespoon plus 1 teaspoon olive oil
- 4 cloves garlic, halved,
- divided
- 1¼ teaspoons kosher salt, divided
- ¾ teaspoon ground black pepper, divided
- 1 cleaned whole red snapper (about 2 pounds / 907 g), scaled and fins removed
- ½–1 lemon, sliced
- 4 cups (4 ounces) baby spinach

1. Preheat the oven to 350°F(180°C). 2. Strip the leaves off 2 sprigs thyme and 1 sprig oregano and chop. In a 9' × 13' baking dish, toss the potatoes and tomatoes with 1 tablespoon of the oil, the chopped thyme and oregano leaves, 2 cloves of the garlic, 1 teaspoon of the salt, and ½ teaspoon of the pepper. 3. Cut 3 or 4 diagonal slashes in the skin on both sides of the snapper. Rub the skin with the remaining 1 teaspoon oil. Sprinkle the cavity of the snapper with the remaining ¼ teaspoon salt and pepper. Fill it with the lemon slices, the remaining thyme and oregano sprigs, and the remaining 2 cloves garlic. Sprinkle the outside of the snapper with a pinch of salt and pepper. Set the fish on the vegetables. 4. Cover the baking dish with foil and bake for 20 minutes. Remove the foil and continue baking until the potatoes are tender and the fish flakes easily with a fork, 20 to 25 minutes. 5. Transfer the fish to a serving platter. Toss the spinach with the tomatoes and potatoes in the baking dish, until wilted. 6. Using forks, peel the skin off the fish fillets. Scatter the vegetables around the fish and serve.

Per Serving:
calories: 345 | fat: 6g | protein: 39g | carbs: 33g | fiber: 5g | sodium: 782mg

Salmon Croquettes

Prep time: 10 minutes | Cook time: 7 to 8 minutes | Serves 4

- 1 tablespoon oil
- ½ cup bread crumbs
- 1 (14¾ -ounce / 418-g) can salmon, drained and all skin and fat removed
- 1 egg, beaten
- ⅓ cup coarsely crushed
- saltine crackers (about 8 crackers)
- ½ teaspoon Old Bay Seasoning
- ½ teaspoon onion powder
- ½ teaspoon Worcestershire sauce

1. Preheat the air fryer to 390ºF (199°C). 2. In a shallow dish, mix oil and bread crumbs until crumbly. 3. In a large bowl, combine the salmon, egg, cracker crumbs, Old Bay, onion powder, and Worcestershire. Mix well and shape into 8 small patties about ½-inch thick. 4. Gently dip each patty into bread crumb mixture and turn to coat well on all sides. 5. Cook for 7 to 8 minutes or until

outside is crispy and browned.

Per Serving:
calories: 250 | fat: 11g | protein: 25g | carbs: 11g | fiber: 1g | sodium: 244mg

Roasted Red Snapper

Prep time: 5 minutes | Cook time: 45 minutes | Serves 4

- 1 (2 to 2½ pounds / 907 g to 1.1 kg) whole red snapper, cleaned and scaled
- 2 lemons, sliced (about 10 slices)
- 3 cloves garlic, sliced
- 4 or 5 sprigs of thyme
- 3 tablespoons cold salted butter, cut into small cubes, divided

1. Preheat the oven to 350°F(180°C). 2. Cut a piece of foil to about the size of your baking sheet; put the foil on the baking sheet. 3. Make a horizontal slice through the belly of the fish to create a pocket. 4. Place 3 slices of lemon on the foil and the fish on top of the lemons. 5. Stuff the fish with the garlic, thyme, 3 lemon slices and butter. Reserve 3 pieces of butter. 6. Place the reserved 3 pieces of butter on top of the fish, and 3 or 4 slices of lemon on top of the butter. Bring the foil together and seal it to make a pocket around the fish. 7. Put the fish in the oven and bake for 45 minutes. Serve with remaining fresh lemon slices.

Per Serving:
calories: 345 | fat: 13g | protein: 54g | carbs: 12g | fiber: 3g | sodium: 170mg

Mediterranean Cod Stew

Prep time: 10 minutes |Cook time: 20 minutes| Serves: 6

- 2 tablespoons extra-virgin olive oil
- 2 cups chopped onion (about 1 medium onion)
- 2 garlic cloves, minced (about 1 teaspoon)
- ¾ teaspoon smoked paprika
- 1 (14½-ounce / 411-g) can diced tomatoes, undrained
- 1 (12-ounce / 340-g) jar roasted red peppers, drained and chopped
- 1 cup sliced olives, green or black
- ⅓ cup dry red wine
- ¼ teaspoon freshly ground black pepper
- ¼ teaspoon kosher or sea salt
- 1½ pounds (680 g) cod fillets, cut into 1-inch pieces
- 3 cups sliced mushrooms (about 8 ounces / 227 g)

1. In a large stockpot over medium heat, heat the oil. Add the onion and cook for 4 minutes, stirring occasionally. Add the garlic and smoked paprika and cook for 1 minute, stirring often. 2. Mix in the tomatoes with their juices, roasted peppers, olives, wine, pepper, and salt, and turn the heat up to medium-high. Bring to a boil. Add the cod and mushrooms, and reduce the heat to medium. 3. Cover and cook for about 10 minutes, stirring a few times, until the cod is cooked through and flakes easily, and serve.

Per Serving:
calories: 209 | fat: 8g | protein: 23g | carbs: 12g | fiber: 4g | sodium: 334mg

Salmon Spring Rolls

Prep time: 20 minutes | Cook time: 8 to 10 minutes | Serves 4

- ½ pound (227 g) salmon fillet
- 1 teaspoon toasted sesame oil
- 1 onion, sliced
- 8 rice paper wrappers
- 1 yellow bell pepper, thinly sliced
- 1 carrot, shredded
- ⅓ cup chopped fresh flat-leaf parsley
- ¼ cup chopped fresh basil

1. Put the salmon in the air fryer basket and drizzle with the sesame oil. Add the onion. Air fry at 370ºF (188ºC) for 8 to 10 minutes, or until the salmon just flakes when tested with a fork and the onion is tender. 2. Meanwhile, fill a small shallow bowl with warm water. One at a time, dip the rice paper wrappers into the water and place on a work surface. 3. Top each wrapper with one-eighth each of the salmon and onion mixture, yellow bell pepper, carrot, parsley, and basil. Roll up the wrapper, folding in the sides, to enclose the ingredients. 4. If you like, bake in the air fryer at 380ºF (193ºC) for 7 to 9 minutes, until the rolls are crunchy. Cut the rolls in half to serve.

Per Serving:
calories: 197 | fat: 4g | protein: 14g | carbs: 26g | fiber: 2g | sodium: 145mg

Chapter 5

Poultry

Chapter 5 Poultry

Broccoli Cheese Chicken

Prep time: 10 minutes | Cook time: 19 to 24 minutes | Serves 6

- 1 tablespoon avocado oil
- ¼ cup chopped onion
- ½ cup finely chopped broccoli
- 4 ounces (113 g) cream cheese, at room temperature
- 2 ounces (57 g) Cheddar cheese, shredded
- 1 teaspoon garlic powder
- ½ teaspoon sea salt, plus additional for seasoning, divided
- ¼ freshly ground black pepper, plus additional for seasoning, divided
- 2 pounds (907 g) boneless, skinless chicken breasts
- 1 teaspoon smoked paprika

1. Heat a medium skillet over medium-high heat and pour in the avocado oil. Add the onion and broccoli and cook, stirring occasionally, for 5 to 8 minutes, until the onion is tender. 2. Transfer to a large bowl and stir in the cream cheese, Cheddar cheese, and garlic powder, and season to taste with salt and pepper. 3. Hold a sharp knife parallel to the chicken breast and cut a long pocket into one side. Stuff the chicken pockets with the broccoli mixture, using toothpicks to secure the pockets around the filling. 4. In a small dish, combine the paprika, ½ teaspoon salt, and ¼ teaspoon pepper. Sprinkle this over the outside of the chicken. 5. Set the air fryer to 400ºF (204ºC). Place the chicken in a single layer in the air fryer basket, cooking in batches if necessary, and cook for 14 to 16 minutes, until an instant-read thermometer reads 160ºF (71ºC). Place the chicken on a plate and tent a piece of aluminum foil over the chicken. Allow to rest for 5 to 10 minutes before serving.

Per Serving:
calorie: 287 | fat: 16g | protein: 32g | carbs: 1g | fiber: 0g | sodium: 291mg

Chicken Jalfrezi

Prep time: 15 minutes | Cook time: 15 minutes | Serves 4

Chicken:
- 1 pound (454 g) boneless, skinless chicken thighs, cut into 2 or 3 pieces each
- 1 medium onion, chopped
- 1 large green bell pepper, stemmed, seeded, and chopped
- 2 tablespoons olive oil
- 1 teaspoon ground turmeric
- 1 teaspoon garam masala
- 1 teaspoon kosher salt
- ½ to 1 teaspoon cayenne pepper

Sauce:
- ¼ cup tomato sauce
- 1 tablespoon water
- 1 teaspoon garam masala
- ½ teaspoon kosher salt
- ½ teaspoon cayenne pepper
- Side salad, rice, or naan bread, for serving

1. For the chicken: In a large bowl, combine the chicken, onion, bell pepper, oil, turmeric, garam masala, salt, and cayenne. Stir and toss until well combined. 2. Place the chicken and vegetables in the air fryer basket. Set the air fryer to 350ºF (177ºC) for 15 minutes, stirring and tossing halfway through the cooking time. Use a meat thermometer to ensure the chicken has reached an internal temperature of 165ºF (74ºC). 3. Meanwhile, for the sauce: In a small microwave-safe bowl, combine the tomato sauce, water, garam masala, salt, and cayenne. Microwave on high for 1 minute. Remove and stir. Microwave for another minute; set aside. 4. When the chicken is cooked, remove and place chicken and vegetables in a large bowl. Pour the sauce over all. Stir and toss to coat the chicken and vegetables evenly. 5. Serve with rice, naan, or a side salad.

Per Serving:
calories: 224 | fat: 12g | protein: 23g | carbs: 6g | fiber: 2g | sodium: 827mg

Chicken and Mushroom Marsala

Prep time: 10 minutes | Cook time: 25 minutes | Serves 4

- 3 tablespoons all-purpose flour
- ½ teaspoon ground black pepper
- ¼ teaspoon salt
- 2 (6-ounce / 170-g) boneless, skinless chicken breasts
- 2 tablespoons olive oil
- 1 medium white onion, peeled and diced
- 1 pound (454 g) sliced button mushrooms
- 2 cloves garlic, peeled and minced
- 2 sprigs thyme
- 2 sprigs oregano
- ¼ cup marsala wine
- ¼ cup low-sodium chicken broth
- ¼ cup chopped fresh parsley

1. Combine flour, pepper, and salt in a shallow dish. Dredge chicken breasts in flour, shaking to remove excess. Press the Sauté button on the Instant Pot® and heat oil. Brown chicken on both sides, about 4 minutes per side. Transfer chicken to a plate and set aside. 2. Add onion to the pot and cook until just tender, about 3 minutes. Add mushrooms and cook, stirring often, until mushrooms are tender, about 8 minutes. Add garlic, thyme, and oregano, and cook until fragrant, about 30 seconds. 3. Stir in wine and chicken broth, and scrape bottom of pot to release any browned bits. Top with chicken. Press the Cancel button, close lid, set steam release to Sealing, press the Manual button, and set time to 5 minutes. 4. When the timer beeps, let pressure release naturally, about 20 minutes. Press the Cancel button and open lid. Transfer chicken breasts to a cutting board and slice into ½" pieces. Arrange on serving platter. Pour mushrooms and cooking liquid over chicken. Sprinkle with parsley and serve hot.

Per Serving:
calories: 525 | fat: 14g | protein: 37g | carbs: 9g | fiber: 8g | sodium: 218mg

Shredded Chicken Souvlaki

Prep time: 10 minutes | Cook time: 6 to 8 hours | Serves 6

- 3 pounds (1.4 kg) boneless, skinless chicken thighs
- ⅓ cup water
- ⅓ cup freshly squeezed lemon juice
- ¼ cup red wine vinegar
- 4 garlic cloves, minced
- 2 tablespoons extra-virgin olive oil
- 2 teaspoons dried oregano
- ¼ teaspoon sea salt
- ¼ teaspoon freshly ground black pepper

1. In a slow cooker, combine the chicken, water, lemon juice, vinegar, garlic, olive oil, oregano, salt, and pepper. Stir to mix well. 2. Cover the cooker and cook for 6 to 8 hours on Low heat. 3. Transfer the chicken from the slow cooker to a work surface. Using 2 forks, shred the chicken, return it to the slow cooker, mix it with the sauce, and keep it warm until ready to serve.

Per Serving:
calories: 462 | fat: 28g | protein: 48g | carbs: 3g | fiber: 1g | sodium: 626mg

Old Delhi Butter Chicken

Prep time: 15 minutes | Cook time: 3 to 7 hours | Serves 6

Tomato Sauce:
- 3 medium red onions, roughly chopped
- 2 to 3 fresh green chiles
- 1 tablespoon freshly grated ginger
- 6 garlic cloves, roughly chopped
- 2¾-inch piece cassia bark
- 5 green cardamom pods
- 4 cloves
- 10 black peppercorns
- 1 teaspoon salt

Chicken:
- 2 tablespoons ghee or butter
- 1 tablespoon cumin seeds
- 12 chicken thighs, skinned, trimmed, and cut into cubes
- 1 to 2 tablespoons honey
- 1 tablespoon dried fenugreek leaves

- 10 ripe red tomatoes, roughly chopped, or 1 (14-ounce / 397-g) can plum tomatoes
- 1 tablespoon tomato paste
- ½ teaspoon turmeric
- 1 tablespoon Kashmiri chili powder
- 2 teaspoons coriander seeds, ground
- 2 cups hot water

- ⅓ cup heavy cream (optional)
- 1 tablespoon butter (optional)
- Coriander leaves to garnish (optional)

Make the Tomato Sauce: 1. Heat the slow cooker to high and add the onion, chiles, ginger, garlic, cassia bark, green cardamom pods, cloves, black peppercorns, salt, tomatoes, tomato paste, turmeric, chili powder, ground coriander seeds, and water. 2. Cover and cook on high for 1 to 2 hours, or on low for 3 hours. By the end, the tomatoes should have broken down. 3. Remove the cassia bark (this is important, because if you grind the cassia in the sauce it will turn out much darker) and blend the sauce with an immersion or regular blender until it's smooth. You can strain this to get a fine, glossy sauce, if you'd like, or leave it as it is. Return the sauce to the slow cooker. Make the Chicken: 4. In a frying pan, heat the ghee. Add cumin seeds and cook until fragrant, about 1 minute. Pour into the sauce in the slow cooker. 5. Add the diced chicken, cover the

slow cooker, and cook on high for 2 hours, or on low for 4 hours. 6. When the chicken is cooked, stir in the honey, dried fenugreek leaves, and cream (if using). If you want to thicken the sauce you can turn the cooker to high and reduce for a while with the cover off. Add some butter, a little extra drizzle of cream, and garnish with coriander leaves (if using) just before serving.

Per Serving:
calories: 600 | fat: 21g | protein: 80g | carbs: 22g | fiber: 5g | sodium: 814mg

Herb-Marinated Chicken Breasts

Prep time: 10 minutes | Cook time: 10 minutes | Serves 4

- ½ cup fresh lemon juice
- ¼ cup extra-virgin olive oil
- 4 cloves garlic, minced
- 2 tablespoons chopped fresh basil
- 1 tablespoon chopped fresh oregano
- 1 tablespoon chopped fresh

- mint
- 2 pounds (907 g) chicken breast tenders
- ½ teaspoon unrefined sea salt or salt
- ¼ teaspoon freshly ground black pepper

1. In a small bowl, whisk the lemon juice, olive oil, garlic, basil, oregano, and mint well to combine. Place the chicken breasts in a large shallow bowl or glass baking pan, and pour dressing over the top. 2. Cover, place in the refrigerator, and allow to marinate for 1 to 2 hours. Remove from the refrigerator, and season with salt and pepper. 3. Heat a large, wide skillet over medium-high heat. Using tongs, place chicken tenders evenly in the bottom of the skillet. Pour the remaining marinade over the chicken. 4. Allow to cook for 3 to 5 minutes each side, or until chicken is golden, juices have been absorbed, and meat is cooked to an internal temperature of 160°F (71°C).

Per Serving:
calories: 521 | fat: 35g | protein: 48g | carbs: 3g | fiber: 0g | sodium: 435mg

Lebanese Grilled Chicken

Prep time: 10 minutes | Cook time: 14 minutes | Serves 4

- ½ cup olive oil
- ¼ cup apple cider vinegar
- Zest and juice of 1 lemon
- 4 cloves garlic, minced
- 1 teaspoon sea salt

- 1 teaspoon Arabic 7 spices (baharaat)
- ½ teaspoon cinnamon
- 1 chicken, cut into 8 pieces

1. Combine all the ingredients except the chicken in a shallow dish or plastic bag. 2. Place the chicken in the bag or dish and marinate overnight, or at least for several hours. 3. Drain, reserving the marinade. Heat the grill to medium-high. 4. Cook the chicken pieces for 10–14 minutes, brushing them with the marinade every 5 minutes or so. 5. The chicken is done when the crust is golden brown and an instant-read thermometer reads 180°F (82°C) in the thickest parts. Remove skin before eating.

Per Serving:
calories: 518 | fat: 34g | protein: 49g | carbs: 4g | fiber: 0g | sodium: 613mg

Calabrian Chicken with Potatoes and Vegetables

Prep time: 10 minutes | Cook time: 45 minutes | Serves 4

- 4 chicken drumsticks
- 4 bone-in, skin-on chicken thighs
- 1 pint cherry tomatoes, halved
- 1 pound (454 g) potatoes, scrubbed and cut into ½' wedges
- 3 red, orange, or yellow bell peppers, seeded and cut into
- ½' strips
- 1 large sweet onion, cut into ½' wedges
- ¼ cup olive oil
- 4 cloves garlic, minced
- 1 teaspoon dried oregano
- 1 teaspoon sweet paprika
- 1 teaspoon kosher salt
- ¼ teaspoon red-pepper flakes

1. Preheat the oven to 400°F(205ºC). 2. On a large rimmed baking sheet, combine the chicken, tomatoes, potatoes, bell peppers, onion, oil, garlic, oregano, paprika, salt, and pepper flakes, tossing to combine and rubbing the chicken with the spices. 3. Arrange the vegetables underneath the chicken pieces. Roast until the vegetables are tender and a thermometer inserted in the thickest part of the chicken, but not touching bone, registers 165°F(74ºC), about 45 minutes, turning the chicken and tossing the vegetables halfway through.

Per Serving:
calories: 571 | fat: 23g | protein: 56g | carbs: 34g | fiber: 6g | sodium: 755mg

Skillet Creamy Tarragon Chicken and Mushrooms

Prep time: 10 minutes | Cook time: 20 minutes | Serves 2

- 2 tablespoons olive oil, divided
- ½ medium onion, minced
- 4 ounces (113 g) baby bella (cremini) mushrooms, sliced
- 2 small garlic cloves, minced
- 8 ounces (227 g) chicken cutlets
- 2 teaspoons tomato paste
- 2 teaspoons dried tarragon
- 2 cups low-sodium chicken stock
- 6 ounces (170 g) pappardelle pasta
- ¼ cup plain full-fat Greek yogurt
- Salt
- Freshly ground black pepper

1. Heat 1 tablespoon of the olive oil in a sauté pan over medium-high heat. Add the onion and mushrooms and sauté for 5 minutes. Add the garlic and cook for 1 minute more. 2. Move the vegetables to the edges of the pan and add the remaining 1 tablespoon of olive oil to the center of the pan. Place the cutlets in the center and let them cook for about 3 minutes, or until they lift up easily and are golden brown on the bottom. 3. Flip the chicken and cook for another 3 minutes. 4. Mix in the tomato paste and tarragon. Add the chicken stock and stir well to combine everything. Bring the stock to a boil. 5. Add the pappardelle. Break up the pasta if needed to fit into the pan. Stir the noodles so they don't stick to the bottom of the pan. 6. Cover the sauté pan and reduce the heat to medium-low. Let the chicken and noodles simmer for 15 minutes, stirring occasionally, until the pasta is cooked and the liquid is mostly absorbed. If the liquid absorbs too quickly and the pasta isn't cooked, add more water or chicken stock, about ¼ cup at a time as needed. 7. Remove the pan from the heat. 8. Stir 2 tablespoons of the hot liquid from the pan into the yogurt. Pour the tempered yogurt into the pan and stir well to mix it into the sauce. Season with salt and pepper. 9. The sauce will tighten up as it cools, so if it seems too thick, add a few tablespoons of water.

Per Serving:
calories: 556 | fat: 18g | protein: 42g | carbs: 56g | fiber: 2g | sodium: 190mg

Chicken Patties

Prep time: 15 minutes | Cook time: 12 minutes | Serves 4

- 1 pound (454 g) ground chicken thigh meat
- ½ cup shredded Mozzarella cheese
- 1 teaspoon dried parsley
- ½ teaspoon garlic powder
- ¼ teaspoon onion powder
- 1 large egg
- 2 ounces (57 g) pork rinds, finely ground

1. In a large bowl, mix ground chicken, Mozzarella, parsley, garlic powder, and onion powder. Form into four patties. 2. Place patties in the freezer for 15 to 20 minutes until they begin to firm up. 3. Whisk egg in a medium bowl. Place the ground pork rinds into a large bowl. 4. Dip each chicken patty into the egg and then press into pork rinds to fully coat. Place patties into the air fryer basket. 5. Adjust the temperature to 360°F (182ºC) and air fry for 12 minutes. 6. Patties will be firm and cooked to an internal temperature of 165ºF (74ºC) when done. Serve immediately.

Per Serving:
calories: 265 | fat: 15g | protein: 29g | carbs: 1g | fiber: 0g | sodium: 285mg

Jerk Chicken Thighs

Prep time: 30 minutes | Cook time: 15 to 20 minutes | Serves 6

- 2 teaspoons ground coriander
- 1 teaspoon ground allspice
- 1 teaspoon cayenne pepper
- 1 teaspoon ground ginger
- 1 teaspoon salt
- 1 teaspoon dried thyme
- ½ teaspoon ground cinnamon
- ½ teaspoon ground nutmeg
- 2 pounds (907 g) boneless chicken thighs, skin on
- 2 tablespoons olive oil

1. In a small bowl, combine the coriander, allspice, cayenne, ginger, salt, thyme, cinnamon, and nutmeg. Stir until thoroughly combined. 2. Place the chicken in a baking dish and use paper towels to pat dry. Thoroughly coat both sides of the chicken with the spice mixture. Cover and refrigerate for at least 2 hours, preferably overnight. 3. Preheat the air fryer to 360ºF (182ºC). 4. Working in batches if necessary, arrange the chicken in a single layer in the air fryer basket and lightly coat with the olive oil. Pausing halfway through the cooking time to flip the chicken, air fry for 15 to 20 minutes, until a thermometer inserted into the thickest part registers 165ºF (74ºC).

Per Serving:
calories: 227 | fat: 11g | protein: 30g | carbs: 1g | fiber: 0g | sodium: 532mg

Chicken Marsala

Prep time: 10 minutes | Cook time: 30 minutes | Serves 4

- ¼ cup olive oil
- 4 boneless, skinless chicken breasts, pounded thin
- Sea salt and freshly ground pepper, to taste
- ¼ cup whole-wheat flour
- ½ pound (227 g) mushrooms, sliced
- 1 cup Marsala wine
- 1 cup chicken broth
- ¼ cup flat-leaf parsley, chopped

1. Heat the olive oil in a large skillet on medium-high heat. 2. Season the chicken breasts with sea salt and freshly ground pepper, then dredge them in flour. 3. Sauté them in the olive oil until golden brown. 4. Transfer to an oven-safe plate, and keep warm in the oven on low. Sauté the mushrooms in the same pan. Add the wine and chicken broth and bring to a simmer. 5. Simmer for 10 minutes, or until the sauce is reduced and thickened slightly. Return the chicken to the pan, and cook it in the sauce for 10 minutes. Transfer to a serving dish and sprinkle with the parsley.

Per Serving:
calories: 543 | fat: 21g | protein: 65g | carbs: 10g | fiber: 2g | sodium: 146mg

Hot Goan-Style Coconut Chicken

Prep time: 20 minutes | Cook time: 4 to 6 hours | Serves 6

Spice Paste:
- 8 dried Kashmiri chiles, broken into pieces
- 2 tablespoons coriander seeds
- 2-inch piece cassia bark, broken into pieces
- 1 teaspoon black peppercorns
- 1 teaspoon cumin seeds

Chicken:
- 12 chicken thigh and drumstick pieces, on the bone, skinless
- 1 teaspoon salt (or to taste)
- 1 teaspoon turmeric
- 2 tablespoons coconut oil
- 2 medium onions, finely sliced

- 1 teaspoon fennel seeds
- 4 cloves
- 2 star anise
- 1 tablespoon poppy seeds
- 1 cup freshly grated coconut, or desiccated coconut shreds
- 6 garlic cloves
- ⅓ cup water

- ⅓ cup water
- ½ teaspoon ground nutmeg
- 2 teaspoons tamarind paste
- Handful fresh coriander leaves, chopped for garnish
- 1 or 2 fresh red chiles, for garnish

Make the Spice Paste: 1. In a dry frying pan, roast the Kashmiri chiles, coriander seeds, cassia bark, peppercorns, cumin seeds, fennel seeds, cloves, and star anise until fragrant, about 1 minute. Add the poppy seeds and continue roasting for a few minutes. Then remove from the heat and leave to cool. 2. Once cooled, grind the toasted spices in your spice grinder and set aside. 3. In the same pan, add the dried coconut and toast it for 5 to 7 minutes, until it just starts to turn golden. 4. Transfer to a blender with the garlic, and add the water. Blend to make a thick, wet paste. 5. Add the ground spices and blend again to mix together. Make the Chicken: 6. In a large bowl, toss the chicken with the salt and turmeric.

Marinate for 15 to 20 minutes. In the meantime, heat the slow cooker to high. 7. Heat the oil in a frying pan (or in the slow cooker if you have a sear setting). Cook the sliced onions for 10 minutes, and then add the spice and coconut paste. Cook until it becomes fragrant. 8. Transfer everything to the slow cooker. Add the chicken, then the water. Cover and cook on low for 6 hours, or on high for 4 hours. 9. Sprinkle in the nutmeg and stir in the tamarind paste. Cover and cook for another 5 minutes. 10. Garnish with fresh coriander leaves and whole red chiles to serve.

Per Serving:
calories: 583 | fat: 26g | protein: 77g | carbs: 7g | fiber: 3g | sodium: 762mg

Blackened Chicken

Prep time: 10 minutes | Cook time: 20 minutes | Serves 4

- 1 large egg, beaten
- ¾ cup Blackened seasoning
- 2 whole boneless, skinless
- chicken breasts (about 1 pound / 454 g each), halved
- 1 to 2 tablespoons oil

1. Place the beaten egg in one shallow bowl and the Blackened seasoning in another shallow bowl. 2. One at a time, dip the chicken pieces in the beaten egg and the Blackened seasoning, coating thoroughly. 3. Preheat the air fryer to 360ºF (182ºC). Line the air fryer basket with parchment paper. 4. Place the chicken pieces on the parchment and spritz with oil. 5. Cook for 10 minutes. Flip the chicken, spritz it with oil, and cook for 10 minutes more until the internal temperature reaches 165ºF (74ºC) and the chicken is no longer pink inside. Let sit for 5 minutes before serving.

Per Serving:
calories: 225 | fat: 10g | protein: 28g | carbs: 8g | fiber: 6g | sodium: 512mg

Turkish Chicken Kebabs

Prep time: 30 minutes | Cook time: 15 minutes | Serves 4

- ¼ cup plain Greek yogurt
- 1 tablespoon minced garlic
- 1 tablespoon tomato paste
- 1 tablespoon fresh lemon juice
- 1 tablespoon vegetable oil
- 1 teaspoon kosher salt
- 1 teaspoon ground cumin
- 1 teaspoon sweet Hungarian
- paprika
- ½ teaspoon ground cinnamon
- ½ teaspoon black pepper
- ½ teaspoon cayenne pepper
- 1 pound (454 g) boneless, skinless chicken thighs, quartered crosswise

1. In a large bowl, combine the yogurt, garlic, tomato paste, lemon juice, vegetable oil, salt, cumin, paprika, cinnamon, black pepper, and cayenne. Stir until the spices are blended into the yogurt. 2. Add the chicken to the bowl and toss until well coated. Marinate at room temperature for 30 minutes, or cover and refrigerate for up to 24 hours. 3. Arrange the chicken in a single layer in the air fryer basket. Set the air fryer to 375ºF (191ºC) for 10 minutes. Turn the chicken and cook for 5 minutes more. Use a meat thermometer to ensure the chicken has reached an internal temperature of 165ºF (74ºC).

Per Serving:
calories: 188 | fat: 8g | protein: 24g | carbs: 4g | fiber: 1g | sodium: 705mg

Chicken and Olives with Couscous

Prep time: 15 minutes | Cook time: 1 hour | Serves 6

- 2 tablespoons olive oil, divided
- 8 bone-in, skin-on chicken thighs
- ½ teaspoon kosher salt
- ¼ teaspoon ground black pepper
- 2 cloves garlic, chopped
- 1 small red onion, chopped
- 1 red bell pepper, seeded and chopped
- 1 green bell pepper, seeded and chopped
- 1 tablespoon fresh thyme
- leaves
- 2 teaspoons fresh oregano leaves
- 1 (28-ounce / 794-g) can no-salt-added diced tomatoes
- 1 cup low-sodium chicken broth
- 1 cup pitted green olives, coarsely chopped
- 2 cups whole wheat couscous
- Chopped flat-leaf parsley, for garnish

1. Preheat the oven to 350°F(180°C). 2. In a large ovenproof or cast-iron skillet over medium heat, warm 1 tablespoon of the oil. Pat the chicken thighs dry with a paper towel, season with the salt and black pepper, and cook, turning once, until golden and crisp, 8 to 10 minutes per side. Remove the chicken from the skillet and set aside. 3. Add the remaining 1 tablespoon oil to the skillet. Cook the garlic, onion, bell peppers, thyme, and oregano until softened, about 5 minutes. Add the tomatoes and broth and bring to a boil. Return the chicken to the skillet, add the olives, cover, and place the skillet in the oven. Roast until the chicken is tender and a thermometer inserted in the thickest part registers 165°F(74°C), 40 to 50 minutes. 4. While the chicken is cooking, prepare the couscous according to package directions. 5. To serve, pile the couscous on a serving platter and nestle the chicken on top. Pour the vegetables and any pan juices over the chicken and couscous. Sprinkle with the parsley and serve.

Per Serving:
calories: 481 | fat: 15g | protein: 29g | carbs: 61g | fiber: 11g | sodium: 893mg

Curried Chicken and Lentil Salad

Prep time: 15 minutes | Cook time: 13 minutes | Serves 8

- 1 teaspoon olive oil
- 2 pounds (907 g) boneless, skinless chicken breasts, cut into ½" pieces
- 1 cup dried lentils, rinsed and drained
- 2 cups water
- 2½ teaspoons curry powder, divided
- 2 small Golden Delicious apples, divided
- 1 teaspoon lemon juice
- 2 cups halved seedless grapes
- 1 cup roasted salted cashews
- 2 stalks celery, diced
- ½ small red onion, peeled and diced
- ¾ cup plain low-fat yogurt
- ¼ cup mayonnaise
- 11 ounces (312 g) baby salad greens

1. Press the Sauté button on the Instant Pot® and heat oil. Add chicken and cook for 5 minutes or until browned. Stir in lentils, water, and 1 teaspoon curry powder. Halve one of the apples; core and dice 1 half and add it to the pot. Coat the cut side of the other half of the apple with lemon juice to prevent it from turning brown and set aside. Press the Cancel button. 2. Close lid, set steam release to Sealing, press the Manual button, and set time to 8 minutes. When the timer beeps, let pressure release naturally, about 20 minutes. Open lid. 3. Transfer the contents of the Instant Pot® to a large bowl and set aside to cool. 4. Dice reserved apple half, and core and dice remaining apple. Add to chicken and lentil mixture along with grapes, cashews, celery, and red onion. 5. In a small bowl, mix together yogurt, mayonnaise, and remaining 1½ teaspoons curry powder. Drizzle over chicken and lentil mixture, and stir to combine. Serve over salad greens.

Per Serving:
calories: 404 | fat: 18g | protein: 41g | carbs: 21g | fiber: 3g | sodium: 177mg

Marinated Chicken

Prep time: 5 minutes | Cook time: 16 minutes | Serves 4

- ½ cup olive oil
- 2 tablespoon fresh rosemary
- 1 teaspoon minced garlic
- Juice and zest of 1 lemon
- ¼ cup chopped flat-leaf
- parsley
- Sea salt and freshly ground pepper, to taste
- 4 boneless, skinless chicken breasts

1. Mix all ingredients except the chicken together in a plastic bag or bowl. 2. Place the chicken in the container and shake/stir so the marinade thoroughly coats the chicken. 3. Refrigerate up to 24 hours. 4. Heat a grill to medium heat and cook the chicken for 6–8 minutes a side. Turn only once during the cooking process. 5. Serve with a Greek salad and brown rice.

Per Serving:
calories: 571 | fat: 34g | protein: 61g | carbs: 1g | fiber: 0g | sodium: 126mg

Chicken in Mango Chutney

Prep time: 10 minutes | Cook time: 6 to 8 hours | Serves 2

- 12 ounces (340 g) boneless, skinless chicken thighs, cut into 1-inch pieces
- ½ cup thinly sliced red onion
- 1 cup canned mango or peaches, drained and diced
- 2 tablespoons golden raisins
- 2 tablespoons apple cider
- vinegar
- 1 teaspoon minced fresh ginger
- ¼ teaspoon red pepper flakes
- 1 teaspoon curry powder
- ¼ teaspoon ground cinnamon
- ⅛ teaspoon sea salt

1. Put all the ingredients to the slow cooker and gently stir to combine. 2. Cover and cook on low for 6 to 8 hours. The chutney should be thick and sweet and the chicken tender and cooked through.

Per Serving:
calories: 278 | fat: 8g | protein: 35g | carbs: 17g | fiber: 3g | sodium: 320mg

Taco Chicken

Prep time: 10 minutes | Cook time: 23 minutes | Serves 4

- 2 large eggs
- 1 tablespoon water
- Fine sea salt and ground black pepper, to taste
- 1 cup pork dust
- 1 teaspoon ground cumin
- 1 teaspoon smoked paprika
- 4 (5 ounces / 142 g) boneless, skinless chicken
- breasts or thighs, pounded to ¼ inch thick
- 1 cup salsa
- 1 cup shredded Monterey Jack cheese (about 4 ounces / 113 g) (omit for dairy-free)
- Sprig of fresh cilantro, for garnish (optional)

1. Spray the air fryer basket with avocado oil. Preheat the air fryer to 400°F (204°C). 2. Crack the eggs into a shallow baking dish, add the water and a pinch each of salt and pepper, and whisk to combine. In another shallow baking dish, stir together the pork dust, cumin, and paprika until well combined. 3. Season the chicken breasts well on both sides with salt and pepper. Dip 1 chicken breast in the eggs and let any excess drip off, then dredge both sides of the chicken breast in the pork dust mixture. Spray the breast with avocado oil and place it in the air fryer basket. Repeat with the remaining 3 chicken breasts. 4. Air fry the chicken in the air fryer for 20 minutes, or until the internal temperature reaches 165°F (74°C) and the breading is golden brown, flipping halfway through. 5. Dollop each chicken breast with ¼ cup of the salsa and top with ¼ cup of the cheese. Return the breasts to the air fryer and cook for 3 minutes, or until the cheese is melted. Garnish with cilantro before serving, if desired. 6. Store leftovers in an airtight container in the refrigerator for up to 4 days. Reheat in a preheated 400°F (204°C) air fryer for 5 minutes, or until warmed through.

Per Serving:
calories: 360 | fat: 15g | protein: 20g | carbs: 4g | fiber: 1g | sodium: 490mg

Turkey Breast in Yogurt Sauce

Prep time: 10 minutes | Cook time: 16 minutes | Serves 6

- 1 cup plain low-fat yogurt
- 1 teaspoon ground turmeric
- 1 teaspoon ground cumin
- 1 teaspoon yellow mustard seeds
- ¼ teaspoon salt
- ½ teaspoon ground black pepper
- 1 pound (454 g) boneless turkey breast, cut into bite-sized pieces
- 1 tablespoon olive oil
- 1 (1-pound / 454-g) bag frozen baby peas and pearl onions, thawed

1. In a large bowl, mix together yogurt, turmeric, cumin, mustard seeds, salt, and pepper. Stir in in turkey. Cover and refrigerate for 4 hours. 2. Press the Sauté button on the Instant Pot® and heat oil. Add turkey and yogurt mixture. Press the Cancel button, close lid, set steam release to Sealing, press the Manual button, and set time to 8 minutes. When the timer beeps, quick-release the pressure and open lid. 3. Stir in peas and onions. Press the Cancel button, then press the Sauté button and simmer until sauce is thickened, about 8 minutes. Serve hot.

Per Serving:
calories: 146 | fat: 6g | protein: 17g | carbs: 7g | fiber: 1g | sodium: 554mg

Greek Chicken Souvlaki

Prep time: 30 minutes | Cook time: 15 minutes | Serves 3 to 4

Chicken:
- Grated zest and juice of 1 lemon
- 2 tablespoons extra-virgin olive oil
- 1 tablespoon Greek souvlaki

seasoning
- 1 pound (454 g) boneless, skinless chicken breast, cut into 2-inch chunks
- Vegetable oil spray

For Serving:
- Warm pita bread or hot cooked rice
- Sliced ripe tomatoes
- Sliced cucumbers
- Thinly sliced red onion
- Kalamata olives
- Tzatziki

1. For the chicken: In a small bowl, combine the lemon zest, lemon juice, olive oil, and souvlaki seasoning. Place the chicken in a gallon-size resealable plastic bag. Pour the marinade over chicken. Seal bag and massage to coat. Place the bag in a large bowl and marinate for 30 minutes, or cover and refrigerate up to 24 hours, turning the bag occasionally. 2. Place the chicken a single layer in the air fryer basket. Set the air fryer to 350°F (177°C) for 10 minutes, turning the chicken and spraying with a little vegetable oil spray halfway through the cooking time. Increase the air fryer temperature to 400°F (204°C) for 5 minutes to allow the chicken to crisp and brown a little. 3. Transfer the chicken to a serving platter and serve with pita bread or rice, tomatoes, cucumbers, onion, olives and tzatziki.

Per Serving:
calories: 198 | fat: 10g | protein: 26g | carbs: 1g | fiber: 0g | sodium: 51mg

Chicken with Dates and Almonds

Prep time: 15 minutes | Cook time: 6 to 8 hours | Serves 4

- 1 onion, sliced
- 1 (15-ounce / 425-g) can reduced-sodium chickpeas, drained and rinsed
- 2½ pounds (1.1 kg) bone-in, skin-on chicken thighs
- ½ cup low-sodium chicken broth
- 2 garlic cloves, minced
- 1 teaspoon sea salt
- 1 teaspoon ground cumin
- ½ teaspoon ground ginger
- ½ teaspoon ground coriander
- ¼ teaspoon ground cinnamon
- ¼ teaspoon freshly ground black pepper
- ½ cup dried dates
- ¼ cup sliced almonds

1. In a slow cooker, gently toss together the onion and chickpeas. 2. Place the chicken on top of the chickpea mixture and pour the chicken broth over the chicken. 3. In a small bowl, stir together the garlic, salt, cumin, ginger, coriander, cinnamon, and pepper. Sprinkle the spice mix over everything. 4. Top with the dates and almonds. 5. Cover the cooker and cook for 6 to 8 hours on Low heat.

Per Serving:
calories: 841 | fat: 48g | protein: 57g | carbs: 41g | fiber: 9g | sodium: 812mg

Chicken Tagine

Prep time: 15 minutes | Cook time: 11 minutes | Serves 4

- 2 (15-ounce / 425-g) cans chickpeas, rinsed, divided
- 1 tablespoon extra-virgin olive oil
- 5 garlic cloves, minced
- 1½ teaspoons paprika
- ½ teaspoon ground turmeric
- ½ teaspoon ground cumin
- ¼ teaspoon ground ginger
- ¼ teaspoon cayenne pepper
- 1 fennel bulb, 1 tablespoon fronds minced, stalks discarded, bulb halved and cut lengthwise into ½-inch-thick wedges
- 1 cup chicken broth
- 3 (2-inch) strips lemon zest, plus lemon wedges for serving
- 4 (5- to 7-ounce / 142- to 198-g) bone-in chicken thighs, skin removed, trimmed
- ½ teaspoon table salt
- ½ cup pitted large brine-cured green or black olives, halved
- ⅓ cup raisins
- 2 tablespoons chopped fresh parsley

1. Using potato masher, mash ½ cup chickpeas in bowl to paste. Using highest sauté function, cook oil, garlic, paprika, turmeric, cumin, ginger, and cayenne in Instant Pot until fragrant, about 1 minute. Turn off Instant Pot, then stir in remaining whole chickpeas, mashed chickpeas, fennel wedges, broth, and zest. 2. Sprinkle chicken with salt. Nestle chicken skinned side up into pot and spoon some of cooking liquid over top. Lock lid in place and close pressure release valve. Select high pressure cook function and cook for 10 minutes. 3. Turn off Instant Pot and quick-release pressure. Carefully remove lid, allowing steam to escape away from you. Discard lemon zest. Stir in olives, raisins, parsley, and fennel fronds. Season with salt and pepper to taste. Serve with lemon wedges.

Per Serving:

calories: 489 | fat: 16g | protein: 41g | carbs: 48g | fiber: 13g | sodium: 717mg

Tahini Chicken Rice Bowls

Prep time: 10 minutes |Cook time: 15 minutes| Serves: 4

- 1 cup uncooked instant brown rice
- ¼ cup tahini or peanut butter (tahini for nut-free)
- ¼ cup 2% plain Greek yogurt
- 2 tablespoons chopped scallions, green and white parts (2 scallions)
- 1 tablespoon freshly squeezed lemon juice (from ½ medium lemon)
- 1 tablespoon water
- 1 teaspoon ground cumin
- ¾ teaspoon ground
- cinnamon
- ¼ teaspoon kosher or sea salt
- 2 cups chopped cooked chicken breast (about 1 pound / 454 g)
- ½ cup chopped dried apricots
- 2 cups peeled and chopped seedless cucumber (1 large cucumber)
- 4 teaspoons sesame seeds
- Fresh mint leaves, for serving (optional)

1. Cook the brown rice according to the package instructions. 2. While the rice is cooking, in a medium bowl, mix together the tahini, yogurt, scallions, lemon juice, water, cumin, cinnamon, and salt. Transfer half the tahini mixture to another medium bowl.

Mix the chicken into the first bowl. 3. When the rice is done, mix it into the second bowl of tahini (the one without the chicken). 4. To assemble, divide the chicken among four bowls. Spoon the rice mixture next to the chicken in each bowl. Next to the chicken, place the dried apricots, and in the remaining empty section, add the cucumbers. Sprinkle with sesame seeds, and top with mint, if desired, and serve.

Per Serving:

calories: 448 | fat: 13g | protein: 30g | carbs: 53g | fiber: 5g | sodium: 243mg

Braised Duck with Fennel Root

Prep time: 10 minutes | Cook time: 50 minutes | Serves 6

- ¼ cup olive oil
- 1 whole duck, cleaned
- 3 teaspoon fresh rosemary
- 2 garlic cloves, minced
- Sea salt and freshly ground
- pepper, to taste
- 3 fennel bulbs, cut into chunks
- ½ cup sherry

1. Preheat the oven to 375ºF (190ºC) 2. Heat the olive oil in a large stew pot or Dutch oven. 3. Season the duck, including the cavity, with the rosemary, garlic, sea salt, and freshly ground pepper. 4. Place the duck in the oil, and cook it for 10–15 minutes, turning as necessary to brown all sides. 5. Add the fennel bulbs and cook an additional 5 minutes. 6. Pour the sherry over the duck and fennel, cover the pot, and cook in the oven for 30–45 minutes, or until internal temperature of the duck is 150ºF (66ºC) at its thickest part. 7. Allow duck to sit for 15 minutes before serving.

Per Serving:

calories: 308 | fat: 23g | protein: 17g | carbs: 9g | fiber: 4g | sodium: 112mg

Pomegranate-Glazed Chicken

Prep time: 10 minutes | Cook time: 30 minutes | Serves 6

- 1 teaspoon cumin
- 1 clove garlic, minced
- Sea salt and freshly ground pepper, to taste
- 6 tablespoons olive oil, divided
- 6 boneless, skinless chicken breasts
- 1 cup pomegranate juice (no sugar added)
- 2 tablespoons honey
- 1 tablespoon Dijon mustard
- ½ teaspoon dried thyme
- 1 fresh pomegranate, seeds removed

1. Mix the cumin, garlic, sea salt, and freshly ground pepper with 2 tablespoons of olive oil, and rub into the chicken. 2. Heat the remaining olive oil in a large skillet over medium heat. 3. Add the chicken breasts and sauté for 10 minutes, turning halfway through the cooking time, so the chicken breasts are golden brown on each side. 4. Add the pomegranate juice, honey, Dijon mustard, and thyme. 5. Lower the heat and simmer for 20 minutes, or until the chicken is cooked through and the sauce reduces by half. 6. Transfer the chicken and sauce to a serving platter, and top with fresh pomegranate seeds.

Per Serving:

calories: 532 | fat: 21g | protein: 62g | carbs: 20g | fiber: 2g | sodium: 157mg

Chicken with Lettuce

Prep time: 15 minutes | Cook time: 14 minutes | Serves 4

- 1 pound (454 g) chicken breast tenders, chopped into bite-size pieces
- ½ onion, thinly sliced
- ½ red bell pepper, seeded and thinly sliced
- ½ green bell pepper, seeded and thinly sliced
- 1 tablespoon olive oil
- 1 tablespoon fajita seasoning
- 1 teaspoon kosher salt
- Juice of ½ lime
- 8 large lettuce leaves
- 1 cup prepared guacamole

1. Preheat the air fryer to 400°F (204°C). 2. In a large bowl, combine the chicken, onion, and peppers. Drizzle with the olive oil and toss until thoroughly coated. Add the fajita seasoning and salt and toss again. 3. Working in batches if necessary, arrange the chicken and vegetables in a single layer in the air fryer basket. Pausing halfway through the cooking time to shake the basket, air fry for 14 minutes, or until the vegetables are tender and a thermometer inserted into the thickest piece of chicken registers 165°F (74°C). 4. Transfer the mixture to a serving platter and drizzle with the fresh lime juice. Serve with the lettuce leaves and top with the guacamole.

Per Serving:
calories: 273 | fat: 15g | protein: 27g | carbs: 9g | fiber: 5g | sodium: 723mg

Chicken Nuggets

Prep time: 10 minutes | Cook time: 15 minutes | Serves 4

- 1 pound (454 g) ground chicken thighs
- ½ cup shredded Mozzarella cheese
- 1 large egg, whisked
- ½ teaspoon salt
- ¼ teaspoon dried oregano
- ¼ teaspoon garlic powder

1. In a large bowl, combine all ingredients. Form mixture into twenty nugget shapes, about 2 tablespoons each. 2. Place nuggets into ungreased air fryer basket, working in batches if needed. Adjust the temperature to 375°F (191°C) and air fry for 15 minutes, turning nuggets halfway through cooking. Let cool 5 minutes before serving.

Per Serving:
calories: 195 | fat: 8g | protein: 28g | carbs: 1g | fiber: 0g | sodium: 419mg

Chicken with Lentils and Butternut Squash

Prep time: 15 minutes | Cook time: 28 minutes | Serves 4

- 2 large shallots, halved and sliced thin, divided
- 5 teaspoons extra-virgin olive oil, divided
- ½ teaspoon grated lemon zest plus 2 teaspoons juice
- 1 teaspoon table salt, divided
- 4 (5 to 7 ounces / 142 to 198 g) bone-in chicken thighs, trimmed
- ¼ teaspoon pepper
- 2 garlic cloves, minced
- 1½ teaspoons caraway seeds
- 1 teaspoon ground coriander
- 1 teaspoon ground cumin
- ½ teaspoon paprika
- ⅛ teaspoon cayenne pepper
- 2 cups chicken broth
- 1 cup French green lentils, picked over and rinsed
- 2 pounds (907 g) butternut squash, peeled, seeded, and cut into 1½-inch pieces
- 1 cup fresh parsley or cilantro leaves

1. Combine half of shallots, 1 tablespoon oil, lemon zest and juice, and ¼ teaspoon salt in bowl; set aside. Pat chicken dry with paper towels and sprinkle with ½ teaspoon salt and pepper. Using highest sauté function, heat remaining 2 teaspoons oil in Instant Pot for 5 minutes (or until just smoking). Place chicken skin side down in pot and cook until well browned on first side, about 5 minutes; transfer to plate. 2. Add remaining shallot and remaining ¼ teaspoon salt to fat left in pot and cook, using highest sauté function, until shallot is softened, about 2 minutes. Stir in garlic, caraway, coriander, cumin, paprika, and cayenne and cook until fragrant, about 30 seconds. Stir in broth, scraping up any browned bits, then stir in lentils. 3. Nestle chicken skin side up into lentils and add any accumulated juices. Arrange squash on top. Lock lid in place and close pressure release valve. Select high pressure cook function and cook for 15 minutes. 4. Turn off Instant Pot and quick-release pressure. Carefully remove lid, allowing steam to escape away from you. Transfer chicken to plate and discard skin, if desired. Season lentil mixture with salt and pepper to taste. Add parsley to shallot mixture and toss to combine. Serve chicken with lentil mixture, topping individual portions with shallot-parsley salad.

Per Serving:
calories: 513 | fat: 14g | protein: 42g | carbs: 60g | fiber: 17g | sodium: 773mg

Chapter

6

Beef, Pork, and Lamb

Chapter 6 Beef, Pork, and Lamb

Smoked Paprika and Lemon Marinated Pork Kabobs

Prep time: 10 minutes | Cook time: 10 minutes | Serves 4

- ⅓ cup finely chopped flat-leaf parsley
- ¼ cup olive oil
- 2 tablespoons minced red onion
- 1 tablespoon lemon juice
- 1 tablespoon smoked paprika
- 2 teaspoons ground cumin
- 1 clove garlic, minced
- ¼ teaspoon cayenne pepper
- ½ teaspoon salt
- 2 pork tenderloins, each about 1 pound (454 g), trimmed of silver skin and any excess fat, cut into 1¼-inch cubes
- 1 lemon, cut into wedges, for serving

1. In a large bowl, whisk together the parsley, olive oil, onion, lemon juice, smoked paprika, cumin, garlic, cayenne, and salt. Add the pork and toss to coat well. Cover and refrigerate, stirring occasionally, for at least 4 hours (or as long as overnight). 2. Soak bamboo skewers in water for 30 minutes. 3. Preheat the grill to high heat. 4. Remove the meat from the marinade, discarding the marinade. Thread the meat onto the soaked skewers and place the skewers on the grill. Cook, with the lid closed, turning occasionally, until the pork is cooked through and browned on all sides, about 8 to 10 minutes total. 5. Transfer the skewers to a serving platter and serve immediately with the lemon wedges.

Per Serving:
calories: 447 | fat: 21g | protein: 60g | carbs: 3g | fiber: 1g | sodium: 426mg

Garlic-Marinated Flank Steak

Prep time: 30 minutes | Cook time: 8 to 10 minutes | Serves 6

- ½ cup avocado oil
- ¼ cup coconut aminos
- 1 shallot, minced
- 1 tablespoon minced garlic
- 2 tablespoons chopped fresh oregano, or 2 teaspoons dried
- 1½ teaspoons sea salt
- 1 teaspoon freshly ground black pepper
- ¼ teaspoon red pepper flakes
- 2 pounds (907 g) flank steak

1. In a blender, combine the avocado oil, coconut aminos, shallot, garlic, oregano, salt, black pepper, and red pepper flakes. Process until smooth. 2. Place the steak in a zip-top plastic bag or shallow dish with the marinade. Seal the bag or cover the dish and marinate in the refrigerator for at least 2 hours or overnight. 3. Remove the steak from the bag and discard the marinade. 4. Set the air fryer to 400ºF (204ºC). Place the steak in the air fryer basket (if needed, cut into sections and work in batches). Air fry for 4 to 6 minutes, flip the steak, and cook for another 4 minutes or until the internal temperature reaches 120ºF (49ºC) in the thickest part for medium-rare (or as desired).

Per Serving:
calories: 373 | fat: 26g | protein: 33g | carbs: 1g | fiber: 0g | sodium: 672mg

Beef, Mushroom, and Green Bean Soup

Prep time: 10 minutes | Cook time: 45 minutes | Serves 4

- 2 tablespoons olive oil
- 1 pound (454 g) chuck or round beef roast, cut into 2-inch pieces
- 1 large onion, diced
- ½ teaspoon sea salt
- ¼ teaspoon freshly ground black pepper
- ½ cup white wine
- 8 cups chicken broth
- 1 pound (454 g) green beans
- 8 ounces (227 g) cremini (baby bella) mushrooms, chopped
- 3 tablespoons tomato paste
- ½ teaspoon dried oregano

1. In a large stockpot, heat the olive oil over medium-high heat. Add the beef and brown, 5 to 7 minutes. Add the onion, salt, and pepper and cook for 5 minutes. Add the wine and cook for 4 minutes. Add the broth, green beans, mushrooms, tomato paste, and oregano and stir to combine. 2. Bring to a boil, reduce the heat to low, cover, and simmer for 35 to 45 minutes, until the meat is cooked through. Serve.

Per Serving:
calories: 307 | fat: 14g | protein: 28g | carbs: 17g | fiber: 5g | sodium: 265mg

Mediterranean Pork with Olives

Prep time: 10 minutes | Cook time: 6 to 8 hours | Serves 4

- 1 small onion, sliced
- 4 thick-cut, bone-in pork chops
- 1 cup low-sodium chicken broth
- Juice of 1 lemon
- 2 garlic cloves, minced
- 1 teaspoon sea salt
- 1 teaspoon dried oregano
- 1 teaspoon dried parsley
- ½ teaspoon freshly ground black pepper
- 2 cups whole green olives, pitted
- 1 pint cherry tomatoes

1. Put the onion in a slow cooker and arrange the pork chops on top. 2. In a small bowl, whisk together the chicken broth, lemon juice, garlic, salt, oregano, parsley, and pepper. Pour the sauce over the pork chops. Top with the olives and tomatoes. 3. Cover the cooker and cook for 6 to 8 hours on Low heat.

Per Serving:
calories: 339 | fat: 14g | protein: 42g | carbs: 6g | fiber: 4g | sodium: 708mg

Stuffed Flank Steak

Prep time: 20 minutes | Cook time: 6 hours | Serves 6

- 2 pounds (907 g) flank steak
- Sea salt and freshly ground pepper, to taste
- 1 tablespoon olive oil
- ¼ cup onion, diced
- 1 clove garlic, minced
- 2 cups baby spinach, chopped
- ½ cup dried tomatoes, chopped
- ½ cup roasted red peppers, diced
- ½ cup almonds, toasted and chopped
- Kitchen twine
- ½ cup chicken stock

1. Lay the flank steak out on a cutting board, and generously season with sea salt and freshly ground pepper 2. Heat the olive oil in a medium saucepan. Add the onion and garlic. 3. Cook 5 minutes on medium heat, or until onion is tender and translucent, stirring frequently. 4. Add the spinach, tomatoes, peppers, and chopped almonds, and cook an additional 3 minutes, or until the spinach wilts slightly. 5. Let the tomato and spinach mixture cool to room temperature. Spread the tomato and spinach mixture evenly over the flank steak. 6. Roll the flank steak up slowly, and tie it securely with kitchen twine on both ends and in the middle. 7. Brown the flank steak in the same pan for 5 minutes, turning it carefully to brown all sides. 8. Place steak in a slow cooker with the chicken stock. Cover and cook on low for 4–6 hours. 9. Cut into rounds, discarding the twine, and serve.

Per Serving:
calories: 287 | fat: 14g | protein: 35g | carbs: 4g | fiber: 2g | sodium: 95mg

Easy Honey-Garlic Pork Chops

Prep time: 15 minutes | Cook time: 25 minutes | Serves 4

- 4 pork chops, boneless or bone-in
- ¼ teaspoon salt
- ⅛ teaspoon freshly ground black pepper
- 3 tablespoons extra-virgin olive oil
- 5 tablespoons low-sodium chicken broth, divided
- 6 garlic cloves, minced
- ¼ cup honey
- 2 tablespoons apple cider vinegar

1. Season the pork chops with salt and pepper and set aside. 2. In a large sauté pan or skillet, heat the oil over medium-high heat. Add the pork chops and sear for 5 minutes on each side, or until golden brown. 3. Once the searing is complete, move the pork to a dish and reduce the skillet heat from medium-high to medium. Add 3 tablespoons of chicken broth to the pan; this will loosen the bits and flavors from the bottom of the skillet. 4. Once the broth has evaporated, add the garlic to the skillet and cook for 15 to 20 seconds, until fragrant. Add the honey, vinegar, and the remaining 2 tablespoons of broth. Bring the heat back up to medium-high and continue to cook for 3 to 4 minutes. 5. Stir periodically; the sauce is ready once it's thickened slightly. Add the pork chops back into the pan, cover them with the sauce, and cook for 2 minutes. Serve.

Per Serving:
calories: 302 | fat: 16g | protein: 22g | carbs: 19g | fiber: 0g | sodium: 753mg

Beef Ragù

Prep time: 15 minutes | Cook time: 4½ hours | Serves 6

- 1 medium yellow onion, diced small
- 3 cloves garlic, minced
- 6 tablespoons tomato paste
- 3 tablespoons chopped fresh oregano leaves (or 3 teaspoons dried oregano)
- 1 (4-pound / 1.8-kg) beef chuck roast, halved
- Coarse sea salt
- Black pepper
- 2 cups beef stock
- 2 tablespoons red wine vinegar

1. Combine the onion, garlic, tomato paste, and oregano in the slow cooker. 2. Season the roast halves with salt and pepper and place on top of the onion mixture in the slow cooker. Add the beef stock. 3. Cover and cook until meat is tender and can easily be pulled apart with a fork, on high for 4½ hours, or on low for 9 hours. Let cool 10 minutes. 4. Shred the meat while it is still in the slow cooker using two forks. Stir the vinegar into the sauce. Serve hot, over pasta.

Per Serving:
calories: 482 | fat: 19g | protein: 67g | carbs: 13g | fiber: 1g | sodium: 292mg

Cheesy Low-Carb Lasagna

Prep time: 10 minutes | Cook time: 10 minutes | Serves 4

Meat Layer:
- Extra-virgin olive oil
- 1 pound (454 g) 85% lean ground beef
- 1 cup prepared marinara sauce
- ¼ cup diced celery
- ¼ cup diced red onion
- ½ teaspoon minced garlic
- Kosher salt and black pepper, to taste

Cheese Layer:
- 8 ounces (227 g) ricotta cheese
- 1 cup shredded Mozzarella cheese
- ½ cup grated Parmesan cheese
- 2 large eggs
- 1 teaspoon dried Italian seasoning, crushed
- ½ teaspoon each minced garlic, garlic powder, and black pepper

1. For the meat layer: Grease a cake pan with 1 teaspoon olive oil. 2. In a large bowl, combine the ground beef, marinara, celery, onion, garlic, salt, and pepper. Place the seasoned meat in the pan. 3. Place the pan in the air fryer basket. Set the air fryer to 375°F (191°C) for 10 minutes. 4. Meanwhile, for the cheese layer: In a medium bowl, combine the ricotta, half the Mozzarella, the Parmesan, lightly beaten eggs, Italian seasoning, minced garlic, garlic powder, and pepper. Stir until well blended. 5. At the end of the cooking time, spread the cheese mixture over the meat mixture. Sprinkle with the remaining ½ cup Mozzarella. Set the air fryer to 375°F (191°C) for 10 minutes, or until the cheese is browned and bubbling. 6. At the end of the cooking time, use a meat thermometer to ensure the meat has reached an internal temperature of 160°F (71°C). 7. Drain the fat and liquid from the pan. Let stand for 5 minutes before serving.

Per Serving:
calories: 555 | fat: 36g | protein: 45g | carbs: 10g | fiber: 2g | sodium: 248mg

Ground Lamb with Lentils and Pomegranate Seeds

Prep time: 15 minutes | Cook time: 15 minutes | Serves 4

- 1 tablespoon extra-virgin olive oil
- ½ pound (227 g) ground lamb
- 1 teaspoon red pepper flakes
- ½ teaspoon ground cumin
- ½ teaspoon kosher salt
- ¼ teaspoon freshly ground black pepper
- 2 garlic cloves, minced
- 2 cups cooked, drained lentils
- 1 hothouse or English cucumber, diced
- ⅓ cup fresh mint, chopped
- ⅓ cup fresh parsley, chopped
- Zest of 1 lemon
- 1 cup plain Greek yogurt
- ½ cup pomegranate seeds

1. Heat the olive oil in a large skillet or sauté pan over medium-high heat. Add the lamb and season with the red pepper flakes, cumin, salt, and black pepper. Cook the lamb without stirring until the bottom is brown and crispy, about 5 minutes. Stir and cook for another 5 minutes. Using a spatula, break up the lamb into smaller pieces. Add the garlic and cook, stirring occasionally, for 1 minute. Transfer the lamb mixture to a medium bowl. 2. Add the lentils to the skillet and cook, stirring occasionally, until brown and crisp, about 5 minutes. Return the lamb to the skillet, mix, and warm through, about 3 minutes. Transfer to the large bowl. Add the cucumber, mint, parsley, and lemon zest, mixing together gently. 3. Spoon the yogurt into 4 bowls and top each with some of the lamb mixture. Garnish with the pomegranate seeds.

Per Serving:
calories: 370 | fat: 18g | protein: 24g | carbs: 30g | fiber: 10g | sodium: 197mg

One-Pan Greek Pork and Vegetables

Prep time: 10 minutes | Cook time: 40 minutes | Serves 3

- 1 pound (454 g) pork shoulder, cut into 1-inch cubes
- ¾ teaspoon fine sea salt, divided
- ½ teaspoon freshly ground black pepper, divided, plus more for serving
- 4 tablespoons extra virgin olive oil, divided
- 1 medium red onion, sliced
- 1 medium green bell pepper, seeded and sliced
- 1 medium carrot, peeled and julienned
- ¼ cup dry red wine
- 15 cherry tomatoes, halved
- 2 tablespoons hot water
- ½ teaspoon dried oregano

1. Scatter the cubed pork onto a cutting board and sprinkle with ¼ teaspoon of sea salt and ¼ teaspoon of black pepper. Flip the pieces over and sprinkle an additional ¼ teaspoon of sea salt and the remaining ¼ teaspoon of black pepper. 2. In a large pan wide enough to hold all the pork in a single layer, heat 3 tablespoons of olive oil over high heat. Once the oil is hot, add the pork pieces and brown for 2 minutes, then flip the pork pieces and brown for 2 more minutes. (Do not stir.) 3. Add the onions and sauté for 2 minutes and then add the bell peppers and carrots and sauté for 2 more minutes, ensuring all vegetables are coated with the oil. Reduce the heat to medium, cover the pan loosely, and cook for 5 minutes, stirring occasionally. 4. Add the wine and continue cooking for about 4 minutes, using a wooden spatula to scrape any browned bits from the bottom of the pan. Add about 20 cherry tomato halves and stir gently, then drizzle with the remaining 1 tablespoon of olive oil and add the hot water. Reduce the heat to low and simmer for 15–20 minutes or until all the liquids are absorbed. Remove the pan from the heat. 5. Sprinkle the oregano over the top. Top with the remaining cherry tomato halves and season to taste with the remaining ¼ teaspoon of sea salt and additional black pepper before serving. Store covered in the refrigerator for up to 3 days.

Per Serving:
calories: 407 | fat: 27g | protein: 30g | carbs: 8g | fiber: 2g | sodium: 700mg

Grilled Kefta

Prep time: 10 minutes | Cook time: 5 minutes | Serves 4

- 1 medium onion
- ⅓ cup fresh Italian parsley
- 1 pound (454 g) ground beef
- ¼ teaspoon ground cumin
- ¼ teaspoon cinnamon
- 1 teaspoon salt
- ½ teaspoon freshly ground black pepper

1. Preheat a grill or grill pan to high. 2. Mince the onion and parsley in a food processor until finely chopped. 3. In a large bowl, using your hands, combine the beef with the onion mix, ground cumin, cinnamon, salt, and pepper. 4. Divide the meat into 6 portions. Form each portion into a flat oval. 5. Place the patties on the grill or grill pan and cook for 3 minutes on each side.

Per Serving:
calories: 203 | fat: 10g | protein: 24g | carbs: 3g | fiber: 1g | sodium: 655mg

Herbed Lamb Steaks

Prep time: 30 minutes | Cook time: 15 minutes | Serves 4

- ½ medium onion
- 2 tablespoons minced garlic
- 2 teaspoons ground ginger
- 1 teaspoon ground cinnamon
- 1 teaspoon onion powder
- 1 teaspoon cayenne pepper
- 1 teaspoon salt
- 4 (6 ounces / 170 g) boneless lamb sirloin steaks
- Oil, for spraying

1. In a blender, combine the onion, garlic, ginger, cinnamon, onion powder, cayenne pepper, and salt and pulse until the onion is minced. 2. Place the lamb steaks in a large bowl or zip-top plastic bag and sprinkle the onion mixture over the top. Turn the steaks until they are evenly coated. Cover with plastic wrap or seal the bag and refrigerate for 30 minutes. 3. Preheat the air fryer to 330°F (166°C). Line the air fryer basket with parchment and spray lightly with oil. 4. Place the lamb steaks in a single layer in the prepared basket, making sure they don't overlap. You may need to work in batches, depending on the size of your air fryer. 5. Cook for 8 minutes, flip, and cook for another 7 minutes, or until the internal temperature reaches 155°F (68°C).

Per Serving:
calories: 255 | fat: 10g | protein: 35g | carbs: 5g | fiber: 1g | sodium: 720mg

Savoy Cabbage Rolls

Prep time: 10 minutes | Cook time: 16 minutes | Serves 10

- 1 medium head savoy cabbage
- 3 cups water, divided
- ½ pound (227 g) ground beef
- 1 cup long-grain rice
- 1 small red bell pepper, seeded and minced
- 1 medium onion, peeled and diced
- 1 cup beef broth
- 1 tablespoon olive oil
- 2 tablespoons minced fresh mint
- 1 teaspoon dried tarragon
- 1 teaspoon salt
- ½ teaspoon ground black pepper
- 2 tablespoons lemon juice

1. Remove the large outer leaves from cabbage and set aside. Remove remaining cabbage leaves and place them in the Instant Pot®. Pour in 1 cup water. 2. Close lid, set steam release to Sealing, press the Steam button, and set time to 1 minute. Press the Adjust button to change the pressure to Low. When the timer beeps, quick-release the pressure until the float valve drops and then open lid. Press the Cancel button. Drain cabbage leaves in a colander and then move them to a kitchen towel. 3. In a medium mixing bowl, add ground beef, rice, bell pepper, onion, broth, olive oil, mint, tarragon, salt, and black pepper. Stir to combine. 4. Place the large uncooked cabbage leaves on the bottom of the Instant Pot®. 5. Remove the stem running down the center of each steamed cabbage leaf and tear each leaf in half lengthwise. Place 1 tablespoon ground beef mixture in the center of each cabbage piece. Loosely fold the sides of the leaf over the filling and then fold the top and bottom of the leaf over the folded sides. As you complete them, place each stuffed cabbage leaf in the pot. 6. Pour remaining 2 cups water and lemon juice over the stuffed cabbage rolls. Close lid, set steam release to Sealing, press the Manual button, and set time to 15 minutes. When the timer beeps, let pressure release naturally for 10 minutes. Quick-release any remaining pressure until the float valve drops and then open lid. 7. Carefully move stuffed cabbage rolls to a serving platter. Serve warm.

Per Serving:
calories: 117 | fat: 3g | protein: 6g | carbs: 15g | fiber: 0g | sodium: 337mg

Lebanese Ground Meat with Rice

Prep time: 10 minutes | Cook time: 35 minutes | Serves 6

- 3 tablespoons olive oil, divided
- 4 ounces (113 g) cremini (baby bella) mushrooms, sliced
- ½ red onion, finely chopped
- 2 garlic cloves, minced
- 1 pound (454 g) lean ground beef
- ¾ teaspoon ground
- cinnamon
- ¼ teaspoon ground cloves
- ¼ teaspoon ground nutmeg
- Sea salt
- Freshly ground black pepper
- 1½ cups basmati rice
- 2¾ cups chicken broth
- ½ cup pine nuts
- ½ cup coarsely chopped fresh Italian parsley

1. In a sauté pan, heat 2 tablespoons of olive oil over medium-high heat. Add the mushrooms, onion, and garlic and sauté until the mushrooms release their liquid and the onion becomes translucent, about 5 minutes. Add the ground beef, cinnamon, cloves, and nutmeg and season with salt and pepper. Reduce the heat to medium and cook, stirring often, for 5 to 7 minutes, until the meat is cooked through. Remove the beef mixture from the pan with a slotted spoon and set aside in a medium bowl. 2. In the same pan, heat the remaining 1 tablespoon of olive oil over medium-high heat. Add the rice and fry for about 5 minutes. Return the meat mixture to the pan and mix well to combine with the rice. Add the broth and bring to a boil, then reduce the heat to low, cover, and simmer for 15 minutes, or until you can fluff the rice with a fork. 3. Add the pine nuts and mix well. Garnish with the parsley and serve.

Per Serving:
calories: 422 | fat: 19g | protein: 22g | carbs: 43g | fiber: 2g | sodium: 81mg

Garlic Balsamic London Broil

Prep time: 30 minutes | Cook time: 8 to 10 minutes | Serves 8

- 2 pounds (907 g) London broil
- 3 large garlic cloves, minced
- 3 tablespoons balsamic vinegar
- 3 tablespoons whole-grain
- mustard
- 2 tablespoons olive oil
- Sea salt and ground black pepper, to taste
- ½ teaspoon dried hot red pepper flakes

1. Score both sides of the cleaned London broil. 2. Thoroughly combine the remaining ingredients; massage this mixture into the meat to coat it on all sides. Let it marinate for at least 3 hours. 3. Set the air fryer to 400°F (204°C); Then cook the London broil for 15 minutes. Flip it over and cook another 10 to 12 minutes. Bon appétit!

Per Serving:
calories: 240 | fat: 15g | protein: 23g | carbs: 2g | fiber: 0g | sodium: 141mg

Beef Burger

Prep time: 20 minutes | Cook time: 12 minutes | Serves 4

- 1¼ pounds (567 g) lean ground beef
- 1 tablespoon coconut aminos
- 1 teaspoon Dijon mustard
- A few dashes of liquid smoke
- 1 teaspoon shallot powder
- 1 clove garlic, minced
- ½ teaspoon cumin powder
- ¼ cup scallions, minced
- ⅓ teaspoon sea salt flakes
- ⅓ teaspoon freshly cracked mixed peppercorns
- 1 teaspoon celery seeds
- 1 teaspoon parsley flakes

1. Mix all of the above ingredients in a bowl; knead until everything is well incorporated. 2. Shape the mixture into four patties. Next, make a shallow dip in the center of each patty to prevent them puffing up during air frying. 3. Spritz the patties on all sides using nonstick cooking spray. Cook approximately 12 minutes at 360°F (182°C). 4. Check for doneness, an instant-read thermometer should read 160°F (71°C). Bon appétit!

Per Serving:
calories: 193 | fat: 7g | protein: 31g | carbs: 1g | fiber: 0g | sodium: 304mg

Smothered Pork Chops with Leeks and Mustard

Prep time: 15 minutes | Cook time: 35 minutes | Serves 4

- 4 (8- to 10-ounce/ 227- to 283-g) bone-in blade-cut pork chops, about ¾ inch thick, trimmed
- ½ teaspoon table salt
- ½ teaspoon pepper
- 4 teaspoons extra-virgin olive oil, divided
- 2 ounces (57 g) pancetta, chopped fine
- 1 tablespoon all-purpose
- flour
- ¾ cup dry white wine
- 1½ pounds (680 g) leeks, ends trimmed, halved lengthwise, sliced into 3-inch lengths, and washed thoroughly
- 1 tablespoon Dijon mustard
- 2 tablespoons chopped fresh parsley

1. Pat pork chops dry with paper towels. Using sharp knife, cut 2 slits, about 2 inches apart, through fat on edge of each chop. Sprinkle with salt and pepper. Using highest sauté function, heat 2 teaspoons oil in Instant Pot for 5 minutes (or until just smoking). Brown 2 chops on both sides, 6 to 8 minutes; transfer to plate. Repeat with remaining 2 teaspoons oil and remaining chops; transfer to plate. 2. Add pancetta to fat left in pot and cook, using highest sauté function, until softened and lightly browned, about 2 minutes. Stir in flour and cook for 30 seconds. Stir in wine, scraping up any browned bits and smoothing any lumps. Stir in leeks and cook until softened, about 3 minutes. Nestle chops into pot (chops will overlap) and add any accumulated juices. Lock lid in place and close pressure release valve. Select high pressure cook function and cook for 10 minutes. 3. Turn off Instant Pot and let pressure release naturally for 15 minutes. Quick-release any remaining pressure, then carefully remove lid, allowing steam to escape away from you. Transfer chops to serving platter, tent with aluminum foil, and let rest while finishing leeks. 4. Using highest sauté function, bring leek mixture to simmer. Stir in mustard and cook until slightly thickened, about 5 minutes. Season with salt and pepper to taste. Spoon leek mixture over chops and sprinkle with parsley. Serve.

Per Serving:
calories: 390 | fat: 17g | protein: 35g | carbs: 13g | fiber: 1g | sodium: 780mg

Pork and Cabbage Egg Roll in a Bowl

Prep time: 10 minutes | Cook time: 10 minutes | Serves 6

- 1 tablespoon light olive oil
- 1 pound (454 g) ground pork
- 1 medium yellow onion, peeled and chopped
- 1 clove garlic, peeled and minced
- 2 teaspoons minced fresh
- ginger
- ¼ cup low-sodium chicken broth
- 2 tablespoons soy sauce
- 2 (10-ounce/ 283-g) bags shredded coleslaw mix
- 1 teaspoon sesame oil
- 1 teaspoon garlic chili sauce

1. Press the Sauté button on the Instant Pot® and heat olive oil. Add pork and sauté until cooked through, about 8 minutes. Add onion, garlic, and ginger, and cook until fragrant, about 2 minutes. Stir in chicken broth and soy sauce. Press the Cancel button. 2. Spread coleslaw mix over pork, but do not mix. Close lid, set steam release to Sealing, press the Manual button, and set time to 0 minutes. 3. When the timer beeps, quick-release the pressure until the float valve drops and open lid. Stir in sesame oil and garlic chili sauce. Serve hot.

Per Serving:
calories: 283 | fat: 24g | protein: 12g | carbs: 5g | fiber: 2g | sodium: 507mg

Beef Bourguignon with Egg Noodles

Prep time: 15 minutes | Cook time: 8 hours | Serves 8

- 2 pounds (907 g) lean beef stew meat
- 6 tablespoons all-purpose flour
- 2 large carrots, cut into 1-inch slices
- 16 ounces (454 g) pearl onions, peeled fresh or frozen, thawed
- 8 ounces (227 g) mushrooms, stems removed
- 2 garlic cloves, minced
- ¾ cup beef stock
- ½ cup dry red wine
- ¼ cup tomato paste
- 1½ teaspoons sea salt
- ½ teaspoon dried rosemary
- ¼ teaspoon dried thyme
- ½ teaspoon black pepper
- 8 ounces (227 g) uncooked egg noodles
- ¼ cup chopped fresh thyme leaves

1. Place the beef in a medium bowl, sprinkle with the flour, and toss well to coat. 2. Place the beef mixture, carrots, onions, mushrooms, and garlic in the slow cooker. 3. Combine the stock, wine, tomato paste, salt, rosemary, thyme, and black pepper in a small bowl. Stir into the beef mixture. 4. Cover and cook on low for 8 hours. 5. Cook the noodles according to package directions, omitting any salt. 6. Serve the beef mixture over the noodles, sprinkled with the thyme.

Per Serving:
calories: 397 | fat: 6g | protein: 34g | carbs: 53g | fiber: 6g | sodium: 592mg

Smoky Pork Tenderloin

Prep time: 5 minutes | Cook time: 19 to 22 minutes | Serves 6

- 1½ pounds (680 g) pork tenderloin
- 1 tablespoon avocado oil
- 1 teaspoon chili powder
- 1 teaspoon smoked paprika
- 1 teaspoon garlic powder
- 1 teaspoon sea salt
- 1 teaspoon freshly ground black pepper

1. Pierce the tenderloin all over with a fork and rub the oil all over the meat. 2. In a small dish, stir together the chili powder, smoked paprika, garlic powder, salt, and pepper. 3. Rub the spice mixture all over the tenderloin. 4. Set the air fryer to 400ºF (204ºC). Place the pork in the air fryer basket and air fry for 10 minutes. Flip the tenderloin and cook for 9 to 12 minutes more, until an instant-read thermometer reads at least 145ºF (63ºC). 5. Allow the tenderloin to rest for 5 minutes, then slice and serve.

Per Serving:
calories: 149 | fat: 5g | protein: 24g | carbs: 1g | fiber: 0g | sodium: 461mg

Greek-Style Ground Beef Pita Sandwiches

Prep timePrep Time: 15 minutes | Cook Time: 10 minutes | Serves 2

For the beef
- 1 tablespoon olive oil
- ½ medium onion, minced
- 2 garlic cloves, minced
- 6 ounces (170 g) lean ground beef
- 1 teaspoon dried oregano
- For the yogurt sauce
- ⅓ cup plain Greek yogurt
- 1 ounce (28 g) crumbled
For the sandwiches
- 2 large Greek-style pitas
- ½ cup cherry tomatoes, halved
- feta cheese (about 3 tablespoons)
- 1 tablespoon minced fresh parsley
- 1 tablespoon minced scallion
- 1 tablespoon freshly squeezed lemon juice
- Pinch salt
- 1 cup diced cucumber
- Salt
- Freshly ground black pepper

Make the beef Heat the olive oil in a sauté pan over medium high-heat. Add the onion, garlic, and ground beef and sauté for 7 minutes, breaking up the meat well. When the meat is no longer pink, drain off any fat and stir in the oregano. Turn off the heat. Make the yogurt sauce In a small bowl, combine the yogurt, feta, parsley, scallion, lemon juice, and salt. To assemble the sandwiches 1. Warm the pitas in the microwave for 20 seconds each. 2. To serve, spread some of the yogurt sauce over each warm pita. Top with the ground beef, cherry tomatoes, and diced cucumber. Season with salt and pepper. Add additional yogurt sauce if desired.

Per Serving:
calories: 541 | fat: 21g | protein: 29g | carbs: 57g | fiber: 4g | sodium: 694mg

Ground Pork and Eggplant Casserole

Prep time: 20 minutes | Cook time: 18 minutes | Serves 8

- 2 pounds (907 g) lean ground pork
- 1 large yellow onion, peeled and diced
- 1 stalk celery, diced
- 1 medium green bell pepper, seeded and diced
- 2 medium eggplants, cut into ½" pieces
- 4 cloves garlic, peeled and minced
- ⅛ teaspoon dried thyme
- 1 tablespoon freeze-dried parsley
- 3 tablespoons tomato paste
- ½ teaspoon hot sauce
- 2 teaspoons Worcestershire sauce
- 1 teaspoon salt
- ½ teaspoon ground black pepper
- 1 large egg, beaten
- ½ cup low-sodium chicken broth

1. Press the Sauté button on the Instant Pot® and add pork, onion, celery, and bell pepper to the pot. Cook until pork is no longer pink, breaking it apart as it cooks, about 8 minutes. 2. Drain and discard any fat rendered from pork. Add eggplant, garlic, thyme, parsley, tomato paste, hot sauce, Worcestershire sauce, salt, pepper, and egg. Stir well, then press the Cancel button. 3. Pour in chicken broth. Close lid, set steam release to Sealing, press the Manual button, and set time to 10 minutes. When the timer beeps, let pressure release

naturally, about 25 minutes. Open lid and serve hot.
Per Serving:
calories: 292 | fat: 18g | protein: 22g | carbs: 10g | fiber: 4g | sodium: 392mg

Pork Loin in Dried Fig Sauce

Prep time: 10 minutes | Cook time: 55 minutes | Serves 6

- 3 teaspoon fresh rosemary
- 1 tablespoon fresh thyme
- Sea salt and freshly ground pepper, to taste
- 1 (3-pound / 1.4-kg) pork loin
- ½ cup olive oil
- 3 carrots, peeled and sliced
- 1 onion, diced
- 1 garlic clove, minced
- 1 cup dried figs, cut into small pieces
- 1 cup white wine
- Juice of 1 lemon

1. Preheat the oven to 300ºF (150ºC). 2. Mix the rosemary, thyme, sea salt, and freshly ground pepper together to make a dry rub. Press the rub into the pork loin. 3. Heat the olive oil in a skillet. 4. Add the pork loin, carrots, onion, and garlic, and cook for 15 minutes, or until the pork is browned. 5. Transfer all to a shallow roasting pan. 6. Add the figs, white wine, and lemon juice. 7. Cover with aluminum foil and bake for 40–50 minutes, or until the meat is tender and internal temperature is about 145ºF (63ºC). 8. Transfer the meat to a serving dish, and cover with aluminum foil. Wait 15 minutes before slicing. 9. In the meantime, pour the vegetables, figs, and liquids into a blender. Process until smooth and strain through a sieve or strainer. 10. Transfer to a gravy dish, or pour directly over the sliced meat.
Per Serving:
calories: 546 | fat: 28g | protein: 52g | carbs: 22g | fiber: 4g | sodium: 139mg

Pork Casserole with Fennel and Potatoes

Prep time: 20 minutes | Cook time: 6 to 8 hours | Serves 6

- 2 large fennel bulbs
- 3 pounds (1.4 kg) pork tenderloin, cut into 1½-inch pieces
- 2 pounds (907 g) red potatoes, quartered
- 1 cup low-sodium chicken broth
- 4 garlic cloves, minced
- 1½ teaspoons dried thyme
- 1 teaspoon dried parsley
- 1 teaspoon sea salt
- Freshly ground black pepper
- ⅓ cup shredded Parmesan cheese

1. Cut the stalks off the fennel bulbs. Trim a little piece from the bottom of the bulbs to make them stable, then cut straight down through the bulbs to halve them. Cut the halves into quarters. Peel off and discard any wilted outer layers. Cut the fennel pieces crosswise into slices. 2. In a slow cooker, combine the fennel, pork, and potatoes. Stir to mix well. 3. In a small bowl, whisk together the chicken broth, garlic, thyme, parsley, and salt until combined. Season with pepper and whisk again. Pour the sauce over the pork. 4. Cover the cooker and cook for 6 to 8 hours on Low heat. 5. Top with Parmesan cheese for serving.
Per Serving:
calories: 412 | fat: 7g | protein: 55g | carbs: 31g | fiber: 5g | sodium: 592mg

Beef Meatballs in Garlic Cream Sauce

Prep time: 15 minutes | Cook time: 6 to 8 hours | Serves 4

For the Sauce:
- 1 cup low-sodium vegetable broth or low-sodium chicken broth
- 1 tablespoon extra-virgin olive oil
- 2 garlic cloves, minced
- 1 tablespoon dried onion flakes
- 1 teaspoon dried rosemary
- 2 tablespoons freshly squeezed lemon juice
- Pinch sea salt
- Pinch freshly ground black pepper

For the Meatballs:
- 1 pound (454 g) raw ground beef
- 1 large egg
- 2 tablespoons bread crumbs
- 1 teaspoon ground cumin
- 1 teaspoon salt
- ½ teaspoon freshly ground black pepper

To Finish
- 2 cups plain Greek yogurt
- 2 tablespoons chopped fresh parsley

Make the Sauce: 1. In a medium bowl, whisk together the vegetable broth, olive oil, garlic, onion flakes, rosemary, lemon juice, salt, and pepper until combined. Make the Meatballs: 2. In a large bowl, mix together the ground beef, egg, bread crumbs, cumin, salt, and pepper until combined. Shape the meat mixture into 10 to 12 (2½-inch) meatballs. 3. Pour the sauce into the slow cooker. 4. Add the meatballs to the slow cooker. 5. Cover the cooker and cook for 6 to 8 hours on Low heat. 6. Stir in the yogurt. Replace the cover on the cooker and cook for 15 to 30 minutes on Low heat, or until the sauce has thickened. 7. Garnish with fresh parsley for serving.

Per Serving:
calories: 345 | fat: 20g | protein: 29g | carbs: 13g | fiber: 1g | sodium: 842mg

Pepper Steak

Prep time: 30 minutes | Cook time: 16 to 20 minutes | Serves 4

- 1 pound (454 g) cube steak, cut into 1-inch pieces
- 1 cup Italian dressing
- 1½ cups beef broth
- 1 tablespoon soy sauce
- ½ teaspoon salt
- ¼ teaspoon freshly ground black pepper
- ¼ cup cornstarch
- 1 cup thinly sliced bell pepper, any color
- 1 cup chopped celery
- 1 tablespoon minced garlic
- 1 to 2 tablespoons oil

1. In a large resealable bag, combine the beef and Italian dressing. Seal the bag and refrigerate to marinate for 8 hours. 2. In a small bowl, whisk the beef broth, soy sauce, salt, and pepper until blended. 3. In another small bowl, whisk ¼ cup water and the cornstarch until dissolved. Stir the cornstarch mixture into the beef broth mixture until blended. 4. Preheat the air fryer to 375ºF (191ºC). 5. Pour the broth mixture into a baking pan. Cook for 4 minutes. Stir and cook for 4 to 5 minutes more. Remove and set aside. 6. Increase the air fryer temperature to 400ºF (204ºC). Line the air fryer basket with parchment paper. 7. Remove the steak from the marinade and place it in a medium bowl. Discard the marinade. Stir in the bell pepper, celery, and garlic. 8. Place the steak and pepper mixture on the parchment. Spritz with oil. 9. Cook for 4 minutes. Shake the basket and cook for 4 to 7 minutes more, until the vegetables are tender and the meat reaches an internal temperature of 145ºF (63ºC). Serve with the gravy.

Per Serving:
calories: 302 | fat: 14g | protein: 27g | carbs: 15g | fiber: 1g | sodium: 635mg

One-Pot Pork Loin Dinner

Prep time: 35 minutes | Cook time: 28 minutes | Serves 6

- 1 tablespoon olive oil
- 1 small onion, peeled and diced
- 1 pound (454 g) boneless pork loin, cut into 1" pieces
- ½ teaspoon salt
- ¼ teaspoon ground black pepper
- ½ cup white wine
- 1 cup low-sodium chicken broth
- 1 large rutabaga, peeled and diced
- 1 large turnip, peeled and diced
- 4 small Yukon Gold or red potatoes, quartered
- 4 medium carrots, peeled and diced
- 1 stalk celery, finely diced
- ½ cup sliced leeks, white part only
- ½ teaspoon mild curry powder
- ¼ teaspoon dried thyme
- 2 teaspoons dried parsley
- 3 tablespoons lemon juice
- 2 large Granny Smith apples, peeled, cored, and diced

1. Press the Sauté button on the Instant Pot® and heat oil. Add onion and cook until tender, about 3 minutes. Add pork and season with salt and pepper. Cook until pork begins to brown, about 5 minutes. Add wine, broth, rutabaga, and turnip and stir well. Add potatoes, carrots, celery, leeks, curry powder, thyme, parsley, and lemon juice to the pot. Stir to combine. Press the Cancel button. 2. Close lid, set steam release to Sealing, press the Manual button, and set time to 15 minutes. When the timer beeps, let pressure release naturally, about 25 minutes. Press the Cancel button. 3. Open lid and add diced apples. Press the Sauté button and simmer for 5 minutes or until apples are tender. Serve immediately in large bowls.

Per Serving:
calories: 271 | fat: 4g | protein: 14g | carbs: 30g | fiber: 5g | sodium: 316mg

Spiced Beef on Whole-Wheat Flatbread

Prep time: 10 minutes | Cook time: 15 minutes | Serves 4

- 6 ounces (170 g) lean ground beef
- 2 garlic cloves, minced
- 1 small onion, grated
- 3 tablespoons tomato paste
- 1 tablespoon minced flat-leaf parsley
- ½ teaspoon salt
- ¼ teaspoon cayenne pepper
- ¼ teaspoon ground cumin
- ¼ teaspoon sweet paprika
- ⅛ teaspoon ground
- cinnamon
- 4 whole-wheat flatbread rounds
- ½ cup plain Greek yogurt, for garnish
- 2 tablespoons cilantro leaves, for garnish
- 1 Persian cucumber, cut lengthwise into thin sheets
- ½ small red onion, thinly sliced
- Lemon wedges, for serving

1. Preheat the oven to 475°F(245ºC). 2 In medium skillet, brown the meat over medium-high heat, breaking up with a spatula, about 4 minutes. When the meat is browned, drain off the excess fat. Add the garlic and grated onion and cook, stirring, 1 minute. Add the tomato paste, parsley, salt, cayenne, cumin, paprika, and cinnamon and cook, stirring, for 1 more minute. 3. Place 2 flatbread rounds onto each of 2 large baking sheets and spoon the meat on top of them, dividing equally. Bake in the preheated oven, rotating the pans halfway through, for 6 to 8 minutes, until the edges of the flatbread are beginning to brown. 4. Remove from the oven and serve with a dollop of yogurt, a sprinkling of cilantro, a few strips of cucumber, and a few slices of red onion on top. Serve lemon wedges on the side for squeezing over the meat.

Per Serving:
calories: 293 | fat: 8g | protein: 21g | carbs: 37g | fiber: 5g | sodium: 793mg

Steak with Bell Pepper

Prep time: 30 minutes | Cook time: 20 to 23 minutes | Serves 6

- ¼ cup avocado oil
- ¼ cup freshly squeezed lime juice
- 2 teaspoons minced garlic
- 1 tablespoon chili powder
- ½ teaspoon ground cumin
- Sea salt and freshly ground black pepper, to taste
- 1 pound (454 g) top sirloin
- steak or flank steak, thinly sliced against the grain
- 1 red bell pepper, cored, seeded, and cut into ½-inch slices
- 1 green bell pepper, cored, seeded, and cut into ½-inch slices
- 1 large onion, sliced

1. In a small bowl or blender, combine the avocado oil, lime juice, garlic, chili powder, cumin, and salt and pepper to taste. 2. Place the sliced steak in a zip-top bag or shallow dish. Place the bell peppers and onion in a separate zip-top bag or dish. Pour half the marinade over the steak and the other half over the vegetables. Seal both bags and let the steak and vegetables marinate in the refrigerator for at least 1 hour or up to 4 hours. 3. Line the air fryer basket with an air fryer liner or aluminum foil. Remove the vegetables from their bag or dish and shake off any excess marinade. Set the air fryer to 400°F (204ºC). Place the vegetables in the air fryer basket and cook for 13 minutes. 4. Remove the steak from its bag or dish and shake off any excess marinade. Place the steak on top of the vegetables in the air fryer, and cook for 7 to 10 minutes or until an instant-read thermometer reads 120ºF (49ºC) for medium-rare (or cook to your desired doneness). 5. Serve with desired fixings, such as keto tortillas, lettuce, sour cream, avocado slices, shredded Cheddar cheese, and cilantro.

Per Serving:
calories: 252 | fat: 18g | protein: 17g | carbs: 6g | fiber: 2g | sodium: 81mg

Pork Tenderloin with Vegetable Ragu

Prep time: 25 minutes | Cook time: 18 minutes | Serves 6

- 2 tablespoons light olive oil, divided
- 1 (1½-pound / 680-g) pork tenderloin
- ¼ teaspoon salt
- ¼ teaspoon ground black pepper
- 1 medium zucchini, trimmed and sliced
- 1 medium yellow squash, sliced
- 1 medium onion, peeled and chopped
- 1 medium carrot, peeled and
- grated
- 1 (14½-ounce / 411-g) can diced tomatoes, drained
- 2 cloves garlic, peeled and minced
- ¼ teaspoon crushed red pepper flakes
- 1 tablespoon chopped fresh basil
- 1 tablespoon chopped fresh oregano
- 1 sprig fresh thyme
- ½ cup red wine

1. Press the Sauté button on the Instant Pot® and heat 1 tablespoon oil. Season pork with salt and black pepper. Brown pork lightly on all sides, about 2 minutes per side. Transfer pork to a plate and set aside. 2. Add remaining 1 tablespoon oil to the pot. Add zucchini and squash, and cook until tender, about 5 minutes. Add onion and carrot, and cook until just softened, about 5 minutes. Add tomatoes, garlic, crushed red pepper flakes, basil, oregano, thyme, and red wine to pot, and stir well. Press the Cancel button. 3. Top vegetable mixture with browned pork. Close lid, set steam release to Sealing, press the Manual button, and set time to 3 minutes. When the timer beeps, quick-release the pressure until the float valve drops and open lid. Transfer pork to a cutting board and cut into 1" slices. Pour sauce on a serving platter and arrange pork slices on top. Serve immediately.

Per Serving:
calories: 190 | fat: 7g | protein: 23g | carbs: 9g | fiber: 2g | sodium: 606mg

Chapter
7

Snacks and Appetizers

Chapter 7 Snacks and Appetizers

Spanish-Style Pan-Roasted Cod

Prep time: 15 minutes | Cook time: 25 minutes | Serves 4

- 4 tablespoons olive oil
- 8 garlic cloves, minced
- ½ small onion, finely chopped
- ½ pound (227 g) small red or new potatoes, quartered
- 1 (14½-ounce / 411-g) can low-sodium diced tomatoes, with their juices
- 16 pimiento-stuffed low-salt Spanish olives, sliced (about ⅓ cup)
- 4 tablespoons finely chopped fresh parsley
- 4 (4-ounce / 113-g) cod fillets, about 1 inch thick
- Salt and freshly ground black pepper (optional)

1. In a 10-inch skillet, heat 2 tablespoons of the olive oil and the garlic over medium heat. Cook, being careful not to let the garlic burn, until it becomes fragrant, 1 to 2 minutes. 2. Raise the temperature to medium-high heat, and add the onion, potatoes, tomatoes with their juices, olives, and 3 tablespoons of the parsley. Bring to a boil. Reduce the heat to maintain a simmer, cover, and cook for 15 to 18 minutes, until the potatoes are tender. Transfer the mixture from the skillet to a large bowl; keep warm. Wipe out the skillet and return it to the stovetop. 3. Heat the remaining 2 tablespoons olive oil in the skillet over medium-high heat. Season the cod with salt and pepper, if desired, and add it to the pan. Cook for 2 to 3 minutes, then carefully flip the fish and cook for 2 to 3 minutes more, until the fish flakes easily with a fork. 4. Divide the tomato mixture evenly among four plates and top each with a cod fillet. Sprinkle evenly with the remaining 1 tablespoon parsley and serve.

Per Serving:
1 cup: calories: 297 | fat: 20g | protein: 9g | carbs: 20g | fiber: 4g | sodium: 557mg

Black Bean Corn Dip

Prep time: 10 minutes | Cook time: 10 minutes | Serves 4

- ½ (15 ounces / 425 g) can black beans, drained and rinsed
- ½ (15 ounces / 425 g) can corn, drained and rinsed
- ¼ cup chunky salsa
- 2 ounces (57 g) reduced-fat

- cream cheese, softened
- ¼ cup shredded reduced-fat Cheddar cheese
- ½ teaspoon ground cumin
- ½ teaspoon paprika
- Salt and freshly ground black pepper, to taste

1. Preheat the air fryer to 325ºF (163ºC). 2. In a medium bowl, mix together the black beans, corn, salsa, cream cheese, Cheddar cheese,

cumin, and paprika. Season with salt and pepper and stir until well combined. 3. Spoon the mixture into a baking dish. 4. Place baking dish in the air fryer basket and bake until heated through, about 10 minutes. 5. Serve hot.

Per Serving:
calories: 119 | fat: 2g | protein: 8g | carbs: 19g | fiber: 6g | sodium: 469mg

Bite-Size Stuffed Peppers

Prep time: 15 minutes | Cook time: 10 minutes | Serves 8 to 10

- 20 to 25 mini sweet bell peppers, assortment of colors
- 1 tablespoon extra-virgin olive oil
- 4 ounces (113 g) goat cheese, at room temperature

- 4 ounces (113 g) mascarpone cheese, at room temperature
- 1 tablespoon fresh chives, chopped
- 1 tablespoon lemon zest

1. Preheat the oven to 400°F(205ºC). 2. Remove the stem, cap, and any seeds from the peppers. Put them into a bowl and toss to coat with the olive oil. 3. Put the peppers onto a baking sheet; bake for 8 minutes. 4. Remove the peppers from the oven and let cool completely. 5. In a medium bowl, add the goat cheese, mascarpone cheese, chives, and lemon zest. Stir to combine, then spoon mixture into a piping bag. 6. Fill each pepper to the top with the cheese mixture, using the piping bag. 7. Chill the peppers in the fridge for at least 30 minutes before serving.

Per Serving:
calories: 141 | fat: 11g | protein: 4g | carbs: 6g | fiber: 2g | sodium: 73mg

Sweet Potato Fries

Prep time: 15 minutes | Cook time: 40 minutes | Serves 4

- 4 large sweet potatoes, peeled and cut into finger-like strips
- 2 tablespoons extra-virgin

- olive oil
- ½ teaspoon salt
- ½ teaspoon freshly ground black pepper

1. Preheat the oven to 350°F(180ºC). Line a baking sheet with aluminum foil. Toss the potatoes in a large bowl with the olive oil, salt, and pepper. 2. Arrange the potatoes in a single layer on the baking sheet and bake until brown at the edges, about 40 minutes. Serve piping hot.

Per Serving:
calories: 171 | fat: 7g | protein: 2g | carbs: 26g | fiber: 4g | sodium: 362mg

Black-Eyed Pea "Caviar"

Prep time: 10 minutes | Cook time: 30 minutes | Makes 5 cups

- 1 cup dried black-eyed peas
- 4 cups water
- 1 pound (454 g) cooked corn kernels
- ½ medium red onion, peeled and diced
- ½ medium green bell pepper, seeded and diced
- 2 tablespoons minced pickled jalapeño pepper
- 1 medium tomato, diced
- 2 tablespoons chopped fresh cilantro
- ¼ cup red wine vinegar
- 2 tablespoons extra-virgin olive oil
- 1 teaspoon salt
- ½ teaspoon ground black pepper
- ½ teaspoon ground cumin

1. Add black-eyed peas and water to the Instant Pot®. Close lid, set steam release to Sealing, press the Manual button, and set time to 30 minutes. 2. When the timer beeps, let pressure release naturally, about 25 minutes, and open lid. Drain peas and transfer to a large mixing bowl. Add all remaining ingredients and stir until thoroughly combined. Cover and refrigerate for 2 hours before serving.

Per Serving:
½ cup: calories: 28 | fat: 1g | protein: 1g | carbs: 4 | fiber: 1g | sodium: 51mg

Mini Lettuce Wraps

Prep time: 10 minutes | Cook time: 0 minutes | Makes about 1 dozen wraps

- 1 tomato, diced
- 1 cucumber, diced
- 1 red onion, sliced
- 1 ounce (28 g) low-fat feta cheese, crumbled
- Juice of 1 lemon
- 1 tablespoon olive oil
- Sea salt and freshly ground pepper, to taste
- 12 small, intact iceberg lettuce leaves

1. Combine the tomato, cucumber, onion, and feta in a bowl with the lemon juice and olive oil. 2. Season with sea salt and freshly ground pepper. 3. Without tearing the leaves, gently fill each leaf with a tablespoon of the veggie mixture. 4. Roll them as tightly as you can, and lay them seam-side-down on a serving platter.

Per Serving:
1 wrap: calories: 26 | fat: 2g | protein: 1g | carbs: 2g | fiber: 1g | sodium: 20mg

Roasted Stuffed Figs

Prep time: 5 minutes | Cook time: 10 minutes | Serves 5

- 10 medium fresh figs
- 1½ tablespoons finely chopped walnuts
- 1½ tablespoons finely chopped almonds
- ½ teaspoon ground cinnamon
- ½ teaspoon sesame seeds
- Pinch of salt
- 1½ teaspoons honey

1. Preheat the oven to 300°F (150ºC). Line a large baking sheet with foil, and grease the foil with olive oil. 2. Using a sharp knife, make a small vertical cut into the side of each fig, making sure not to cut all the way through the fig. Set aside. 3. In a small bowl, combine the walnuts, almonds, cinnamon, sesame seeds, and salt. Mix well. 4. Stuff each fig with 1 teaspoon of the filling, gently pressing the filling into the figs. Place the figs on the prepared baking sheet, and bake for 10 minutes. 5. While the figs are baking, add the honey to a small saucepan over medium heat. Heat the honey for 30 seconds or until it becomes thin and watery. 6. Transfer the roasted figs to a plate. Drizzle a few drops of the warm honey over each fig before serving. Store in an airtight container in the refrigerator for up to 2 weeks.

Per Serving:
calories: 114 | fat: 3g | protein: 2g | carbs: 22g | fiber: 4g | sodium: 2mg

Pesto Cucumber Boats

Prep time: 10 minutes | Cook time: 0 minutes | Serves 4 to 6

- 3 medium cucumbers
- ¼ teaspoon salt
- 1 packed cup fresh basil leaves
- 1 garlic clove, minced
- ¼ cup walnut pieces
- ¼ cup grated Parmesan cheese
- ¼ cup extra-virgin olive oil
- ½ teaspoon paprika

1. Cut each cucumber in half lengthwise and again in half crosswise to make 4 stocky pieces. Use a spoon to remove the seeds and hollow out a shallow trough in each piece. Lightly salt each piece and set aside on a platter. 2. In a blender or food processor, combine the basil, garlic, walnuts, Parmesan cheese, and olive oil and blend until smooth. 3. Use a spoon to spread pesto into each cucumber "boat" and sprinkle each with paprika. Serve.

Per Serving:
calories: 143 | fat: 14g | protein: 3g | carbs: 4g | fiber: 1g | sodium: 175mg

Sfougato

Prep time: 10 minutes | Cook time: 8 minutes | Serves 4

- ½ cup crumbled feta cheese
- ¼ cup bread crumbs
- 1 medium onion, peeled and minced
- 4 tablespoons all-purpose flour
- 2 tablespoons minced fresh
- mint
- ½ teaspoon salt
- ½ teaspoon ground black pepper
- 1 tablespoon dried thyme
- 6 large eggs, beaten
- 1 cup water

1. In a medium bowl, mix cheese, bread crumbs, onion, flour, mint, salt, pepper, and thyme. Stir in eggs. 2. Spray an 8" round baking dish with nonstick cooking spray. Pour egg mixture into dish. 3. Place rack in the Instant Pot® and add water. Fold a long piece of foil in half lengthwise. Lay foil over rack to form a sling and top with dish. Cover loosely with foil. Close lid, set steam release to Sealing, press the Manual button, and set time to 8 minutes. 4. When the timer beeps, quick-release the pressure until the float valve drops. Open lid. Let stand 5 minutes, then remove dish from pot.

Per Serving:
calories: 226 | fat: 12g | protein: 14g | carbs: 15g | fiber: 1g | sodium: 621mg

Bravas-Style Potatoes

Prep time: 15 minutes | Cook time: 50 minutes | Serves 8

- 4 large russet potatoes (about 2½ pounds / 1.1 kg), scrubbed and cut into 1' cubes
- 1 teaspoon kosher salt, divided
- ½ teaspoon ground black pepper
- ¼ teaspoon red-pepper flakes
- ½ small yellow onion, chopped
- 1 large tomato, chopped
- 1 tablespoon sherry vinegar
- 1 teaspoon hot paprika
- 1 tablespoon chopped fresh flat-leaf parsley Hot sauce (optional)

1. Preheat the oven to 450°F(235ºC). Bring a large pot of well-salted water to a boil. 2. Boil the potatoes until just barely tender, 5 to 8 minutes. Drain and transfer the potatoes to a large rimmed baking sheet. Add 1 tablespoon of the oil, ½ teaspoon of the salt, the black pepper, and pepper flakes. With 2 large spoons, toss very well to coat the potatoes in the oil. Spread the potatoes out on the baking sheet. Roast until the bottoms are starting to brown and crisp, 20 minutes. Carefully flip the potatoes and roast until the other side is golden and crisp, 15 to 20 minutes. 3. Meanwhile, in a small skillet over medium heat, warm the remaining 1 teaspoon oil. Cook the onion until softened, 3 to 4 minutes. Add the tomato and cook until it's broken down and saucy, 5 minutes. Stir in the vinegar, paprika, and the remaining ½ teaspoon salt. Cook for 30 seconds, remove from the heat, and cover to keep warm. 4. Transfer the potatoes to a large serving bowl. Drizzle the tomato mixture over the potatoes. Sprinkle with the parsley. Serve with hot sauce, if using.

Per Serving:
calories: 173 | fat: 2g | protein: 4g | carbs: 35g | fiber: 3g | sodium: 251mg

Pea and Arugula Crostini with Pecorino Romano

Prep time: 10 minutes | Cook time: 15 minutes | Serves 6 to 8

- 1½ cups fresh or frozen peas
- 1 loaf crusty whole-wheat bread, cut into thin slices
- 3 tablespoons olive oil, divided
- 1 small garlic clove, finely mined or pressed
- Juice of ½ lemon
- ½ teaspoon salt
- ¼ teaspoon freshly ground black pepper
- 1 cup (packed) baby arugula
- ¼ cup thinly shaved Pecorino Romano

1. Preheat the oven to 350°F(180ºC). 2. Fill a small saucepan with about ½ inch of water. Bring to a boil over medium-high heat. Add the peas and cook for 3 to 5 minutes, until tender. Drain and rinse with cold water. 3. Arrange the bread slices on a large baking sheet and brush the tops with 2 tablespoons olive oil. Bake in the preheated oven for about 8 minutes, until golden brown. 4. Meanwhile, in a medium bowl, mash the peas gently with the back of a fork. They should be smashed but not mashed into a paste. Add the remaining 1 tablespoon olive oil, lemon juice, garlic, salt, and pepper and stir to mix. 5. Spoon the pea mixture onto the toasted bread slices and top with the arugula and cheese. Serve immediately.

Per Serving:
calories: 301 | fat: 13g | protein: 14g | carbs: 32g | fiber: 6g | sodium: 833mg

Fig-Pecan Energy Bites

Prep time: 20 minutes |Cook time: 0 minutes| Serves: 6

- ¾ cup diced dried figs (6 to 8)
- ½ cup chopped pecans
- ¼ cup rolled oats (old-fashioned or quick oats)
- 2 tablespoons ground
- flaxseed or wheat germ (flaxseed for gluten-free)
- 2 tablespoons powdered or regular peanut butter
- 2 tablespoons honey

1. In a medium bowl, mix together the figs, pecans, oats, flaxseed, and peanut butter. Drizzle with the honey, and mix everything together. A wooden spoon works well to press the figs and nuts into the honey and powdery ingredients. (If you're using regular peanut butter instead of powdered, the dough will be stickier to handle, so freeze the dough for 5 minutes before making the bites.) 2. Divide the dough evenly into four sections in the bowl. Dampen your hands with water—but don't get them too wet or the dough will stick to them. Using your hands, roll three bites out of each of the four sections of dough, making 12 total energy bites. 3. Enjoy immediately or chill in the freezer for 5 minutes to firm up the bites before serving. The bites can be stored in a sealed container in the refrigerator for up to 1 week.

Per Serving:
calories: 196 | fat: 10g | protein: 4g | carbs: 26g | fiber: 4g | sodium: 13mg

Manchego Crackers

Prep time: 15 minutes | Cook time: 15 minutes | Makes 40 crackers

- 4 tablespoons butter, at room temperature
- 1 cup finely shredded Manchego cheese
- 1 cup almond flour
- 1 teaspoon salt, divided
- ¼ teaspoon freshly ground black pepper
- 1 large egg

1. Using an electric mixer, cream together the butter and shredded cheese until well combined and smooth. 2. In a small bowl, combine the almond flour with ½ teaspoon salt and pepper. Slowly add the almond flour mixture to the cheese, mixing constantly until the dough just comes together to form a ball. 3. Transfer to a piece of parchment or plastic wrap and roll into a cylinder log about 1½ inches thick. Wrap tightly and refrigerate for at least 1 hour. 4. Preheat the oven to 350°F(180ºC). Line two baking sheets with parchment paper or silicone baking mats. 5. To make the egg wash, in a small bowl, whisk together the egg and remaining ½ teaspoon salt. 6. Slice the refrigerated dough into small rounds, about ¼ inch thick, and place on the lined baking sheets. 7. Brush the tops of the crackers with egg wash and bake until the crackers are golden and crispy, 12 to 15 minutes. Remove from the oven and allow to cool on a wire rack. 8. Serve warm or, once fully cooled, store in an airtight container in the refrigerator for up to 1 week.

Per Serving:
2 crackers: calories: 73 | fat: 7g | protein: 3g | carbs: 1g | fiber: 1g | sodium: 154mg

Savory Lentil Dip

Prep time: 10 minutes | Cook time: 32 minutes | Serves 16

- 2 tablespoons olive oil
- ½ medium yellow onion, peeled and diced
- 3 cloves garlic, peeled and minced
- 2 cups dried red lentils, rinsed and drained
- 4 cups water
- 1 teaspoon salt
- ¼ teaspoon ground black pepper
- 2 tablespoons minced fresh flat-leaf parsley

1. Press the Sauté button on the Instant Pot® and heat oil. Add onion and cook 2–3 minutes, or until translucent. Add garlic and cook until fragrant, about 30 seconds. Add lentils, water, and salt to pot, and stir to combine. Close lid, set steam release to Sealing, press the Bean button, and cook for the default time of 30 minutes. 2. When the timer beeps, let pressure release naturally for 10 minutes. Quick-release any remaining pressure until the float valve drops, then open lid. Transfer lentil mixture to a food processor and blend until smooth. Season with pepper and garnish with parsley. Serve warm.

Per Serving:
calories: 76 | fat: 2g | protein: 5g | carbs: 11g | fiber: 2g | sodium: 145mg

Ranch Oyster Snack Crackers

Prep time: 3 minutes | Cook time: 12 minutes | Serves 6

- Oil, for spraying
- ¼ cup olive oil
- 2 teaspoons dry ranch seasoning
- 1 teaspoon chili powder
- ½ teaspoon dried dill
- ½ teaspoon granulated garlic
- ½ teaspoon salt
- 1 (9 ounces / 255 g) bag oyster crackers

1. Preheat the air fryer to 325ºF (163ºC). Line the air fryer basket with parchment and spray lightly with oil. 2. In a large bowl, mix together the olive oil, ranch seasoning, chili powder, dill, garlic, and salt. Add the crackers and toss until evenly coated. 3. Place the mixture in the prepared basket. 4. Cook for 10 to 12 minutes, shaking or stirring every 3 to 4 minutes, or until crisp and golden brown.

Per Serving:
calories: 261 | fat: 13g | protein: 4g | carbs: 32g | fiber: 1g | sodium: 621mg

Asian Five-Spice Wings

Prep time: 30 minutes | Cook time: 13 to 15 minutes | Serves 4

- 2 pounds (907 g) chicken wings
- ½ cup Asian-style salad dressing
- 2 tablespoons Chinese five-spice powder

1. Cut off wing tips and discard or freeze for stock. Cut remaining wing pieces in two at the joint. 2. Place wing pieces in a large sealable plastic bag. Pour in the Asian dressing, seal bag, and massage the marinade into the wings until well coated. Refrigerate for at least an hour. 3. Remove wings from bag, drain off excess marinade, and place wings in air fryer basket. 4. Air fry at 360ºF (182ºC) for 13 to 15 minutes or until juices run clear. About halfway through cooking time, shake the basket or stir wings for more even cooking. 5. Transfer cooked wings to plate in a single layer. Sprinkle half of the Chinese five-spice powder on the wings, turn, and sprinkle other side with remaining seasoning.

Per Serving:
calories: 357 | fat: 12g | protein: 51g | carbs: 9g | fiber: 2g | sodium: 591mg

Nutty Apple Salad

Prep time: 25 minutes | Cook time: 0 minutes | Serves 4

- 6 firm apples, such as Gala or Golden Delicious, peeled, cored, and sliced
- 1 tablespoon freshly squeezed lemon juice
- 2 kiwis, peeled and diced
- ½ cup sliced strawberries
- ½ cup packaged shredded coleslaw mix, without dressing
- ½ cup walnut halves
- ¼ cup slivered almonds
- ¼ cup balsamic vinegar
- ¼ cup extra-virgin olive oil
- 2 tablespoons sesame seeds, plus more for garnish (optional)
- ¼ teaspoon salt
- ¼ teaspoon freshly ground black pepper

1. In a medium bowl, toss the apple slices with the lemon juice to prevent browning. Add the kiwis, strawberries, coleslaw mix, walnuts, and almonds and toss well to mix. 2. In a small bowl, whisk together the balsamic vinegar, olive oil, and sesame seeds and season with salt and pepper. 3. Pour the dressing over the salad and toss to coat. 4. To serve, spoon into small bowls and top with additional sesame seeds if desired.

Per Serving:
calories: 371 | fat: 21g | protein: 3g | carbs: 49g | fiber: 9g | sodium: 155mg

Crispy Spiced Chickpeas

Prep time: 5 minutes | Cook time: 25 minutes | Serves 6

- 3 cans (15 ounces / 425 g each) chickpeas, drained and rinsed
- 1 cup olive oil
- 1 teaspoon paprika
- ½ teaspoon ground cumin
- ½ teaspoon kosher salt
- ¼ teaspoon ground cinnamon
- ¼ teaspoon ground black pepper

1. Spread the chickpeas on paper towels and pat dry. 2. In a large saucepan over medium-high heat, warm the oil until shimmering. Add 1 chickpea; if it sizzles right away, the oil is hot enough to proceed. 3. Add enough chickpeas to form a single layer in the saucepan. Cook, occasionally gently shaking the saucepan until golden brown, about 8 minutes. With a slotted spoon, transfer to a paper towel–lined plate to drain. Repeat with the remaining chickpeas until all the chickpeas are fried. Transfer to a large bowl. 4. In a small bowl, combine the paprika, cumin, salt, cinnamon, and pepper. Sprinkle all over the fried chickpeas and toss to coat. The chickpeas will crisp as they cool.

Per Serving:
calories: 175 | fat: 9g | protein: 6g | carbs: 20g | fiber: 5g | sodium: 509mg

Classic Hummus with Tahini

Prep time: 5 minutes | Cook time: 0 minutes | Makes about 2 cups

- 2 cups drained canned chickpeas, liquid reserved
- ½ cup tahini
- ¼ cup olive oil, plus more for garnish
- 2 cloves garlic, peeled, or to taste
- Juice of 1 lemon, plus more as needed
- 1 tablespoon ground cumin
- Salt
- Freshly ground black pepper
- 1 teaspoon paprika, for garnish
- 2 tablespoons chopped flat-leaf parsley, for garnish
- 4 whole-wheat pita bread or flatbread rounds, warmed

1. In a food processor, combine the chickpeas, tahini, oil, garlic, lemon juice, and cumin. Season with salt and pepper, and process until puréed. With the food processor running, add the reserved chickpea liquid until the mixture is smooth and reaches the desired consistency. 2. Spoon the hummus into a serving bowl, drizzle with a bit of olive oil, and sprinkle with the paprika and parsley. 3. Serve immediately, with warmed pita bread or flatbread, or cover and refrigerate for up to 2 days. Bring to room temperature before serving.

Per Serving:
¼ cup: calories: 309 | fat: 16g | protein: 9g | carbs: 36g | fiber: 7g | sodium: 341mg

Mediterranean-Style Stuffed Mushrooms

Prep time: 10 minutes | Cook time: 20 minutes | Serves 4

- 2 ounces (57 g) feta
- 1 tablespoon cream cheese
- 2 teaspoons dried oregano
- 1 tablespoon finely chopped fresh parsley
- 2 tablespoons finely chopped fresh basil
- 2 tablespoons finely chopped fresh mint
- ¼ teaspoon freshly ground black pepper
- 3 tablespoons unseasoned breadcrumbs, divided
- 2 tablespoons extra virgin olive oil, divided
- 20 medium button mushrooms, washed, dried, and stems removed

1. Preheat the oven to 400°F (205°C). Line a large baking pan with foil. 2. In a medium bowl, combine the feta, cream cheese, oregano, parsley, basil, mint, black pepper, 2 tablespoons of the breadcrumbs, and 1 tablespoon of the olive oil. Use a fork to mash the ingredients until they're combined and somewhat creamy. 3. Stuff the mushrooms with the filling and then place them in the prepared pan. 4. Sprinkle the remaining 1 tablespoon of breadcrumbs over the mushrooms and then drizzle the remaining olive oil over the top. 5. Bake for 15–20 minutes or until the tops are golden brown. Serve promptly.

Per Serving:
calories: 151 | fat: 12g | protein: 6g | carbs: 8g | fiber: 1g | sodium: 186mg

Sardine and Herb Bruschetta

Prep time: 5 minutes | Cook time: 10 minutes | Serves 4

- 8 (1-inch) thick whole-grain baguette slices
- 1½ tablespoons extra virgin olive oil
- 4 ounces (113 g) olive oil–packed sardines
- 2 tablespoons fresh lemon juice
- 1 teaspoon red wine vinegar
- 2 tablespoons capers, drained
- 3 tablespoons finely chopped onion (any variety)
- ½ teaspoon dried oregano
- 1 tablespoon finely chopped fresh mint
- 1 garlic clove, halved

1. Preheat the oven to 400°F (205°C). 2. Place the baguette slices on a large baking sheet and brush them with the olive oil. Transfer to the oven and toast until the slices are golden, about 10 minutes. 3. While the baguette slices are toasting, make the sardine topping by combining the sardines, lemon juice, and vinegar in a medium bowl. Mash with a fork. Add the capers, onions, oregano, and mint, and stir to combine. 4. When the baguette slices are done toasting, remove them from the oven and rub them with the garlic. 5. Transfer the slices to a serving platter. Place 1 heaping tablespoon of the topping onto each baguette slice. Store the sardine topping in the refrigerator for up to 3 days.

Per Serving:
calories: 249 | fat: 11g | protein: 14g | carbs: 24g | fiber: 4g | sodium: 387mg

Pita Pizza with Olives, Feta, and Red Onion

Prep time: 15 minutes | Cook time: 10 minutes | Serves 4

- 4 (6-inch) whole-wheat pitas
- 1 tablespoon extra-virgin olive oil
- ½ cup hummus
- ½ bell pepper, julienned
- ½ red onion, julienned
- ¼ cup olives, pitted and
- chopped
- ¼ cup crumbled feta cheese
- ¼ teaspoon red pepper flakes
- ¼ cup fresh herbs, chopped (mint, parsley, oregano, or a mix)

1. Preheat the broiler to low. Line a baking sheet with parchment paper or foil. 2. Place the pitas on the prepared baking sheet and brush both sides with the olive oil. Broil 1 to 2 minutes per side until starting to turn golden brown. 3. Spread 2 tablespoons hummus on each pita. Top the pitas with bell pepper, onion, olives, feta cheese, and red pepper flakes. Broil again until the cheese softens and starts to get golden brown, 4 to 6 minutes, being careful not to burn the pitas. 4. Remove from broiler and top with the herbs.

Per Serving:
calories: 185 | fat: 11g | protein: 5g | carbs: 17g | fiber: 3g | sodium: 285mg

Chapter

8

Vegetables and Sides

Chapter 8 Vegetables and Sides

Roasted Acorn Squash

Prep time: 10 minutes | Cook time: 35 minutes | Serves 6

- 2 acorn squash, medium to large
- 2 tablespoons extra-virgin olive oil
- 1 teaspoon salt, plus more for seasoning
- 5 tablespoons unsalted
- butter
- ¼ cup chopped sage leaves
- 2 tablespoons fresh thyme leaves
- ½ teaspoon freshly ground black pepper

1. Preheat the oven to 400°F(205°C). 2. Cut the acorn squash in half lengthwise. Scrape out the seeds with a spoon and cut it horizontally into ¾-inch-thick slices. 3. In a large bowl, drizzle the squash with the olive oil, sprinkle with salt, and toss together to coat. 4. Lay the acorn squash flat on a baking sheet. 5. Put the baking sheet in the oven and bake the squash for 20 minutes. Flip squash over with a spatula and bake for another 15 minutes. 6. Melt the butter in a medium saucepan over medium heat. 7. Add the sage and thyme to the melted butter and let them cook for 30 seconds. 8. Transfer the cooked squash slices to a plate. Spoon the butter/herb mixture over the squash. Season with salt and black pepper. Serve warm.

Per Serving:
calories: 188 | fat: 15g | protein: 1g | carbs: 16g | fiber: 3g | sodium: 393mg

Citrus Asparagus with Pistachios

Prep time: 10 minutes | Cook time: 15 minutes | Serves 4

- 5 tablespoons extra-virgin olive oil, divided
- Zest and juice of 2 clementines or 1 orange (about ¼ cup juice and 1 tablespoon zest)
- Zest and juice of 1 lemon
- 1 tablespoon red wine
- vinegar
- 1 teaspoon salt, divided
- ¼ teaspoon freshly ground black pepper
- ½ cup shelled pistachios
- 1 pound (454 g) fresh asparagus
- 1 tablespoon water

1. In a small bowl, whisk together 4 tablespoons olive oil, the clementine and lemon juices and zests, vinegar, ½ teaspoon salt, and pepper. Set aside. 2. In a medium dry skillet, toast the pistachios over medium-high heat until lightly browned, 2 to 3 minutes, being careful not to let them burn. Transfer to a cutting board and coarsely chop. Set aside. 3. Trim the rough ends off the asparagus, usually the last 1 to 2 inches of each spear. In a skillet, heat the remaining 1 tablespoon olive oil over medium-high heat. Add the asparagus and sauté for 2 to 3 minutes. Sprinkle with the remaining ½ teaspoon salt and add the water. Reduce the heat to

medium-low, cover, and cook until tender, another 2 to 4 minutes, depending on the thickness of the spears. 4. Transfer the cooked asparagus to a serving dish. Add the pistachios to the dressing and whisk to combine. Pour the dressing over the warm asparagus and toss to coat.

Per Serving:
calories: 271 | fat: 24g | protein: 6g | carbs: 12g | fiber: 4g | sodium: 585mg

Spinach and Sweet Pepper Poppers

Prep time: 10 minutes | Cook time: 8 minutes | Makes 16 poppers

- 4 ounces (113 g) cream cheese, softened
- 1 cup chopped fresh spinach leaves
- ½ teaspoon garlic powder
- 8 mini sweet bell peppers, tops removed, seeded, and halved lengthwise

1. In a medium bowl, mix cream cheese, spinach, and garlic powder. Place 1 tablespoon mixture into each sweet pepper half and press down to smooth. 2. Place poppers into ungreased air fryer basket. Adjust the temperature to 400°F (204°C) and air fry for 8 minutes. Poppers will be done when cheese is browned on top and peppers are tender-crisp. Serve warm.

Per Serving:
calories: 31 | fat: 2g | protein: 1g | carbs: 3g | fiber: 0g | sodium: 34mg

Creamed Spinach

Prep time: 10 minutes | Cook time: 15 minutes | Serves 4

- Vegetable oil spray
- 1 (10-ounce / 283-g) package frozen spinach, thawed and squeezed dry
- ½ cup chopped onion
- 2 cloves garlic, minced
- 4 ounces (113 g) cream
- cheese, diced
- ½ teaspoon ground nutmeg
- 1 teaspoon kosher salt
- 1 teaspoon black pepper
- ½ cup grated Parmesan cheese

1. Spray a baking pan with vegetable oil spray. 2. In a medium bowl, combine the spinach, onion, garlic, cream cheese, nutmeg, salt, and pepper. Transfer to the prepared pan. 3. Place the pan in the air fryer basket. Set the air fryer to 350°F (177°C) for 10 minutes. Open and stir to thoroughly combine the cream cheese and spinach. 4. Sprinkle the Parmesan cheese on top. Set the air fryer to 400°F (204°C) for 5 minutes, or until the cheese has melted and browned.

Per Serving:
calories: 185 | fat: 14g | protein: 10g | carbs: 7g | fiber: 3g | sodium: 746mg

Stuffed Artichokes

Prep time: 20 minutes | Cook time: 5 to 7 hours | Serves 4 to 6

- 4 to 6 fresh large artichokes
- ½ cup bread crumbs
- ½ cup grated Parmesan cheese or Romano cheese
- 4 garlic cloves, minced
- ½ teaspoon sea salt
- ½ teaspoon freshly ground
- black pepper
- ¼ cup water
- 2 tablespoons extra-virgin olive oil
- 2 tablespoons chopped fresh parsley for garnish (optional)

1. To trim and prepare the artichokes, cut off the bottom along with 1 inch from the top of each artichoke. Pull off and discard the lowest leaves nearest the stem end. Trim off any pointy tips of artichoke leaves that are poking out. Set aside. 2. In a small bowl, stir together the bread crumbs, Parmesan cheese, garlic, salt, and pepper. 3. Spread apart the artichoke leaves and stuff the bread-crumb mixture into the spaces, down to the base. 4. Pour the water into a slow cooker. 5. Place the artichokes in the slow cooker in a single layer. Drizzle the olive oil over the artichokes. 6. Cover the cooker and cook for 5 to 7 hours on Low heat, or until the artichokes are tender. 7. Garnish with fresh parsley if desired.

Per Serving:
calories: 224 | fat: 12g | protein: 12g | carbs: 23g | fiber: 8g | sodium: 883mg

Roasted Vegetables with Lemon Tahini

Prep time: 15 minutes | Cook time: 25 minutes | Serves 4

For the Dressing:
- ½ cup tahini
- ½ cup water, as needed
- 3 tablespoons freshly

For the Vegetables:
- 8 ounces (227 g) baby potatoes, halved
- 8 ounces (227 g) baby carrots
- 1 head cauliflower, cored and cut into large chunks
- 2 red bell peppers, quartered
- 1 zucchini, cut into 1-inch

- squeezed lemon juice
- Sea salt

- pieces
- ¼ cup olive oil
- 1½ teaspoons garlic powder
- ¼ teaspoon dried oregano
- ¼ teaspoon dried thyme
- Sea salt
- Freshly ground black pepper
- Red pepper flakes (optional)

Make the Dressing: 1. In a small bowl, stir together the tahini, water, and lemon juice until well blended. 2. Taste, season with salt, and set aside. Make the Vegetables: 3. Preheat the oven to 425°F(220°C). Line a baking sheet with parchment paper. 4. Place the potatoes in a microwave-safe bowl with 3 tablespoons water, cover with a paper plate, and microwave on high for 4 minutes. Drain any excess water. 5. Transfer the potatoes to a large bowl and add the carrots, cauliflower, bell peppers, zucchini, olive oil, garlic powder, oregano, and thyme. Season with salt and black pepper. 6. Spread the vegetables in a single layer on the prepared baking sheet and roast until fork-tender and a little charred, about 25 minutes. 7. Transfer the vegetables to a large bowl and add the dressing and red pepper flakes, if desired. Toss to coat. 8. Serve the roasted vegetables alongside your favorite chicken or fish dish.

Per Serving:
calories: 412 | fat: 30g | protein: 9g | carbs: 31g | fiber: 9g | sodium: 148mg

Greek Stewed Zucchini

Prep time: 5 minutes | Cook time: 40 minutes | Serves 4 to 6

- ¼ cup extra-virgin olive oil
- 1 small yellow onion, peeled and slivered
- 4 medium zucchini squash, cut into ½-inch-thick rounds
- 4 small garlic cloves, minced
- 1 to 2 teaspoons dried

- oregano
- 2 cups chopped tomatoes
- ½ cup halved and pitted Kalamata olives
- ¾ cup crumbled feta cheese
- ¼ cup chopped fresh flat-leaf Italian parsley, for garnish (optional)

1. In a large skillet, heat the oil over medium-high heat. Add the slivered onion and sauté until just tender, 6 to 8 minutes. Add the zucchini, garlic, and oregano and sauté another 6 to 8 minutes, or until zucchini is just tender. 2. Add the tomatoes and bring to a boil. Reduce the heat to low and add the olives. Cover and simmer on low heat for 20 minutes, or until the flavors have developed and the zucchini is very tender. 3. Serve warm topped with feta and parsley (if using).

Per Serving:
calories: 183 | fat: 15g | protein: 5g | carbs: 10g | fiber: 3g | sodium: 269mg

Roasted Brussels Sprouts with Delicata Squash and Balsamic Glaze

Prep time: 10 minutes | Cook time: 30 minutes | Serves 2

- ½ pound (227 g) Brussels sprouts, ends trimmed and outer leaves removed
- 1 medium delicata squash, halved lengthwise, seeded, and cut into 1-inch pieces
- 1 cup fresh cranberries
- 2 teaspoons olive oil

- Salt
- Freshly ground black pepper
- ½ cup balsamic vinegar
- 2 tablespoons roasted pumpkin seeds
- 2 tablespoons fresh pomegranate arils (seeds)

1. Preheat oven to 400°F (205°C) and set the rack to the middle position. Line a sheet pan with parchment paper. 2. Combine the Brussels sprouts, squash, and cranberries in a large bowl. Drizzle with olive oil, and season liberally with salt and pepper. Toss well to coat and arrange in a single layer on the sheet pan. 3. Roast for 30 minutes, turning vegetables halfway through, or until Brussels sprouts turn brown and crisp in spots and squash has golden-brown spots. 4. While vegetables are roasting, prepare the balsamic glaze by simmering the vinegar for 10 to 12 minutes, or until mixture has reduced to about ¼ cup and turns a syrupy consistency. 5. Remove the vegetables from the oven, drizzle with balsamic syrup, and sprinkle with pumpkin seeds and pomegranate arils before serving.

Per Serving:
calories: 201 | fat: 7g | protein: 6g | carbs: 21g | fiber: 8g | sodium: 34mg

Roasted Brussels Sprouts with Tahini-Yogurt Sauce

Prep time: 10 minutes | Cook time: 35 minutes | Serves 4

- 1 pound (454 g) Brussels sprouts, trimmed and halved lengthwise
- 6 tablespoons extra-virgin olive oil, divided
- 1 teaspoon salt, divided
- ½ teaspoon garlic powder
- ¼ teaspoon freshly ground black pepper
- ¼ cup plain whole-milk Greek yogurt
- ¼ cup tahini
- Zest and juice of 1 lemon

1. Preheat the oven to 425ºF (220ºC). Line a baking sheet with aluminum foil or parchment paper and set aside. 2. Place the Brussels sprouts in a large bowl. Drizzle with 4 tablespoons olive oil, ½ teaspoon salt, the garlic powder, and pepper and toss well to coat. 3. Place the Brussels sprouts in a single layer on the baking sheet, reserving the bowl, and roast for 20 minutes. Remove from the oven and give the sprouts a toss to flip. Return to the oven and continue to roast until browned and crispy, another 10 to 15 minutes. Remove from the oven and return to the reserved bowl. 4. In a small bowl, whisk together the yogurt, tahini, lemon zest and juice, remaining 2 tablespoons olive oil, and remaining ½ teaspoon salt. Drizzle over the roasted sprouts and toss to coat. Serve warm.

Per Serving:
calories: 330 | fat: 29g | protein: 7g | carbs: 15g | fiber: 6g | sodium: 635mg

Zucchini Fritters with Manchego and Smoked Paprika Yogurt

Prep time: 10 minutes | Cook time: 10 minutes | Serves 4 to 6

- 6 small zucchini, grated on the large holes of a box grater
- 1¼ teaspoons salt, divided
- 1 cup plain Greek yogurt
- 2 teaspoons smoked paprika
- Juice of ½ lemon
- 4 ounces (113 g) manchego cheese, grated
- ¼ cup finely chopped fresh parsley
- 4 scallions, thinly sliced
- 3 eggs, beaten
- ½ cup all-purpose flour
- ¼ teaspoon freshly ground black pepper
- Neutral-flavored oil (such as grapeseed, safflower, or sunflower seed) for frying

1. Put the grated zucchini in a colander. Sprinkle 1 teaspoon of salt over the top and then toss to combine. Let sit over the sink for at least 20 minutes to drain. Transfer the zucchini to a clean dishtowel and squeeze out as much of the water as you can. 2. Meanwhile, make the yogurt sauce. In a small bowl, stir together the yogurt, smoked paprika, lemon juice, and the remaining ¼ teaspoon of salt. 3. In a large bowl, combine the zucchini, cheese, parsley, scallions, eggs, flour, and pepper and stir to mix. 4. Fill a large saucepan with ½ inch of oil and heat over medium-high heat. When the oil is very hot, drop the batter in by rounded tablespoons, cooking 4 or 5 fritters at a time, flattening each dollop with the back of the spoon. Cook until golden on the bottom, about 2 minutes, then flip and cook on the second side until golden, about 2 minutes more. Transfer the cooked fritters to a plate lined with paper towels to drain and repeat until all of the batter has been cooked.

Per Serving:
calories: 237 | fat: 14g | protein: 11g | carbs: 18g | fiber: 3g | sodium: 655mg

Glazed Carrots

Prep time: 10 minutes | Cook time: 8 to 10 minutes | Serves 4

- 2 teaspoons honey
- 1 teaspoon orange juice
- ½ teaspoon grated orange rind
- ⅛ teaspoon ginger
- 1 pound (454 g) baby carrots
- 2 teaspoons olive oil
- ¼ teaspoon salt

1. Combine honey, orange juice, grated rind, and ginger in a small bowl and set aside. 2. Toss the carrots, oil, and salt together to coat well and pour them into the air fryer basket. 3. Roast at 390ºF (199ºC) for 5 minutes. Shake basket to stir a little and cook for 2 to 4 minutes more, until carrots are barely tender. 4. Pour carrots into a baking pan. 5. Stir the honey mixture to combine well, pour glaze over carrots, and stir to coat. 6. Roast at 360ºF (182ºC) for 1 minute or just until heated through.

Per Serving:
calories: 71 | fat: 2g | protein: 1g | carbs: 12g | fiber: 3g | sodium: 234mg

Garlic-Parmesan Crispy Baby Potatoes

Prep time: 10 minutes | Cook time: 15 minutes | Serves 4

- Oil, for spraying
- 1 pound (454 g) baby potatoes
- ½ cup grated Parmesan cheese, divided
- 3 tablespoons olive oil
- 2 teaspoons granulated garlic
- ½ teaspoon onion powder
- ½ teaspoon salt
- ¼ teaspoon freshly ground black pepper
- ¼ teaspoon paprika
- 2 tablespoons chopped fresh parsley, for garnish

1. Line the air fryer basket with parchment and spray lightly with oil. 2. Rinse the potatoes, pat dry with paper towels, and place in a large bowl. 3. In a small bowl, mix together ¼ cup of Parmesan cheese, the olive oil, garlic, onion powder, salt, black pepper, and paprika. Pour the mixture over the potatoes and toss to coat. 4. Transfer the potatoes to the prepared basket and spread them out in an even layer, taking care to keep them from touching. You may need to work in batches, depending on the size of your air fryer. 5. Air fry at 400ºF (204ºC) for 15 minutes, stirring after 7 to 8 minutes, or until easily pierced with a fork. Continue to cook for another 1 to 2 minutes, if needed. 6. Sprinkle with the parsley and the remaining Parmesan cheese and serve.

Per Serving:
calories: 234 | fat: 14g | protein: 6g | carbs: 22g | fiber: 3g | sodium: 525mg

Spinach and Paneer Cheese

Prep time: 15 minutes | Cook time: 2 to 4 hours | Serves 6

- 2 pounds (907 g) fresh spinach
- 1½-inch piece fresh ginger, roughly chopped
- 5 garlic cloves, whole
- 2 fresh green chiles, roughly chopped
- 1 onion, roughly chopped
- 1 teaspoon salt
- ½ teaspoon turmeric
- 4 tomatoes, finely chopped
- 1 to 2 tablespoons cornstarch to thicken (if required)
- 4 tablespoons butter
- 1 teaspoon cumin seeds
- 3 garlic cloves, minced
- 1 tablespoon dried fenugreek leaves
- 2 tablespoons rapeseed oil
- 12 ounces (340 g) paneer, cut into cubes

1. Heat the slow cooker to high and add the spinach, ginger, garlic, chiles, onion, salt, turmeric, and tomatoes. 2. Cover and cook on high for 3 hours, or on low for 6 hours. 3. Using your immersion blender or a food processor, purée the greens to a fine, glossy consistency. The aim is to have a thick and bright-green purée. If it's a little watery you may need to reduce it on the stove to thicken, or if your slow cooker has a boil function, use it to boil off a little of the liquid. You can also thicken it up by sprinkling with some cornstarch. 4. Heat the butter in a pan and add the cumin seeds until they sizzle. Then add the minced garlic and stir until it just browns. Remove from the heat. Add the dried fenugreek leaves and pour everything into the saag that's in the slow cooker. Whisk through. 5. Fry the cubes of paneer in a little oil in the same pan, until they are golden brown. Stir into the saag. Replace the lid and let everything sit for another 10 minutes before serving.

Per Serving:
calories: 252 | fat: 17g | protein: 10g | carbs: 20g | fiber: 6g | sodium: 682mg

Beet and Watercress Salad with Orange and Dill

Prep time: 20 minutes | Cook time: 8 minutes | Serves 4

- 2 pounds (907 g) beets, scrubbed, trimmed, and cut into ¾-inch pieces
- ½ cup water
- 1 teaspoon caraway seeds
- ½ teaspoon table salt
- 1 cup plain Greek yogurt
- 1 small garlic clove, minced to paste
- 5 ounces (142 g) watercress, torn into bite-size pieces
- 1 tablespoon extra-virgin
- olive oil, divided, plus extra for drizzling
- 1 tablespoon white wine vinegar, divided
- 1 teaspoon grated orange zest plus 2 tablespoons juice
- ¼ cup hazelnuts, toasted, skinned, and chopped
- ¼ cup coarsely chopped fresh dill
- Coarse sea salt

1. Combine beets, water, caraway seeds, and table salt in Instant Pot. Lock lid in place and close pressure release valve. Select high pressure cook function and cook for 8 minutes. Turn off Instant Pot and quick-release pressure. Carefully remove lid, allowing steam to escape away from you. 2. Using slotted spoon, transfer beets to plate; set aside to cool slightly. Combine yogurt, garlic,

and 3 tablespoons beet cooking liquid in bowl; discard remaining cooking liquid. In large bowl toss watercress with 2 teaspoons oil and 1 teaspoon vinegar. Season with table salt and pepper to taste. 3. Spread yogurt mixture over surface of serving dish. Arrange watercress on top of yogurt mixture, leaving 1-inch border of yogurt mixture. Add beets to now-empty large bowl and toss with orange zest and juice, remaining 2 teaspoons vinegar, and remaining 1 teaspoon oil. Season with table salt and pepper to taste. Arrange beets on top of watercress mixture. Drizzle with extra oil and sprinkle with hazelnuts, dill, and sea salt. Serve.

Per Serving:
calories: 240 | fat: 15g | protein: 9g | carbs: 19g | fiber: 5g | sodium: 440mg

Braised Eggplant and Tomatoes

Prep time: 10 minutes | Cook time: 40 minutes | Serves 4

- 1 large eggplant, peeled and diced
- Pinch sea salt
- 1 (15-ounce / 425-g) can chopped tomatoes and juices
- 1 cup chicken broth
- 2 garlic cloves, smashed
- 1 tablespoon Italian seasoning
- 1 bay leaf
- Sea salt and freshly ground pepper, to taste

1. Cut the eggplant, and salt both sides to remove bitter juices. Let the eggplant sit for 20 minutes before rinsing and patting dry. 2. Dice eggplant. 3. Put eggplant, tomatoes, chicken broth, garlic, seasoning, and bay leaf in a large saucepot. 4. Bring to a boil and reduce heat to simmer. 5. Cover and simmer for about 30–40 minutes until eggplant is tender. Remove garlic cloves and bay leaf, season to taste, and serve.

Per Serving:
calories: 70 | fat: 1g | protein: 4g | carbs: 14g | fiber: 6g | sodium: 186mg

Garlicky Sautéed Zucchini with Mint

Prep time: 5 minutes | Cook time: 10 minutes | Serves 4

- 3 large green zucchini
- 3 tablespoons extra-virgin olive oil
- 1 large onion, chopped
- 3 cloves garlic, minced
- 1 teaspoon salt
- 1 teaspoon dried mint

1. Cut the zucchini into ½-inch cubes. 2. In a large skillet over medium heat, cook the olive oil, onions, and garlic for 3 minutes, stirring constantly. 3. Add the zucchini and salt to the skillet and toss to combine with the onions and garlic, cooking for 5 minutes. 4. Add the mint to the skillet, tossing to combine. Cook for another 2 minutes. Serve warm.

Per Serving:
calories: 147 | fat: 11g | protein: 4g | carbs: 12g | fiber: 3g | sodium: 607mg

Tingly Chili-Roasted Broccoli

Prep time: 5 minutes | Cook time: 10 minutes | Serves 2

- 12 ounces (340 g) broccoli florets
- 2 tablespoons Asian hot chili oil
- 1 teaspoon ground Sichuan peppercorns (or black pepper)
- 2 garlic cloves, finely
- chopped
- 1 (2-inch) piece fresh ginger, peeled and finely chopped
- Kosher salt and freshly ground black pepper, to taste

1. In a bowl, toss together the broccoli, chili oil, Sichuan peppercorns, garlic, ginger, and salt and black pepper to taste. 2. Transfer to the air fryer and roast at 375ºF (191ºC), shaking the basket halfway through, until lightly charred and tender, about 10 minutes. Remove from the air fryer and serve warm.

Per Serving:
calories: 141 | fat: 9g | protein: 5g | carbs: 13g | fiber: 5g | sodium: 57mg

Parmesan Mushrooms

Prep time: 5 minutes | Cook time: 15 minutes | Serves 4

- Oil, for spraying
- 1 pound (454 g) cremini mushrooms, stems trimmed
- 2 tablespoons olive oil
- 2 teaspoons granulated garlic
- 1 teaspoon dried onion soup
- mix
- ½ teaspoon salt
- ¼ teaspoon freshly ground black pepper
- ⅓ cup grated Parmesan cheese, divided

1. Line the air fryer basket with parchment and spray lightly with oil. 2. In a large bowl, toss the mushrooms with the olive oil, garlic, onion soup mix, salt, and black pepper until evenly coated. 3. Place the mushrooms in the prepared basket. 4. Roast at 370ºF (188ºC) for 13 minutes. 5. Sprinkle half of the cheese over the mushrooms and cook for another 2 minutes. 6. Transfer the mushrooms to a serving bowl, add the remaining Parmesan cheese, and toss until evenly coated. Serve immediately.

Per Serving:
calories: 89 | fat: 9g | protein: 5g | carbs: 7g | fiber: 1g | sodium: 451mg

Lemony Orzo

Prep time: 5 minutes | Cook time: 5 minutes | Yield 2 cups

- 1 cup dry orzo
- 1 cup halved grape tomatoes
- 1 (6-ounce / 170-g) bag baby spinach
- 2 tablespoons extra-virgin
- olive oil
- ¼ teaspoon salt
- Freshly ground black pepper
- ¾ cup crumbled feta cheese
- 1 lemon, juiced and zested

1. Bring a medium pot of water to a boil. Stir in the orzo and cook uncovered for 8 minutes. Drain the water, then return the orzo to medium heat. 2. Add in the tomatoes and spinach and cook until the spinach is wilted. Add the oil, salt, and pepper and mix well. Top the dish with feta, lemon juice, and lemon zest, then toss one or two more times and enjoy!

Per Serving:
½ cup: calories: 273 | fat: 13g | protein: 10g | carbs: 32g | fiber: 6g | sodium: 445mg

Hearty Minestrone Soup

Prep time: 20 minutes | Cook time: 20 minutes | Serves 8

- 2 cups dried Great Northern beans, soaked overnight and drained
- 1 cup orzo
- 2 large carrots, peeled and diced
- 1 bunch Swiss chard, ribs removed and roughly chopped
- 1 medium zucchini, trimmed and diced
- 2 stalks celery, diced
- 1 medium onion, peeled and
- diced
- 1 teaspoon minced garlic
- 1 tablespoon Italian seasoning
- 1 teaspoon salt
- ½ teaspoon ground black pepper
- 2 bay leaves
- 1 (14½-ounce / 411-g) can diced tomatoes, including juice
- 4 cups vegetable broth
- 1 cup tomato juice

1. Place all ingredients in the Instant Pot® and stir to combine. Close lid, set steam release to Sealing, press the Soup button, and cook for the default time of 20 minutes. 2. When the timer beeps, let pressure release naturally for 10 minutes. Quick-release any remaining pressure until the float valve drops and open lid. Remove and discard bay leaves. 3. Ladle into bowls and serve warm.

Per Serving:
calories: 207 | fat: 1g | protein: 12g | carbs: 47g | fiber: 10g | sodium: 814mg

Roasted Cherry Tomato Caprese

Prep time: 15 minutes | Cook time: 30 minutes | Serves 4

- 2 pints (about 20 ounces / 567 g) cherry tomatoes
- 6 thyme sprigs
- 6 garlic cloves, smashed
- 2 tablespoons extra-virgin olive oil
- ½ teaspoon kosher salt
- 8 ounces (227 g) fresh, unsalted Mozzarella, cut into bite-size slices
- ¼ cup basil, chopped or cut into ribbons
- Loaf of crusty whole-wheat bread, for serving

1. Preheat the oven to 350ºF (180ºC). Line a baking sheet with parchment paper or foil. 2. Put the tomatoes, thyme, garlic, olive oil, and salt into a large bowl and mix together. Place on the prepared baking sheet in a single layer. Roast for 30 minutes, or until the tomatoes are bursting and juicy. 3. Place the Mozzarella on a platter or in a bowl. Pour all the tomato mixture, including the juices, over the Mozzarella. Garnish with the basil. 4. Serve with crusty bread.

Per Serving:
calories: 250 | fat: 17g | protein: 17g | carbs: 9g | fiber: 2g | sodium: 157mg

Broccoli Salad

Prep time: 5 minutes | Cook time: 7 minutes | Serves 4

- 2 cups fresh broccoli florets, chopped
- 1 tablespoon olive oil
- ¼ teaspoon salt
- ⅛ teaspoon ground black pepper
- ¼ cup lemon juice, divided
- ¼ cup shredded Parmesan cheese
- ¼ cup sliced roasted almonds

1. In a large bowl, toss broccoli and olive oil together. Sprinkle with salt and pepper, then drizzle with 2 tablespoons lemon juice. 2. Place broccoli into ungreased air fryer basket. Adjust the temperature to 350ºF (177ºC) and set the timer for 7 minutes, shaking the basket halfway through cooking. Broccoli will be golden on the edges when done. 3. Place broccoli into a large serving bowl and drizzle with remaining lemon juice. Sprinkle with Parmesan and almonds. Serve warm.

Per Serving:
calories: 76 | fat: 5g | protein: 3g | carbs: 5g | fiber: 1g | sodium: 273mg

Roasted Harissa Carrots

Prep time: 10 minutes | Cook time: 15 minutes | Serves 4

- 1 pound (454 g) carrots, peeled and sliced into 1-inch-thick rounds
- 2 tablespoons extra-virgin olive oil
- 2 tablespoons harissa
- 1 teaspoon honey
- 1 teaspoon ground cumin
- ½ teaspoon kosher salt
- ½ cup fresh parsley, chopped

1. Preheat the oven to 450ºF (235ºC). Line a baking sheet with parchment paper or foil. 2. In a large bowl, combine the carrots, olive oil, harissa, honey, cumin, and salt. Arrange in a single layer on the baking sheet. Roast for 15 minutes. Remove from the oven, add the parsley, and toss together.

Per Serving:
calories: 120 | fat: 8g | protein: 1g | carbs: 13g | fiber: 4g | sodium: 255mg

Air-Fried Okra

Prep time: 10 minutes | Cook time: 10 minutes | Serves 4

- 1 egg
- ½ cup almond milk
- ½ cup crushed pork rinds
- ¼ cup grated Parmesan cheese
- ¼ cup almond flour
- 1 teaspoon garlic powder
- ¼ teaspoon freshly ground black pepper
- ½ pound (227 g) fresh okra, stems removed and chopped into 1-inch slices

1. Preheat the air fryer to 400ºF (204ºC). 2. In a shallow bowl, whisk together the egg and milk. 3. In a second shallow bowl, combine the pork rinds, Parmesan, almond flour, garlic powder, and black pepper. 4. Working with a few slices at a time, dip the okra into the egg mixture followed by the crumb mixture. Press lightly

to ensure an even coating. 5. Working in batches if necessary, arrange the okra in a single layer in the air fryer basket and spray lightly with olive oil. Pausing halfway through the cooking time to turn the okra, air fry for 10 minutes until tender and golden brown. Serve warm.

Per Serving:
calories: 200 | fat: 16g | protein: 6g | carbs: 8g | fiber: 2g | sodium: 228mg

Herb Vinaigrette Potato Salad

Prep time: 10 minutes | Cook time: 4 minutes | Serves 10

- ¼ cup olive oil
- 3 tablespoons red wine vinegar
- ¼ cup chopped fresh flat-leaf parsley
- 2 tablespoons chopped fresh dill
- 2 tablespoons chopped fresh chives
- 1 clove garlic, peeled and
- minced
- ½ teaspoon dry mustard powder
- ¼ teaspoon ground black pepper
- 2 pounds (907 g) baby Yukon Gold potatoes
- 1 cup water
- 1 teaspoon salt

1. Whisk together oil, vinegar, parsley, dill, chives, garlic, mustard, and pepper in a small bowl. Set aside. 2. Place potatoes in a steamer basket. Place the rack in the Instant Pot®, add water and salt, then top with the steamer basket. Close lid, set steam release to Sealing, press the Manual button, and set time to 4 minutes. When the timer beeps, quick-release the pressure until the float valve drops. Press the Cancel button and open lid. 3. Transfer hot potatoes to a serving bowl. Pour dressing over potatoes and gently toss to coat. Serve warm or at room temperature.

Per Serving:
calories: 116 | fat: 6g | protein: 2g | carbs: 16g | fiber: 1g | sodium: 239mg

Five-Spice Roasted Sweet Potatoes

Prep time: 10 minutes | Cook time: 12 minutes | Serves 4

- ½ teaspoon ground cinnamon
- ¼ teaspoon ground cumin
- ¼ teaspoon paprika
- 1 teaspoon chile powder
- ⅛ teaspoon turmeric
- ½ teaspoon salt (optional)
- Freshly ground black pepper, to taste
- 2 large sweet potatoes, peeled and cut into ¾-inch cubes (about 3 cups)
- 1 tablespoon olive oil

1. In a large bowl, mix together cinnamon, cumin, paprika, chile powder, turmeric, salt, and pepper to taste. 2. Add potatoes and stir well. 3. Drizzle the seasoned potatoes with the olive oil and stir until evenly coated. 4. Place seasoned potatoes in a baking pan or an ovenproof dish that fits inside your air fryer basket. 5. Cook for 6 minutes at 390ºF (199ºC), stop, and stir well. 6. Cook for an additional 6 minutes.

Per Serving:
calories: 14 | fat: 3g | protein: 1g | carbs: 14g | fiber: 2g | sodium: 327mg

Greek Fasolakia (Green Beans)

Prep time: 10 minutes | Cook time: 6 to 8 hours | Serves 6

- 2 pounds (907 g) green beans, trimmed
- 1 (15-ounce / 425-g) can no-salt-added diced tomatoes, with juice
- 1 large onion, chopped
- 4 garlic cloves, chopped
- Juice of 1 lemon
- 1 teaspoon dried dill
- 1 teaspoon ground cumin
- 1 teaspoon dried oregano
- 1 teaspoon sea salt
- ½ teaspoon freshly ground black pepper
- ¼ cup feta cheese, crumbled

1. In a slow cooker, combine the green beans, tomatoes and their juice, onion, garlic, lemon juice, dill, cumin, oregano, salt, and pepper. Stir to mix well. 2. Cover the cooker and cook for 6 to 8 hours on Low heat. 3. Top with feta cheese for serving.

Per Serving:
calories: 94 | fat: 2g | protein: 5g | carbs: 18g | fiber: 7g | sodium: 497mg

Polenta with Mushroom Bolognese

Prep time: 5 minutes |Cook time: 25 minutes| Serves: 4

- 2 (8-ounce / 227-g) packages white button mushrooms
- 3 tablespoons extra-virgin olive oil, divided
- 1½ cups finely chopped onion (about ¾ medium onion)
- ½ cup finely chopped carrot (about 1 medium carrot)
- 4 garlic cloves, minced (about 2 teaspoons)
- 1 (18-ounce / 510-g) tube plain polenta, cut into 8
- slices
- ¼ cup tomato paste
- 1 tablespoon dried oregano, crushed between your fingers
- ¼ teaspoon ground nutmeg
- ¼ teaspoon kosher or sea salt
- ¼ teaspoon freshly ground black pepper
- ½ cup dry red wine
- ½ cup whole milk
- ½ teaspoon sugar

1. Put half the mushrooms in a food processor bowl and pulse about 15 times until finely chopped but not puréed, similar to the texture of ground meat. Repeat with the remaining mushrooms and set aside. (You can also use the food processor to chop the onion, carrot, and garlic, instead of chopping with a knife.) 2. In a large stockpot over medium-high heat, heat 2 tablespoons of oil. Add the onion and carrot and cook for 5 minutes, stirring occasionally. Add the mushrooms and garlic and cook for 5 minutes, stirring frequently. 3. While the vegetables are cooking, add the remaining 1 tablespoon of oil to a large skillet and heat over medium-high heat. Add 4 slices of polenta to the skillet and cook for 3 to 4 minutes, until golden; flip and cook for 3 to 4 minutes more. Remove the polenta from the skillet, place it on a shallow serving dish, and cover with aluminum foil to keep warm. Repeat with the remaining 4 slices of polenta. 4. To the mushroom mixture in the stockpot, add the tomato paste, oregano, nutmeg, salt, and pepper and stir. Continue cooking for another 2 to 3 minutes, until the vegetables have softened and begun to brown. Add the wine and cook for 1 to 2 minutes, scraping up any bits from the bottom of the pan while stirring with a wooden spoon. Cook until the wine

is nearly all evaporated. Lower the heat to medium. 5. Meanwhile, in a small, microwave-safe bowl, mix the milk and sugar together and microwave on high for 30 to 45 seconds, until very hot. Slowly stir the milk into the mushroom mixture and simmer for 4 more minutes, until the milk is absorbed. To serve, pour the mushroom veggie sauce over the warm polenta slices.

Per Serving:
calories: 313 | fat: 12g | protein: 7g | carbs: 41g | fiber: 4g | sodium: 467mg

Cucumbers with Feta, Mint, and Sumac

Prep time: 15 minutes | Cook time: 0 minutes | Serves 4

- 1 tablespoon extra-virgin olive oil
- 1 tablespoon lemon juice
- 2 teaspoons ground sumac
- ½ teaspoon kosher salt
- 2 hothouse or English cucumbers, diced
- ¼ cup crumbled feta cheese
- 1 tablespoon fresh mint, chopped
- 1 tablespoon fresh parsley, chopped
- ⅛ teaspoon red pepper flakes

1. In a large bowl, whisk together the olive oil, lemon juice, sumac, and salt. Add the cucumber and feta cheese and toss well. 2. Transfer to a serving dish and sprinkle with the mint, parsley, and red pepper flakes.

Per Serving:
calories: 85 | fat: 6g | protein: 3g | carbs: 8g | fiber: 1g | sodium: 230mg

Crispy Roasted Red Potatoes with Garlic, Rosemary, and Parmesan

Prep time: 10 minutes | Cook time: 55 minutes | Serves 2

- 12 ounces (340 g) red potatoes (3 to 4 small potatoes)
- 1 tablespoon olive oil
- ½ teaspoon garlic powder
- ¼ teaspoon salt
- 1 tablespoon grated Parmesan cheese
- 1 teaspoon minced fresh rosemary (from 1 sprig)

1. Preheat the oven to 425°F(220°C) and set the rack to the bottom position. Line a baking sheet with parchment paper. (Do not use foil, as the potatoes will stick.) 2. Scrub the potatoes and dry them well. Dice into 1-inch pieces. 3. In a mixing bowl, combine the potatoes, olive oil, garlic powder, and salt. Toss well to coat. 4. Lay the potatoes on the parchment paper and roast for 10 minutes. Flip the potatoes over and return to the oven for 10 more minutes. 5. Check the potatoes to make sure they are golden brown on the top and bottom. Toss them again, turn the heat down to 350°F(180°C), and roast for 30 minutes more. 6. When the potatoes are golden, crispy, and cooked through, sprinkle the Parmesan cheese over them and toss again. Return to the oven for 3 minutes to let the cheese melt a bit. 7. Remove from the oven and sprinkle with the fresh rosemary.

Per Serving:
calories: 193 | fat: 8g | protein: 5g | carbs: 28g | fiber: 3g | sodium: 334mg

Chapter
9

Vegetarian Mains

Chapter 9 Vegetarian Mains

Cauliflower Steak with Gremolata

Prep time: 15 minutes | Cook time: 25 minutes | Serves 4

- 2 tablespoons olive oil
- 1 tablespoon Italian seasoning
- 1 large head cauliflower, outer leaves removed and

Gremolata:
- 1 bunch Italian parsley (about 1 cup packed)
- 2 cloves garlic
- Zest of 1 small lemon, plus

sliced lengthwise through the core into thick "steaks"
- Salt and freshly ground black pepper, to taste
- ¼ cup Parmesan cheese

1 to 2 teaspoons lemon juice
- ½ cup olive oil
- Salt and pepper, to taste

1. Preheat the air fryer to 400°F (204°C). 2. In a small bowl, combine the olive oil and Italian seasoning. Brush both sides of each cauliflower "steak" generously with the oil. Season to taste with salt and black pepper. 3. Working in batches if necessary, arrange the cauliflower in a single layer in the air fryer basket. Pausing halfway through the cooking time to turn the "steaks," air fry for 15 to 20 minutes until the cauliflower is tender and the edges begin to brown. Sprinkle with the Parmesan and air fry for 5 minutes longer. 4. To make the gremolata: In a food processor fitted with a metal blade, combine the parsley, garlic, and lemon zest and juice. With the motor running, add the olive oil in a steady stream until the mixture forms a bright green sauce. Season to taste with salt and black pepper. Serve the cauliflower steaks with the gremolata spooned over the top.

Per Serving:
calories: 336 | fat: 30g | protein: 7g | carbs: 15g | fiber: 5g | sodium: 340mg

Root Vegetable Soup with Garlic Aioli

Prep time: 10 minutes | Cook time 25 minutes | Serves 4

For the Soup:
- 8 cups vegetable broth
- ½ teaspoon salt
- 1 medium leek, cut into thick rounds
- 1 pound (454 g) carrots, peeled and diced
- 1 pound (454 g) potatoes,

For the Aioli:
- 5 garlic cloves, minced
- ¼ teaspoon salt

peeled and diced
- 1 pound (454 g) turnips, peeled and cut into 1-inch cubes
- 1 red bell pepper, cut into strips
- 2 tablespoons fresh oregano

- ⅔ cup olive oil
- 1 drop lemon juice

1. Bring the broth and salt to a boil and add the vegetables one at

a time, letting the water return to a boil after each addition. Add the carrots first, then the leeks, potatoes, turnips, and finally the red bell peppers. Let the vegetables cook for about 3 minutes after adding the green beans and bringing to a boil. The process will take about 20 minutes in total. 2. Meanwhile, make the aioli. In a mortar and pestle, grind the garlic to a paste with the salt. Using a whisk and whisking constantly, add the olive oil in a thin stream. Continue whisking until the mixture thickens to the consistency of mayonnaise. Add the lemon juice. 3. Serve the vegetables in the broth, dolloped with the aioli and garnished with the fresh oregano.

Per Serving:
calories: 538 | fat: 37g | protein: 5g | carbs: 50g | fiber: 9g | sodium: 773mg

Beet and Carrot Fritters with Yogurt Sauce

Prep time: 15 minutes | Cook time: 15 minutes | Serves 2

For the Yogurt Sauce :
- ⅓ cup plain Greek yogurt
- 1 tablespoon freshly squeezed lemon juice

For the Fritters :
- 1 large carrot, peeled
- 1 small potato, peeled
- 1 medium golden or red beet, peeled
- 1 scallion, minced
- 2 tablespoons fresh minced parsley
- ¼ cup brown rice flour or

- Zest of ½ lemon
- ¼ teaspoon garlic powder
- ¼ teaspoon salt

unseasoned bread crumbs
- ¼ teaspoon garlic powder
- ¼ teaspoon salt
- 1 large egg, beaten
- ¼ cup feta cheese, crumbled
- 2 tablespoons olive oil (more if needed)

Make the Yogurt Sauce: 1. In a small bowl, mix together the yogurt, lemon juice and zest, garlic powder, and salt. Set aside. Make the Fritters: 1. Shred the carrot, potato, and beet in a food processor with the shredding blade. You can also use a mandoline with a julienne shredding blade or a vegetable peeler. Squeeze out any moisture from the vegetables and place them in a large bowl. 2. Add the scallion, parsley, rice flour, garlic powder, salt, and egg. Stir the mixture well to combine. Add the feta cheese and stir briefly, leaving chunks of feta cheese throughout. 3. Heat a large nonstick sauté pan over medium-high heat and add 1 tablespoon of the olive oil. 4. Make the fritters by scooping about 3 tablespoons of the vegetable mixture into your hands and flattening it into a firm disc about 3 inches in diameter. 5. Place 2 fritters at a time in the pan and let them cook for about two minutes. Check to see if the underside is golden, and then flip and repeat on the other side. Remove from the heat, add the rest of the olive oil to the pan, and repeat with the remaining vegetable mixture. 6. To serve, spoon about 1 tablespoon of the yogurt sauce on top of each fritter.

Per Serving:
calories: 295 | fat: 14g | protein: 6g | carbs: 44g | fiber: 5g | sodium: 482mg

Stuffed Pepper Stew

Prep time: 20 minutes | Cook time: 50 minutes | Serves 2

- 2 tablespoons olive oil
- 2 sweet peppers, diced (about 2 cups)
- ½ large onion, minced
- 1 garlic clove, minced
- 1 teaspoon oregano
- 1 tablespoon gluten-free vegetarian Worcestershire

- sauce
- 1 cup low-sodium vegetable stock
- 1 cup low-sodium tomato juice
- ¼ cup brown lentils
- ¼ cup brown rice
- Salt

1. Heat olive oil in a Dutch oven over medium-high heat. Add the sweet peppers and onion and sauté for 10 minutes, or until the peppers are wilted and the onion starts to turn golden. 2. Add the garlic, oregano, and Worcestershire sauce, and cook for another 30 seconds. Add the vegetable stock, tomato juice, lentils, and rice. 3. Bring the mixture to a boil. Cover, and reduce the heat to medium-low. Simmer for 45 minutes, or until the rice is cooked and the lentils are softened. Season with salt.

Per Serving:
calories: 379 | fat: 16g | protein: 11g | carbs: 53g | fiber: 7g | sodium: 392mg

Mushroom Ragù with Parmesan Polenta

Prep time: 20 minutes | Cook time: 30 minutes | Serves 2

- ½ ounce (14 g) dried porcini mushrooms (optional but recommended)
- 2 tablespoons olive oil
- 1 pound (454 g) baby bella (cremini) mushrooms, quartered
- 1 large shallot, minced (about ⅓ cup)
- 1 garlic clove, minced
- 1 tablespoon flour
- 2 teaspoons tomato paste

- ½ cup red wine
- 1 cup mushroom stock (or reserved liquid from soaking the porcini mushrooms, if using)
- ½ teaspoon dried thyme
- 1 fresh rosemary sprig
- 1½ cups water
- ½ teaspoon salt
- ⅓ cup instant polenta
- 2 tablespoons grated Parmesan cheese

1. If using the dried porcini mushrooms, soak them in 1 cup of hot water for about 15 minutes to soften them. When they're softened, scoop them out of the water, reserving the soaking liquid. (I strain it through a coffee filter to remove any possible grit.) Mince the porcini mushrooms. 2. Heat the olive oil in a large sauté pan over medium-high heat. Add the mushrooms, shallot, and garlic, and sauté for 10 minutes, or until the vegetables are wilted and starting to caramelize. 3. Add the flour and tomato paste, and cook for another 30 seconds. Add the red wine, mushroom stock or porcini soaking liquid, thyme, and rosemary. Bring the mixture to a boil, stirring constantly until it thickens. Reduce the heat and let it simmer for 10 minutes. 4. While the mushrooms are simmering, bring the water to a boil in a saucepan and add salt. 5. Add the instant polenta and stir quickly while it thickens. Stir in the Parmesan cheese. Taste and add additional salt if needed.

Per Serving:
calories: 451 | fat: 16g | protein: 14g | carbs: 58g | fiber: 5g | sodium: 165mg

Eggs Poached in Moroccan Tomato Sauce

Prep time: 10 minutes | Cook time: 35 minutes | Serves 4

- 1 tablespoon olive oil
- 1 medium yellow onion, diced
- 2 red bell peppers, seeded and diced
- 1¾ teaspoons sweet paprika
- 1 teaspoon ras al hanout

- ½ teaspoon cayenne pepper
- 1 teaspoon salt
- ¼ cup tomato paste
- 1 (28-ounce / 794-g) can diced tomatoes, drained
- 8 eggs
- ¼ cup chopped cilantro

1. Heat the olive oil in a skillet over medium-high heat. Add the onion and bell peppers and cook, stirring frequently, until softened, about 5 minutes. Stir in the paprika, ras al hanout, cayenne, salt, and tomato paste and cook, stirring occasionally, for 5 minutes. 2. Stir in the diced tomatoes, reduce the heat to medium-low, and simmer for about 15 minutes, until the tomatoes break down and the sauce thickens. 3. Make 8 wells in the sauce and drop one egg into each. Cover the pan and cook for about 10 minutes, until the whites are fully set, but the yolks are still runny. 4. Spoon the sauce and eggs into serving bowls and serve hot, garnished with cilantro.

Per Serving:
calories: 238 | fat: 13g | protein: 15g | carbs: 18g | fiber: 5g | sodium: 735mg

Creamy Chickpea Sauce with Whole-Wheat Fusilli

Prep time: 15 minutes | Cook time: 20 minutes | Serves 4

- ¼ cup extra-virgin olive oil
- ½ large shallot, chopped
- 5 garlic cloves, thinly sliced
- 1 (15-ounce / 425-g) can chickpeas, drained and rinsed, reserving ½ cup canning liquid
- Pinch red pepper flakes
- 1 cup whole-grain fusilli pasta

- ¼ teaspoon salt
- ⅛ teaspoon freshly ground black pepper
- ¼ cup shaved fresh Parmesan cheese
- ¼ cup chopped fresh basil
- 2 teaspoons dried parsley
- 1 teaspoon dried oregano
- Red pepper flakes

1. In a medium pan, heat the oil over medium heat, and sauté the shallot and garlic for 3 to 5 minutes, until the garlic is golden. Add ¾ of the chickpeas plus 2 tablespoons of liquid from the can, and bring to a simmer. 2. Remove from the heat, transfer into a standard blender, and blend until smooth. At this point, add the remaining chickpeas. Add more reserved chickpea liquid if it becomes thick. 3. Bring a large pot of salted water to a boil and cook pasta until al dente, about 8 minutes. Reserve ½ cup of the pasta water, drain the pasta, and return it to the pot. 4. Add the chickpea sauce to the hot pasta and add up to ¼ cup of the pasta water. You may need to add more pasta water to reach your desired consistency. 5. Place the pasta pot over medium heat and mix occasionally until the sauce thickens. Season with salt and pepper. 6. Serve, garnished with Parmesan, basil, parsley, oregano, and red pepper flakes.

Per Serving:
1 cup pasta: calories: 310 | fat: 17g | protein: 10g | carbs: 33g | fiber: 7g | sodium: 243mg

Baked Tofu with Sun-Dried Tomatoes and Artichokes

Prep time: 15 minutes | Cook time: 30 minutes | Serves 4

- 1 (16-ounce / 454-g) package extra-firm tofu, drained and patted dry, cut into 1-inch cubes
- 2 tablespoons extra-virgin olive oil, divided
- 2 tablespoons lemon juice, divided
- 1 tablespoon low-sodium soy sauce or gluten-free tamari
- 1 onion, diced
- ½ teaspoon kosher salt
- 2 garlic cloves, minced
- 1 (14-ounce / 397-g) can artichoke hearts, drained
- 8 sun-dried tomato halves packed in oil, drained and chopped
- ¼ teaspoon freshly ground black pepper
- 1 tablespoon white wine vinegar
- Zest of 1 lemon
- ¼ cup fresh parsley, chopped

1. Preheat the oven to 400ºF (205ºC). Line a baking sheet with foil or parchment paper. 2. In a bowl, combine the tofu, 1 tablespoon of the olive oil, 1 tablespoon of the lemon juice, and the soy sauce. Allow to sit and marinate for 15 to 30 minutes. Arrange the tofu in a single layer on the prepared baking sheet and bake for 20 minutes, turning once, until light golden brown. 3. Heat the remaining 1 tablespoon olive oil in a large skillet or sauté pan over medium heat. Add the onion and salt; sauté until translucent, 5 to 6 minutes. Add the garlic and sauté for 30 seconds. Add the artichoke hearts, sun-dried tomatoes, and black pepper and sauté for 5 minutes. Add the white wine vinegar and the remaining 1 tablespoon lemon juice and deglaze the pan, scraping up any brown bits. Remove the pan from the heat and stir in the lemon zest and parsley. Gently mix in the baked tofu.

Per Serving:
calories: 230 | fat: 14g | protein: 14g | carbs: 13g | fiber: 5g | sodium: 500mg

Roasted Portobello Mushrooms with Kale and Red Onion

Prep time: 15 minutes | Cook time: 30 minutes | Serves 4

- ¼ cup white wine vinegar
- 3 tablespoons extra-virgin olive oil, divided
- ½ teaspoon honey
- ¾ teaspoon kosher salt, divided
- ¼ teaspoon freshly ground black pepper
- 4 large (4 to 5 ounces / 113 to 142 g each) portobello
- mushrooms, stems removed
- 1 red onion, julienned
- 2 garlic cloves, minced
- 1 (8-ounce / 227-g) bunch kale, stemmed and chopped small
- ¼ teaspoon red pepper flakes
- ¼ cup grated Parmesan or Romano cheese

1. Line a baking sheet with parchment paper or foil. In a medium bowl, whisk together the vinegar, 1½ tablespoons of the olive oil, honey, ¼ teaspoon of the salt, and the black pepper. Arrange the mushrooms on the baking sheet and pour the marinade over them. Marinate for 15 to 30 minutes. 2. Meanwhile, preheat the oven to

400ºF (205ºC). 3. Bake the mushrooms for 20 minutes, turning over halfway through. 4. Heat the remaining 1½ tablespoons olive oil in a large skillet or ovenproof sauté pan over medium-high heat. Add the onion and the remaining ½ teaspoon salt and sauté until golden brown, 5 to 6 minutes. Add the garlic and sauté for 30 seconds. Add the kale and red pepper flakes and sauté until the kale cooks down, about 5 minutes. 5. Remove the mushrooms from the oven and increase the temperature to broil. 6. Carefully pour the liquid from the baking sheet into the pan with the kale mixture; mix well. 7. Turn the mushrooms over so that the stem side is facing up. Spoon some of the kale mixture on top of each mushroom. Sprinkle 1 tablespoon Parmesan cheese on top of each. 8. Broil until golden brown, 3 to 4 minutes.

Per Serving:
calories: 200 | fat: 13g | protein: 8g | carbs: 16g | fiber: 4g | sodium: 365mg

Zucchini Lasagna

Prep time: 15 minutes | Cook time: 1 hour | Serves 8

- ½ cup extra-virgin olive oil, divided
- 4 to 5 medium zucchini squash
- 1 teaspoon salt
- 8 ounces (227 g) frozen spinach, thawed and well drained (about 1 cup)
- 2 cups whole-milk ricotta cheese
- ¼ cup chopped fresh basil or 2 teaspoons dried basil
- 1 teaspoon garlic powder
- ½ teaspoon freshly ground black pepper
- 2 cups shredded fresh whole-milk mozzarella cheese
- 1¾ cups shredded Parmesan cheese
- ½ (24 ounces / 680 g) jar low-sugar marinara sauce (less than 5 grams sugar)

1. Preheat the oven to 425ºF (220ºC). 2. Line two baking sheets with parchment paper or aluminum foil and drizzle each with 2 tablespoons olive oil, spreading evenly. 3. Slice the zucchini lengthwise into ¼-inch-thick long slices and place on the prepared baking sheet in a single layer. Sprinkle with ½ teaspoon salt per sheet. Bake until softened, but not mushy, 15 to 18 minutes. Remove from the oven and allow to cool slightly before assembling the lasagna. 4. Reduce the oven temperature to 375ºF (190ºC). 5. While the zucchini cooks, prep the filling. In a large bowl, combine the spinach, ricotta, basil, garlic powder, and pepper. In a small bowl, mix together the mozzarella and Parmesan cheeses. In a medium bowl, combine the marinara sauce and remaining ¼ cup olive oil and stir to fully incorporate the oil into sauce. 6. To assemble the lasagna, spoon a third of the marinara sauce mixture into the bottom of a 9-by-13-inch glass baking dish and spread evenly. Place 1 layer of softened zucchini slices to fully cover the sauce, then add a third of the ricotta-spinach mixture and spread evenly on top of the zucchini. Sprinkle a third of the mozzarella-Parmesan mixture on top of the ricotta. Repeat with 2 more cycles of these layers: marinara, zucchini, ricotta-spinach, then cheese blend. 7. Bake until the cheese is bubbly and melted, 30 to 35 minutes. Turn the broiler to low and broil until the top is golden brown, about 5 minutes. Remove from the oven and allow to cool slightly before slicing.

Per Serving:
calories: 473 | fat: 36g | protein: 23g | carbs: 17g | fiber: 3g | sodium: 868mg

Turkish Red Lentil and Bulgur Kofte

Prep time: 10 minutes | Cook time: 45 minutes | Serves 4

- ⅓ cup olive oil, plus 2 tablespoons, divided, plus more for brushing
- 1 cup red lentils
- ½ cup bulgur
- 1 teaspoon salt
- 1 medium onion, finely diced
- 2 tablespoons tomato paste
- 1 teaspoon ground cumin
- ¼ cup finely chopped flat-leaf parsley
- 3 scallions, thinly sliced
- Juice of ½ lemon

1. Preheat the oven to 400°F(205ºC). 2. Brush a large, rimmed baking sheet with olive oil. 3. In a medium saucepan, combine the lentils with 2 cups water and bring to a boil. Reduce the heat to low and cook, stirring occasionally, for about 15 minutes, until the lentils are tender and have soaked up most of the liquid. Remove from the heat, stir in the bulgur and salt, cover, and let sit for 15 minutes or so, until the bulgur is tender. 4. Meanwhile, heat ⅓ cup olive oil in a medium skillet over medium-high heat. Add the onion and cook, stirring frequently, until softened, about 5 minutes. Stir in the tomato paste and cook for 2 minutes more. Remove from the heat and stir in the cumin. 5. Add the cooked onion mixture to the lentil-bulgur mixture and stir to combine. Add the parsley, scallions, and lemon juice and stir to mix well. 6. Shape the mixture into walnut-sized balls and place them on the prepared baking sheet. Brush the balls with the remaining 2 tablespoons of olive oil and bake for 15 to 20 minutes, until golden brown. Serve hot.

Per Serving:
calories: 460 | fat: 25g | protein: 16g | carbs: 48g | fiber: 19g | sodium: 604mg

Provençal Ratatouille with Herbed Breadcrumbs and Goat Cheese

Prep time: 10 minutes | Cook time: 1 hour 5 minutes | Serves 4

- 6 tablespoons olive oil, divided
- 2 medium onions, diced
- 2 cloves garlic, minced
- 2 medium eggplants, halved lengthwise and cut into ¾-inch thick half rounds
- 3 medium zucchini, halved lengthwise and cut into ¾-inch thick half rounds
- 2 red bell peppers, seeded and cut into 1½-inch pieces
- 1 green bell pepper, seeded and cut into 1½-inch pieces
- 1 (14-ounce / 397-g) can diced tomatoes, drained
- 1 teaspoon salt
- ½ teaspoon freshly ground black pepper
- 8 ounces (227 g) fresh breadcrumbs
- 1 tablespoon chopped fresh parsley
- 1 tablespoon chopped fresh basil
- 1 tablespoon chopped fresh chives
- 6 ounces (170 g) soft, fresh goat cheese

1. Preheat the oven to 375°F(190ºC). 2. Heat 5 tablespoons of the olive oil in a large skillet over medium heat. Add the onions and garlic and cook, stirring frequently, until the onions are soft and beginning to turn golden, about 8 minutes. Add the eggplant, zucchini, and bell peppers and cook, turning the vegetables occasionally, for another 10 minutes. Stir in the tomatoes, salt, and pepper and let simmer for 15 minutes. 3. While the vegetables are simmering, stir together the breadcrumbs, the remaining tablespoon of olive oil, the parsley, basil, and chives. 4. Transfer the vegetable mixture to a large baking dish, spreading it out into an even layer. Crumble the goat cheese over the top, then sprinkle the breadcrumb mixture evenly over the top. Bake in the preheated oven for about 30 minutes, until the topping is golden brown and crisp. Serve hot.

Per Serving:
calories: 644 | fat: 37g | protein: 21g | carbs: 63g | fiber: 16g | sodium: 861mg

Tortellini in Red Pepper Sauce

Prep time: 15 minutes | Cook time: 10 minutes | Serves 4

- 1 (16-ounce / 454-g) container fresh cheese tortellini (usually green and white pasta)
- 1 (16-ounce / 454-g) jar roasted red peppers, drained
- 1 teaspoon garlic powder
- ¼ cup tahini
- 1 tablespoon red pepper oil (optional)

1. Bring a large pot of water to a boil and cook the tortellini according to package directions. 2. In a blender, combine the red peppers with the garlic powder and process until smooth. Once blended, add the tahini until the sauce is thickened. If the sauce gets too thick, add up to 1 tablespoon red pepper oil (if using). 3. Once tortellini are cooked, drain and leave pasta in colander. Add the sauce to the bottom of the empty pot and heat for 2 minutes. Then, add the tortellini back into the pot and cook for 2 more minutes. Serve and enjoy!

Per Serving:
calories: 350 | fat: 11g | protein: 12g | carbs: 46g | fiber: 4g | sodium: 192mg

Pesto Spinach Flatbread

Prep time: 10 minutes | Cook time: 8 minutes | Serves 4

- 1 cup blanched finely ground almond flour
- 2 ounces (57 g) cream cheese
- 2 cups shredded Mozzarella
- cheese
- 1 cup chopped fresh spinach leaves
- 2 tablespoons basil pesto

1. Place flour, cream cheese, and Mozzarella in a large microwave-safe bowl and microwave on high 45 seconds, then stir. 2. Fold in spinach and microwave an additional 15 seconds. Stir until a soft dough ball forms. 3. Cut two pieces of parchment paper to fit air fryer basket. Separate dough into two sections and press each out on ungreased parchment to create 6-inch rounds. 4. Spread 1 tablespoon pesto over each flatbread and place rounds on parchment into ungreased air fryer basket. Adjust the temperature to 350ºF (177ºC) and air fry for 8 minutes, turning crusts halfway through cooking. Flatbread will be golden when done. 5. Let cool 5 minutes before slicing and serving.

Per Serving:
calories: 387 | fat: 28g | protein: 28g | carbs: 10g | fiber: 5g | sodium: 556mg

Three-Cheese Zucchini Boats

Prep time: 15 minutes | Cook time: 20 minutes | Serves 2

- 2 medium zucchini
- 1 tablespoon avocado oil
- ¼ cup low-carb, no-sugar-added pasta sauce
- ¼ cup full-fat ricotta cheese
- ¼ cup shredded Mozzarella
- cheese
- ¼ teaspoon dried oregano
- ¼ teaspoon garlic powder
- ½ teaspoon dried parsley
- 2 tablespoons grated vegetarian Parmesan cheese

1. Cut off 1 inch from the top and bottom of each zucchini. Slice zucchini in half lengthwise and use a spoon to scoop out a bit of the inside, making room for filling. Brush with oil and spoon 2 tablespoons pasta sauce into each shell. 2. In a medium bowl, mix ricotta, Mozzarella, oregano, garlic powder, and parsley. Spoon the mixture into each zucchini shell. Place stuffed zucchini shells into the air fryer basket. 3. Adjust the temperature to 350ºF (177ºC) and air fry for 20 minutes. 4. To remove from the basket, use tongs or a spatula and carefully lift out. Top with Parmesan. Serve immediately.

Per Serving:
calories: 208 | fat: 14g | protein: 12g | carbs: 11g | fiber: 3g | sodium: 247mg

Balsamic Marinated Tofu with Basil and Oregano

Prep time: 10 minutes | Cook time: 30 minutes | Serves 4

- ¼ cup extra-virgin olive oil
- ¼ cup balsamic vinegar
- 2 tablespoons low-sodium soy sauce or gluten-free tamari
- 3 garlic cloves, grated
- 2 teaspoons pure maple syrup
- Zest of 1 lemon
- 1 teaspoon dried basil
- 1 teaspoon dried oregano
- ½ teaspoon dried thyme
- ½ teaspoon dried sage
- ¼ teaspoon kosher salt
- ¼ teaspoon freshly ground black pepper
- ¼ teaspoon red pepper flakes (optional)
- 1 (16-ounce / 454-g) block extra firm tofu, drained and patted dry, cut into ½-inch or 1-inch cubes

1. In a bowl or gallon zip-top bag, mix together the olive oil, vinegar, soy sauce, garlic, maple syrup, lemon zest, basil, oregano, thyme, sage, salt, black pepper, and red pepper flakes, if desired. Add the tofu and mix gently. Put in the refrigerator and marinate for 30 minutes, or up to overnight if you desire. 2. Preheat the oven to 425ºF (220ºC). Line a baking sheet with parchment paper or foil. Arrange the marinated tofu in a single layer on the prepared baking sheet. Bake for 20 to 30 minutes, turning over halfway through, until slightly crispy on the outside and tender on the inside.

Per Serving:
calories: 225 | fat: 16g | protein: 13g | carbs: 9g | fiber: 2g | sodium: 265mg

Eggplant Parmesan

Prep time: 15 minutes | Cook time: 17 minutes | Serves 4

- 1 medium eggplant, ends trimmed, sliced into ½-inch rounds
- ¼ teaspoon salt
- 2 tablespoons coconut oil
- ½ cup grated Parmesan cheese
- 1 ounce (28 g) 100% cheese crisps, finely crushed
- ½ cup low-carb marinara sauce
- ½ cup shredded Mozzarella cheese

1. Sprinkle eggplant rounds with salt on both sides and wrap in a kitchen towel for 30 minutes. Press to remove excess water, then drizzle rounds with coconut oil on both sides. 2. In a medium bowl, mix Parmesan and cheese crisps. Press each eggplant slice into mixture to coat both sides. 3. Place rounds into ungreased air fryer basket. Adjust the temperature to 350ºF (177ºC) and air fry for 15 minutes, turning rounds halfway through cooking. They will be crispy around the edges when done. 4. Spoon marinara over rounds and sprinkle with Mozzarella. Continue cooking an additional 2 minutes at 350ºF (177ºC) until cheese is melted. Serve warm.

Per Serving:
calories: 208 | fat: 13g | protein: 12g | carbs: 13g | fiber: 5g | sodium: 531mg

Spinach-Artichoke Stuffed Mushrooms

Prep time: 10 minutes | Cook time: 10 to 14 minutes | Serves 4

- 2 tablespoons olive oil
- 4 large portobello mushrooms, stems removed and gills scraped out
- ½ teaspoon salt
- ¼ teaspoon freshly ground pepper
- 4 ounces (113 g) goat cheese, crumbled
- ½ cup chopped marinated artichoke hearts
- 1 cup frozen spinach, thawed and squeezed dry
- ½ cup grated Parmesan cheese
- 2 tablespoons chopped fresh parsley

1. Preheat the air fryer to 400ºF (204ºC). 2. Rub the olive oil over the portobello mushrooms until thoroughly coated. Sprinkle both sides with the salt and black pepper. Place top-side down on a clean work surface. 3. In a small bowl, combine the goat cheese, artichoke hearts, and spinach. Mash with the back of a fork until thoroughly combined. Divide the cheese mixture among the mushrooms and sprinkle with the Parmesan cheese. 4. Air fry for 10 to 14 minutes until the mushrooms are tender and the cheese has begun to brown. Top with the fresh parsley just before serving.

Per Serving:
calories: 284 | fat: 21g | protein: 16g | carbs: 10g | fiber: 4g | sodium: 686mg

Cheese Stuffed Zucchini

Prep time: 20 minutes | Cook time: 8 minutes | Serves 4

- 1 large zucchini, cut into four pieces
- 2 tablespoons olive oil
- 1 cup Ricotta cheese, room temperature
- 2 tablespoons scallions, chopped
- 1 heaping tablespoon fresh parsley, roughly chopped
- 1 heaping tablespoon coriander, minced
- 2 ounces (57 g) Cheddar cheese, preferably freshly grated
- 1 teaspoon celery seeds
- ½ teaspoon salt
- ½ teaspoon garlic pepper

1. Cook your zucchini in the air fryer basket for approximately 10 minutes at 350ºF (177ºC). Check for doneness and cook for 2-3 minutes longer if needed. 2. Meanwhile, make the stuffing by mixing the other items. 3. When your zucchini is thoroughly cooked, open them up. Divide the stuffing among all zucchini pieces and bake an additional 5 minutes.

Per Serving:
calories: 242 | fat: 20g | protein: 12g | carbs: 5g | fiber: 1g | sodium: 443mg

Mozzarella and Sun-Dried Portobello Mushroom Pizza

Prep time: 10 minutes | Cook time: 10 minutes | Serves 4

- 4 large portobello mushroom caps
- 3 tablespoons extra-virgin olive oil
- Salt
- Freshly ground black pepper
- 4 sun-dried tomatoes
- 1 cup mozzarella cheese, divided
- ½ to ¾ cup low-sodium tomato sauce

1. Preheat the broiler on high. 2. On a baking sheet, drizzle the mushroom caps with the olive oil and season with salt and pepper. Broil the portobello mushrooms for 5 minutes on each side, flipping once, until tender. 3. Fill each mushroom cap with 1 sun-dried tomato, 2 tablespoons of cheese, and 2 to 3 tablespoons of sauce. Top each with 2 tablespoons of cheese. Place the caps back under the broiler for a final 2 to 3 minutes, then quarter the mushrooms and serve.

Per Serving:
calories: 218| fat: 16g | protein: 11g | carbs: 12g | fiber: 2g | sodium: 244mg

Chapter

10

Salads

Chapter 10 Salads

Roasted Golden Beet, Avocado, and Watercress Salad

Prep time: 15 minutes | Cook time: 1 hour | Serves 4

- 1 bunch (about 1½ pounds / 680 g) golden beets
- 1 tablespoon extra-virgin olive oil
- 1 tablespoon white wine vinegar
- ½ teaspoon kosher salt
- ¼ teaspoon freshly ground black pepper
- 1 bunch (about 4 ounces / 113 g) watercress
- 1 avocado, peeled, pitted, and diced
- ¼ cup crumbled feta cheese
- ¼ cup walnuts, toasted
- 1 tablespoon fresh chives, chopped

1. Preheat the oven to 425ºF (220ºC). Wash and trim the beets (cut an inch above the beet root, leaving the long tail if desired), then wrap each beet individually in foil. Place the beets on a baking sheet and roast until fully cooked, 45 to 60 minutes depending on the size of each beet. Start checking at 45 minutes; if easily pierced with a fork, the beets are cooked. 2. Remove the beets from the oven and allow them to cool. Under cold running water, slough off the skin. Cut the beets into bite-size cubes or wedges. 3. In a large bowl, whisk together the olive oil, vinegar, salt, and black pepper. Add the watercress and beets and toss well. Add the avocado, feta, walnuts, and chives and mix gently.

Per Serving:
calories: 235 | fat: 16g | protein: 6g | carbs: 21g | fiber: 8g | sodium: 365mg

Simple Insalata Mista (Mixed Salad) with Honey Balsamic Dressing

Prep time: 15 minutes | Cook time: 0 minutes | Serves 2

For the Dressing:
- ¼ cup balsamic vinegar
- ¼ cup olive oil
- 1 tablespoon honey
- 1 teaspoon Dijon mustard
- ¼ teaspoon salt, plus more
- to taste
- ¼ teaspoon garlic powder
- Pinch freshly ground black pepper

For the Salad:
- 4 cups chopped red leaf lettuce
- ½ cup cherry or grape tomatoes, halved
- ½ English cucumber, sliced in quarters lengthwise and
- then cut into bite-size pieces
- Any combination fresh, torn herbs (parsley, oregano, basil, chives, etc.)
- 1 tablespoon roasted sunflower seeds

Make the Dressing: Combine the vinegar, olive oil, honey, mustard, salt, garlic powder, and pepper in a jar with a lid. Shake well. Make the Salad: 1. In a large bowl, combine the lettuce, tomatoes, cucumber, and herbs. 2. Toss well to combine. 3. Pour all or as much dressing as desired over the tossed salad and toss again to coat the salad with dressing. 4. Top with the sunflower seeds.

Per Serving:
calories: 339 | fat: 26g | protein: 4g | carbs: 24g | fiber: 3g | sodium: 171mg

Tricolor Tomato Summer Salad

Prep time: 10 minutes | Cook time: 0 minutes | Serves 3 to 4

- ¼ cup while balsamic vinegar
- 2 tablespoons Dijon mustard
- 1 tablespoon sugar
- ½ teaspoon freshly ground black pepper
- ½ teaspoon garlic salt
- ¼ cup extra-virgin olive oil
- 1½ cups chopped orange, yellow, and red tomatoes
- ½ cucumber, peeled and diced
- 1 small red onion, thinly sliced
- ¼ cup crumbled feta (optional)

1. In a small bowl, whisk the vinegar, mustard, sugar, pepper, and garlic salt. Next, slowly whisk in the olive oil. 2. In a large bowl, add the tomatoes, cucumber, and red onion. Add the dressing. Toss once or twice, and serve with feta crumbles (if using) on top.

Per Serving:
calories: 246 | fat: 18g | protein: 1g | carbs: 19g | fiber: 2g | sodium: 483mg

Insalata Caprese

Prep time: 5 minutes | Cook time: 0 minutes | Serves 2

- 2 firm medium tomatoes (any variety), cut into ¼-inch slices
- ¼ teaspoon kosher salt
- 8 fresh basil leaves
- 7 ounces (198 g) fresh
- mozzarella, cut into ¼-inch slices
- ¼ teaspoon dried oregano
- 3 teaspoons extra virgin olive oil

1. Place the sliced tomatoes on a cutting board and sprinkle them with the kosher salt. Set aside. 2. Arrange 4 basil leaves in a circular pattern on a large, round serving plate. (Tear the leaves into 2 pieces if they're large.) 3. Assemble the tomato slices and mozzarella slices on top of the basil leaves, alternating a tomato slice and then a mozzarella slice, adding a basil leaf between every 3–4 slices of tomato and mozzarella. 4. Sprinkle the oregano over the top and then drizzle the olive oil over the entire salad. Serve promptly. (This salad is best served fresh.)

Per Serving:
calories: 361 | fat: 24g | protein: 28g | carbs: 8g | fiber: 2g | sodium: 313mg

Grain-Free Kale Tabbouleh

Prep time: 15 minutes | Cook time: 0 minutes | Serves 8

- 2 plum tomatoes, seeded and chopped
- ½ cup finely chopped fresh parsley
- 4 scallions (green onions), finely chopped
- 1 head kale, finely chopped (about 2 cups)
- 1 cup finely chopped fresh
- mint
- 1 small Persian cucumber, peeled, seeded, and diced
- 3 tablespoons extra-virgin olive oil
- 2 tablespoons fresh lemon juice
- Coarsely ground black pepper (optional)

1. Place the tomatoes in a strainer set over a bowl and set aside to drain as much liquid as possible. 2. In a large bowl, stir to combine the parsley, scallions, kale, and mint. 3. Shake any remaining liquid from the tomatoes and add them to the kale mixture. Add the cucumber. 4. Add the olive oil and lemon juice and toss to combine. Season with pepper, if desired.

Per Serving:
1 cup: calories: 65 | fat: 5g | protein: 1g | carbs: 4g | fiber: 1g | sodium: 21mg

Chopped Greek Antipasto Salad

Prep time: 20 minutes |Cook time: 0 minutes| Serves: 6

For the Salad:
- 1 head Bibb lettuce or ½ head romaine lettuce, chopped (about 2½ cups)
- ¼ cup loosely packed chopped basil leaves
- 1 (15 ounces / 425 g) can chickpeas, drained and rinsed
- 1 (14 ounces / 397 g) can artichoke hearts, drained and halved

For the Dressing:
- 3 tablespoons extra-virgin olive oil
- 1 tablespoon red wine vinegar
- 1 tablespoon freshly squeezed lemon juice (from about ½ small lemon)

- 1 pint grape tomatoes, halved (about 1½ cups)
- 1 seedless cucumber, peeled and chopped (about 1½ cups)
- ½ cup cubed feta cheese (about 2 ounces / 57 g)
- 1 (2¼ ounces / 35 g) can sliced black olives (about ½ cup)

- 1 tablespoon chopped fresh oregano or ½ teaspoon dried oregano
- 1 teaspoon honey
- ¼ teaspoon freshly ground black pepper

1. In a medium bowl, toss the lettuce and basil together. Spread out on a large serving platter or in a large salad bowl. Arrange the chickpeas, artichoke hearts, tomatoes, cucumber, feta, and olives in piles next to each other on top of the lettuce layer. 2. In a small pitcher or bowl, whisk together the oil, vinegar, lemon juice, oregano, honey, and pepper. Serve on the side with the salad, or drizzle over all the ingredients right before serving.

Per Serving:
calories: 267 | fat: 13g | protein: 11g | carbs: 31g | fiber: 11g | sodium: 417mg

Endive with Shrimp

Prep time: 15 minutes | Cook time: 2 minutes | Serves 4

- ¼ cup olive oil
- 1 small shallot, minced
- 1 tablespoon Dijon mustard
- Juice and zest of 1 lemon
- Sea salt and freshly ground pepper, to taste
- 2 cups salted water
- 14 shrimp, peeled and deveined
- 1 head endive
- ½ cup tart green apple, diced
- 2 tablespoons toasted walnuts

1. For the vinaigrette, whisk together the first five ingredients in a small bowl until creamy and emulsified. 2. Refrigerate for at least 2 hours for best flavor. 3. In a small pan, boil salted water. Add the shrimp and cook 1–2 minutes, or until the shrimp turns pink. Drain and cool under cold water. 4. To assemble the salad, wash and break the endive. Place on serving plates and top with the shrimp, green apple, and toasted walnuts. 5. Drizzle with the vinaigrette before serving.

Per Serving:
calories: 194 | fat: 16g | protein: 6g | carbs: 8g | fiber: 5g | sodium: 191mg

Wild Rice Salad with Chickpeas and Pickled Radish

Prep time: 20 minutes | Cook time: 45 minutes | Serves 6

For the Rice:
- 1 cup water
- 4 ounces (113 g) wild rice
- ¼ teaspoon kosher salt
- For the Pickled Radish:

For the Dressing:
- 2 tablespoons extra-virgin olive oil
- 2 tablespoons white wine vinegar
- ½ teaspoon pure maple

For the Salad:
- 1 (15-ounce / 425-g) can no-salt-added or low-sodium chickpeas, rinsed and drained
- 1 bulb fennel, diced
- ¼ cup walnuts, chopped and

- 1 bunch radishes (6 to 8 small), thinly sliced
- ½ cup white wine vinegar
- ½ teaspoon kosher salt

syrup
- ½ teaspoon kosher salt
- ¼ teaspoon freshly ground black pepper

toasted
- ¼ cup crumbled feta cheese
- ¼ cup currants
- 2 tablespoons fresh dill, chopped

Make the Rice: 1. Bring the water, rice, and salt to a boil in a medium saucepan. Cover, reduce the heat, and simmer for 45 minutes. Make the Pickled Radish: 1. In a medium bowl, combine the radishes, vinegar, and salt. Let sit for 15 to 30 minutes. Make the Dressing: 1. In a large bowl, whisk together the olive oil, vinegar, maple syrup, salt, and black pepper. Make the Salad: 1. While still warm, add the rice to the bowl with the dressing and mix well. 2. Add the chickpeas, fennel, walnuts, feta, currants, and dill. Mix well. 3. Garnish with the pickled radishes before serving.

Per Serving:
calories: 310 | fat: 16g | protein: 10g | carbs: 36g | fiber: 7g | sodium: 400mg

Raw Zucchini Salad

Prep time: 15 minutes | Cook time: 0 minutes | Serves 2

- 1 medium zucchini, shredded or sliced paper thin
- 6 cherry tomatoes, halved
- 3 tablespoons olive oil
- Juice of 1 lemon
- Sea salt and freshly ground pepper, to taste
- 3–4 basil leaves, thinly sliced
- 2 tablespoons freshly grated, low-fat Parmesan cheese

1. Layer the zucchini slices on 2 plates in even layers. Top with the tomatoes. 2. Drizzle with the olive oil and lemon juice. Season to taste. 3. Top with the basil and sprinkle with cheese before serving.

Per Serving:
calories: 256 | fat: 21g | protein: 2g | carbs: 19g | fiber: 3g | sodium: 3mg

Warm Fennel, Cherry Tomato, and Spinach Salad

Prep time: 15 minutes | Cook time: 0 minutes | Serves 2

- 4 tablespoons chicken broth
- 4 cups baby spinach leaves
- 10 cherry tomatoes, halved
- Sea salt and freshly ground
- pepper, to taste
- 1 fennel bulb, sliced
- ¼ cup olive oil
- Juice of 2 lemons

1. In a large sauté pan, heat the chicken broth over medium heat. Add the spinach and tomatoes and cook until spinach is wilted. Season with sea salt and freshly ground pepper to taste. 2. Remove from heat and toss fennel slices in with the spinach and tomatoes. Let the fennel warm in the pan, then transfer to a large bowl. 3. Drizzle with the olive oil and lemon juice, and serve immediately.

Per Serving:
calories: 319 | fat: 28g | protein: 5g | carbs: 18g | fiber: 6g | sodium: 123mg

Pistachio-Parmesan Kale-Arugula Salad

Prep time: 20 minutes |Cook time: 0 minutes| Serves: 6

- 6 cups raw kale, center ribs removed and discarded, leaves coarsely chopped
- ¼ cup extra-virgin olive oil
- 2 tablespoons freshly squeezed lemon juice (from about 1 small lemon)
- ½ teaspoon smoked paprika
- 2 cups arugula
- ⅓ cup unsalted shelled pistachios
- 6 tablespoons grated Parmesan or Pecorino Romano cheese

1. In a large salad bowl, combine the kale, oil, lemon juice, and smoked paprika. With your hands, gently massage the leaves for about 15 seconds or so, until all are thoroughly coated. Let the kale sit for 10 minutes. 2. When you're ready to serve, gently mix in the arugula and pistachios. Divide the salad among six serving bowls, sprinkle 1 tablespoon of grated cheese over each, and serve.

Per Serving:
calories: 150 | fat: 14g | protein: 4g | carbs: 5g | fiber: 1g | sodium: 99mg

French Lentil Salad with Parsley and Mint

Prep time: 20 minutes | Cook time:25 minutes | Serves 6

For the Lentils:
- 1 cup French lentils
- 1 garlic clove, smashed
- 1 dried bay leaf

For the Salad:
- 2 tablespoons extra-virgin olive oil
- 2 tablespoons red wine vinegar
- ½ teaspoon ground cumin
- ½ teaspoon kosher salt
- ¼ teaspoon freshly ground
- black pepper
- 2 celery stalks, diced small
- 1 bell pepper, diced small
- ½ red onion, diced small
- ¼ cup fresh parsley, chopped
- ¼ cup fresh mint, chopped

Make the Lentils: 1. Put the lentils, garlic, and bay leaf in a large saucepan. Cover with water by about 3 inches and bring to a boil. Reduce the heat, cover, and simmer until tender, 20 to 30 minutes. 2. Drain the lentils to remove any remaining water after cooking. Remove the garlic and bay leaf. Make the Salad: 3. In a large bowl, whisk together the olive oil, vinegar, cumin, salt, and black pepper. Add the celery, bell pepper, onion, parsley, and mint and toss to combine. 4. Add the lentils and mix well.

Per Serving:
calories: 200 | fat: 8g | protein: 10g | carbs: 26g | fiber: 10g | sodium: 165mg

Orange-Tarragon Chicken Salad Wrap

Prep time: 15 minutes | Cook time: 0 minutes | Serves 4

- ½ cup plain whole-milk Greek yogurt
- 2 tablespoons Dijon mustard
- 2 tablespoons extra-virgin olive oil
- 2 tablespoons chopped fresh tarragon or 1 teaspoon dried tarragon
- ½ teaspoon salt
- ¼ teaspoon freshly ground black pepper
- 2 cups cooked shredded chicken
- ½ cup slivered almonds
- 4 to 8 large Bibb lettuce leaves, tough stem removed
- 2 small ripe avocados, peeled and thinly sliced
- Zest of 1 clementine, or ½ small orange (about 1 tablespoon)

1. In a medium bowl, combine the yogurt, mustard, olive oil, tarragon, orange zest, salt, and pepper and whisk until creamy. 2. Add the shredded chicken and almonds and stir to coat. 3. To assemble the wraps, place about ½ cup chicken salad mixture in the center of each lettuce leaf and top with sliced avocados.

Per Serving:
calories: 491 | fat: 38g | protein: 28g | carbs: 14g | fiber: 9g | sodium: 454mg

Israeli Salad with Nuts and Seeds

Prep time: 15 minutes | Cook time: 0 minutes | Serves 4

- ¼ cup pine nuts
- ¼ cup shelled pistachios
- ¼ cup coarsely chopped walnuts
- ¼ cup shelled pumpkin seeds
- ¼ cup shelled sunflower seeds
- 2 large English cucumbers, unpeeled and finely chopped
- 1 pint cherry tomatoes, finely chopped

- ½ small red onion, finely chopped
- ½ cup finely chopped fresh flat-leaf Italian parsley
- ¼ cup extra-virgin olive oil
- 2 to 3 tablespoons freshly squeezed lemon juice (from 1 lemon)
- 1 teaspoon salt
- ¼ teaspoon freshly ground black pepper
- 4 cups baby arugula

1. In a large dry skillet, toast the pine nuts, pistachios, walnuts, pumpkin seeds, and sunflower seeds over medium-low heat until golden and fragrant, 5 to 6 minutes, being careful not to burn them. Remove from the heat and set aside. 2. In a large bowl, combine the cucumber, tomatoes, red onion, and parsley. 3. In a small bowl, whisk together olive oil, lemon juice, salt, and pepper. Pour over the chopped vegetables and toss to coat. 4. Add the toasted nuts and seeds and arugula and toss with the salad to blend well. Serve at room temperature or chilled.

Per Serving:
calories: 404 | fat: 36g | protein: 10g | carbs: 16g | fiber: 5g | sodium: 601mg

Pear-Fennel Salad with Pomegranate

Prep time: 15 minutes | Cook time: 5 minutes | Serves 6

Dressing:
- 2 tablespoons red wine vinegar
- 1½ tablespoons pomegranate molasses
- 2 teaspoons finely chopped shallot
- ½ teaspoon Dijon mustard

Salad:
- ¼ cup walnuts, coarsely chopped, or pine nuts
- 2 red pears, halved, cored, and very thinly sliced
- 1 bulb fennel, halved, cored, and very thinly sliced, fronds reserved
- 1 tablespoon fresh lemon juice

- ½ teaspoon kosher salt
- ¼ teaspoon ground black pepper
- ¼ cup extra-virgin olive oil

- 4 cups baby arugula
- ½ cup pomegranate seeds
- ⅓ cup crumbled feta cheese or shaved Parmigiano-Reggiano cheese

1. Make the Dressing: In a small bowl or jar with a lid, combine the vinegar, pomegranate molasses, shallot, mustard, salt, and pepper. Add the oil and whisk until emulsified (or cap the jar and shake vigorously). Set aside. 2. Make the Salad: In a small skillet over medium heat, toast the nuts until golden and fragrant, 4 to 5 minutes. Remove from the skillet to cool. 3. In a large bowl, combine the pears and fennel. Sprinkle with the lemon juice and toss gently. 4. Add the arugula and toss again to evenly distribute. Pour over 3 to 4 tablespoons of the dressing, just enough to moisten the arugula, and toss. Add the pomegranate seeds, cheese, and nuts and toss again. Add more dressing, if necessary, or store remainder in the refrigerator for up to 1 week. Serve the salad topped with the reserved fennel fronds.

Per Serving:
calories: 165 | fat: 10g | protein:31g | carbs: 18g | fiber: 4g | sodium: 215mg

Italian White Bean Salad with Bell Peppers

Prep time: 15 minutes | Cook time: 0 minutes | Serves 4

- 2 tablespoons extra-virgin olive oil
- 2 tablespoons white wine vinegar
- ½ shallot, minced
- ½ teaspoon kosher salt
- ¼ teaspoon freshly ground black pepper
- 3 cups cooked cannellini beans, or 2 (15-ounce / 425-g) cans

no-salt-added or low-sodium cannellini beans, drained and rinsed
- 2 celery stalks, diced
- ½ red bell pepper, diced
- ¼ cup fresh parsley, chopped
- ¼ cup fresh mint, chopped

1. In a large bowl, whisk together the olive oil, vinegar, shallot, salt, and black pepper. 2. Add the beans, celery, red bell pepper, parsley, and mint; mix well.

Per Serving:
calories: 300 | fat: 8g | protein: 15g | carbs: 46g | fiber: 11g | sodium: 175mg

Chapter
11

Desserts

Chapter 11 Desserts

Steamed Dessert Bread

Prep time: 5 minutes | Cook time: 1 hour | Serves 8

- ½ cup all-purpose flour
- ½ cup stone-ground cornmeal
- ½ cup whole-wheat flour
- ½ teaspoon baking powder
- ¼ teaspoon salt
- ¼ teaspoon baking soda
- ½ cup maple syrup
- ½ cup buttermilk
- 1 large egg
- 1 cup water

1. Grease the inside of a 6-cup heatproof pudding mold or baking pan. 2. Add flour, cornmeal, whole-wheat flour, baking powder, salt, and baking soda to a medium mixing bowl. Stir to combine. Add maple syrup, buttermilk, and egg to another mixing bowl or measuring cup. Whisk to mix and then pour into the flour mixture. Mix until a thick batter is formed. 3. Pour enough batter into prepared baking pan to fill it three-quarters full. 4. Butter one side of a piece of heavy-duty aluminum foil large enough to cover the top of the baking dish. Place the foil butter side down over the pan and crimp the edges to seal. 5. Add water to the Instant Pot® and place the rack inside. Fold a long piece of aluminum foil in half lengthwise. Lay foil over rack to form a sling. Place pan on rack so it rests on the sling. 6. Close lid, set steam release to Sealing, press the Manual button, set time to 1 hour, and press the Adjust button and set pressure to Low. When the timer beeps, let pressure release naturally, about 25 minutes. 7. Open lid, lift pan from Instant Pot® using the sling, and place on a cooling rack. Remove foil. Test bread with a toothpick. If the toothpick comes out wet, place the foil over the pan and return it to the Instant Pot® to cook for 10 additional minutes. If the bread is done, use a knife to loosen it and invert it onto the cooling rack. Serve warm.

Per Serving:
calories: 175 | fat: 1g | protein: 4g | carbs: 37g | fiber: 2g | sodium: 102mg

Blueberry Panna Cotta

Prep time: 5 minutes | Cook time: 0 minutes | Serves 6

- 1 tablespoon gelatin powder
- 2 tablespoons water
- 2 cups goat's cream, coconut cream, or heavy whipping cream
- 2 cups wild blueberries,
- fresh or frozen, divided
- ½ teaspoon vanilla powder or 1½ teaspoons unsweetened vanilla extract
- Optional: low-carb sweetener, to taste

1. In a bowl, sprinkle the gelatin powder over the cold water. Set aside to let it bloom. 2. Place the goat's cream, half of the blueberries, and the vanilla in a blender and process until smooth and creamy. Alternatively, use an immersion blender. 3. Pour the blueberry cream into a saucepan. Gently heat; do not boil. Scrape the gelatin into the hot cream mixture together with the sweetener,

if using. Mix well until all the gelatin has dissolved. 4. Divide among 6 (4-ounce / 113-g) jars or serving glasses and fill them about two-thirds full, leaving enough space for the remaining blueberries. Place in the fridge for 3 to 4 hours, or until set. 5. When the panna cotta has set, evenly distribute the remaining blueberries among the jars. Serve immediately or store in the fridge for up to 4 days.

Per Serving:
calories: 172 | fat: 15g | protein: 2g | carbs: 8g | fiber: 2g | sodium: 19mg

Date and Honey Almond Milk Ice Cream

Prep time: 10 minutes | Cook time: 5 minutes | Serves 4

- ¾ cup (about 4 ounces/ 113 g) pitted dates
- ¼ cup honey
- ½ cup water
- 2 cups cold unsweetened almond milk
- 2 teaspoons vanilla extract

1. Combine the dates and water in a small saucepan and bring to a boil over high heat. Remove the pan from the heat, cover, and let stand for 15 minutes. 2. In a blender, combine the almond milk, dates, the date soaking water, honey, and the vanilla and process until very smooth. 3. Cover the blender jar and refrigerate the mixture until cold, at least 1 hour. 4. Transfer the mixture to an electric ice cream maker and freeze according to the manufacturer's instructions. 5. Serve immediately or transfer to a freezer-safe storage container and freeze for 4 hours (or longer). Serve frozen.

Per Serving:
calories: 106 | fat: 2g | protein: 1g | carbs: 23g | fiber: 3g | sodium: 92mg

Greek Yogurt with Honey and Pomegranates

Prep time: 5 minutes | Cook time: 0 minutes | Serves 4

- 4 cups plain full-fat Greek yogurt
- ½ cup pomegranate seeds
- ¼ cup honey
- Sugar, for topping (optional)

1. Evenly divide the yogurt among four bowls. Evenly divide the pomegranate seeds among the bowls and drizzle each with the honey. 2. Sprinkle each bowl with a pinch of sugar, if desired, and serve.

Per Serving:
calories: 232 | fat: 8g | protein: 9g | carbs: 33g | fiber: 1g | sodium: 114mg

Mascarpone and Fig Crostini

Prep time: 10 minutes | Cook time: 10 minutes | Serves 6 to 8

- 1 long French baguette
- 4 tablespoons (½ stick) salted butter, melted
- 1 (8-ounce / 227-g) tub mascarpone cheese
- 1 (12-ounce / 340-g) jar fig jam

1. Preheat the oven to 350°F(180°C). 2. Slice the bread into ¼-inch-thick slices. 3. Arrange the sliced bread on a baking sheet and brush each slice with the melted butter. 4. Put the baking sheet in the oven and toast the bread for 5 to 7 minutes, just until golden brown. 5. Let the bread cool slightly. Spread about a teaspoon or so of the mascarpone cheese on each piece of bread. 6. Top with a teaspoon or so of the jam. Serve immediately.
Per Serving:
calories: 445 | fat: 24g | protein: 3g | carbs: 48g | fiber: 5g | sodium: 314mg

Figs with Mascarpone and Honey

Prep time: 5 minutes | Cook time: 5 minutes | Serves 4

- ⅓ cup walnuts, chopped
- 8 fresh figs, halved
- ¼ cup mascarpone cheese
- 1 tablespoon honey
- ¼ teaspoon flaked sea salt

1. In a skillet over medium heat, toast the walnuts, stirring often, 3 to 5 minutes. 2. Arrange the figs cut-side up on a plate or platter. Using your finger, make a small depression in the cut side of each fig and fill with mascarpone cheese. Sprinkle with a bit of the walnuts, drizzle with the honey, and add a tiny pinch of sea salt.
Per Serving:
calories: 200 | fat: 13g | protein: 3g | carbs: 24g | fiber: 3g | sodium: 105mg

Red Grapefruit Granita

Prep time: 5 minutes | Cook time: 0 minutes | Serves 4 to 6

- 3 cups red grapefruit sections
- 1 cup freshly squeezed red grapefruit juice
- ¼ cup honey
- 1 tablespoon freshly squeezed lime juice
- Fresh basil leaves for garnish

1. Remove as much pith (white part) and membrane as possible from the grapefruit segments. 2. Combine all ingredients except the basil in a blender or food processor and pulse just until smooth. 3. Pour the mixture into a shallow glass baking dish and place in the freezer for 1 hour. Stir with a fork and freeze for another 30 minutes, then repeat. To serve, scoop into small dessert glasses and garnish with fresh basil leaves.
Per Serving:
calories: 94 | fat: 0g | protein: 1g | carbs: 24g | fiber: 1g | sodium: 1mg

Chocolate Lava Cakes

Prep time: 5 minutes | Cook time: 15 minutes | Serves 2

- 2 large eggs, whisked
- ¼ cup blanched finely ground almond flour
- ½ teaspoon vanilla extract
- 2 ounces (57 g) low-carb chocolate chips, melted

1. In a medium bowl, mix eggs with flour and vanilla. Fold in chocolate until fully combined. 2. Pour batter into two ramekins greased with cooking spray. Place ramekins into air fryer basket. Adjust the temperature to 320°F (160°C) and bake for 15 minutes. Cakes will be set at the edges and firm in the center when done. Let cool 5 minutes before serving.
Per Serving:
calories: 313 | fat: 23g | protein: 11g | carbs: 16g | fiber: 5g | sodium: 77mg

Lightened-Up Baklava Rolls

Prep time: 2 minutes | Cook time: 1 hour 15 minutes | Serves 12

- 4 ounces (113 g) shelled walnuts
- 1¼ teaspoons ground cinnamon
- 1½ teaspoons granulated sugar

Syrup:
- ¼ cup water
- ½ cup granulated sugar
- 5 teaspoons unseasoned breadcrumbs
- 1 teaspoon extra virgin olive oil plus 2 tablespoons for brushing
- 6 phyllo sheets, defrosted
- 1½ tablespoons fresh lemon juice

1. Preheat the oven to 350°F (180°C). 2. Make the syrup by combining the water and sugar in a small pan placed over medium heat. Bring to a boil, cook for 2 minutes, then remove the pan from the heat. Add the lemon juice, and stir. Set aside to cool. 3. In a food processor, combine the walnuts, cinnamon, sugar, breadcrumbs, and 1 teaspoon of the olive oil. Pulse until combined and grainy, but not chunky. 4. Place 1 phyllo sheet on a clean working surface and brush with the olive oil. Place a second sheet on top of the first sheet, brush with olive oil, and repeat the process with a third sheet. Cut the sheets in half crosswise, and then cut each half into 3 pieces crosswise. 5. Scatter 1 tablespoon of the walnut mixture over the phyllo sheet. Start rolling the phyllo and filling into a log shape while simultaneously folding the sides in (like a burrito) until the filling is encased in each piece of dough. The rolls should be about 3½ inches long. Place the rolls one next to the other in a large baking pan, then repeat the process with the remaining 3 phyllo sheets. You should have a total of 12 rolls. 6. Lightly brush the rolls with the remaining olive oil. Place in the oven to bake for 30 minutes or until the rolls turn golden brown, then remove from the oven and promptly drizzle the cold syrup over the top. 7. Let the rolls sit for 20 minutes, then flip them over and let them sit for an additional 20 minutes. Turn them over once more and sprinkle any remining walnut mixture over the rolls before serving. Store uncovered at room temperature for 2 days (to retain crispiness) and then cover with plastic wrap and store at room temperature for up to 10 days.
Per Serving:
calories: 148 | fat: 9g | protein: 2g | carbs: 16g | fiber: 1g | sodium: 53mg

Blueberry Compote

Prep time: 10 minutes | Cook time: 5 minutes | Serves 8

- 1 (16-ounce/ 454-g) bag frozen blueberries, thawed
- ¼ cup sugar
- 1 tablespoon lemon juice
- 2 tablespoons cornstarch
- 2 tablespoons water
- ¼ teaspoon vanilla extract
- ¼ teaspoon grated lemon zest

1. Add blueberries, sugar, and lemon juice to the Instant Pot®. Close lid, set steam release to Sealing, press the Manual button, and set time to 1 minute. 2. When the timer beeps, quick-release the pressure until the float valve drops. Press the Cancel button and open lid. 3. Press the Sauté button. In a small bowl, combine cornstarch and water. Stir into blueberry mixture and cook until mixture comes to a boil and thickens, about 3–4 minutes. Press the Cancel button and stir in vanilla and lemon zest. Serve immediately or refrigerate until ready to serve.

Per Serving:
calories: 57 | fat: 0g | protein: 0g | carbs: 14g | fiber: 2g | sodium: 0mg

Red-Wine Poached Pears

Prep time: 10 minutes | Cook time: 20 minutes | Serves 2

- 2 cups red wine, such as Merlot or Zinfandel, more if necessary
- 2 firm pears, peeled
- 2 to3 cardamom pods, split
- 1 cinnamon stick
- 2 peppercorns
- 1 bay leaf

1. Put all ingredients in a large pot and bring to a boil. Make sure the pears are submerged in the wine. 2. Reduce heat and simmer for 15–20 minutes until the pears are tender when poked with a fork. 3. Remove the pears from the wine, and allow to cool. 4. Bring the wine to a boil, and cook until it reduces to a syrup. 5. Strain and drizzle the pears with the warmed syrup before serving.

Per Serving:
calories: 268 | fat: 0g | protein: 1g | carbs: 22g | fiber: 6g | sodium: 0mg

Apricot and Mint No-Bake Parfait

Prep time: 10 minutes | Cook time: 0 minutes | Serves 6

- 4 ounces (113 g) Neufchâtel or other light cream cheese
- 1 (7-ounce / 198-g) container 2% Greek yogurt
- ½ cup plus 2 tablespoons sugar
- 2 teaspoons vanilla extract
- 1 tablespoon fresh lemon
- juice
- 1 pound (454 g) apricots, rinsed, pitted, and cut into bite-size pieces
- 2 tablespoons finely chopped fresh mint, plus whole leaves for garnish if desired

1. In the bowl of a stand mixer fitted with the paddle attachment, beat the Neufchâtel cheese and yogurt on low speed until well combined, about 2 minutes, scraping down the bowl as needed. Add ½ cup of the sugar, the vanilla, and the lemon juice. Mix until smooth and free of lumps, 2 to 3 minutes; set aside. 2. In a medium bowl, combine the apricots, mint, and remaining 2 tablespoons sugar. Stir occasionally, waiting to serve until after the apricots have released their juices and have softened. 3. Line up six 6-to 8-ounce (170-to 227-g) glasses. Using an ice cream scoop, spoon 3 to 4 tablespoons of the cheesecake mixture evenly into the bottom of each glass. (Alternatively, transfer the cheesecake mixture to a piping bag or a small zip-top bag with one corner snipped and pipe the mixture into the glasses.) Add a layer of the same amount of apricots to each glass. Repeat so you have two layers of cheesecake mixture and two layers of the apricots, ending with the apricots.) Garnish with the mint, if desired, and serve.

Per Serving:
calories: 132 | fat: 2g | protein: 5g | carbs: 23g | fiber: 2g | sodium: 35mg

Lemon Coconut Cake

Prep time: 5 minutes | Cook time: 40 minutes | Serves 9

Base:
- 6 large eggs, separated
- ⅓ cup melted ghee or virgin coconut oil
- 1 tablespoon fresh lemon juice
- Zest of 2 lemons
- 2 cups almond flour
- ½ cup coconut flour
- ¼ cup collagen powder
- 1 teaspoon baking soda
- 1 teaspoon vanilla powder or 1 tablespoon unsweetened vanilla extract
- Optional: low-carb sweetener, to taste

Topping:
- ½ cup unsweetened large coconut flakes
- 1 cup heavy whipping cream or coconut cream
- ¼ cup mascarpone, more
- heavy whipping cream, or coconut cream
- ½ teaspoon vanilla powder or 1½ teaspoons unsweetened vanilla extract

1. Preheat the oven to 285°F (140°C) fan assisted or 320°F (160°C) conventional. Line a baking tray with parchment paper (or use a silicone tray). A square 8 × 8–inch (20 × 20 cm) or a rectangular tray of similar size will work best. 2. To make the base: Whisk the egg whites in a bowl until stiff peaks form. In a separate bowl, whisk the egg yolks, melted ghee, lemon juice, and lemon zest. In a third bowl, mix the almond flour, coconut flour, collagen, baking soda, vanilla and optional sweetener. 3. Add the whisked egg yolk–ghee mixture into the dry mixture and combine well. Gently fold in the egg whites, trying not to deflate them. 4. Pour into the baking tray. Bake for 35 to 40 minutes, until lightly golden on top and set inside. Remove from the oven and let cool completely before adding the topping. 5. To make the topping: Preheat the oven to 350°F (175°C) fan assisted or 380°F (195°C) conventional. Place the coconut flakes on a baking tray and bake for 2 to 3 minutes. Remove from the oven and set aside to cool. 6. Once the cake is cool, place the cream, mascarpone, and vanilla in a bowl. Whip until soft peaks form. Spread on top of the cooled cake and top with the toasted coconut flakes. 7. To store, refrigerate for up to 5 days or freeze for up to 3 months. Coconut flakes will soften in the fridge. If you want to keep them crunchy, sprinkle on top of each slice before serving.

Per Serving:
calories: 342 | fat: 31g | protein: 9g | carbs: 10g | fiber: 4g | sodium: 208mg

Creamy Rice Pudding

Prep time: 5 minutes | Cook time: 45 minutes | Serves 6

- 1¼ cups long-grain rice
- 5 cups whole milk
- 1 cup sugar
- 1 tablespoon rose water or orange blossom water
- 1 teaspoon cinnamon

1. Rinse the rice under cold water for 30 seconds. 2. Put the rice, milk, and sugar in a large pot. Bring to a gentle boil while continually stirring. 3. Turn the heat down to low and let simmer for 40 to 45 minutes, stirring every 3 to 4 minutes so that the rice does not stick to the bottom of the pot. 4. Add the rose water at the end and simmer for 5 minutes. 5. Divide the pudding into 6 bowls. Sprinkle the top with cinnamon. Cool for at least 1 hour before serving. Store in the fridge.

Per Serving:
calories: 394 | fat: 7g | protein: 9g | carbs: 75g | fiber: 1g | sodium: 102mg

Grilled Pineapple and Melon

Prep time: 10 minutes | Cook time: 7 minutes | Serves 4

- 8 fresh pineapple rings, rind removed
- 8 watermelon triangles, with rind
- 1 tablespoon honey
- ½ teaspoon freshly ground black pepper

1. Preheat an outdoor grill or a grill pan over high heat. 2. Drizzle the fruit slices with honey and sprinkle one side of each piece with pepper. Grill for 5 minutes, turn, and grill for another 2 minutes. Serve.

Per Serving:
calories: 244 | fat: 1g | protein: 4g | carbs: 62g | fiber: 4g | sodium: 7mg

Brown Betty Apple Dessert

Prep time: 15 minutes | Cook time: 10 minutes | Serves 8

- 2 cups dried bread crumbs
- ½ cup sugar
- 1 teaspoon ground cinnamon
- 3 tablespoons lemon juice
- 1 tablespoon grated lemon
- zest
- 1 cup olive oil, divided
- 8 medium apples, peeled, cored, and diced
- 2 cups water

1. Combine crumbs, sugar, cinnamon, lemon juice, lemon zest, and ½ cup oil in a medium mixing bowl. Set aside. 2. In a greased oven-safe dish that will fit in your cooker loosely, add a thin layer of crumbs, then one diced apple. Continue filling the container with alternating layers of crumbs and apples until all ingredients are finished. Pour remaining ½ cup oil on top. 3. Add water to the Instant Pot® and place rack inside. Make a foil sling by folding a long piece of foil in half lengthwise and lower the uncovered container into the pot using the sling. 4. Close lid, set steam release to Sealing, press the Manual button, and set time to 10 minutes. When the timer beeps, let pressure release naturally, about 20 minutes. Press the Cancel button and open lid. 5. Using the sling,

remove the baking dish from the pot and let stand for 5 minutes before serving.

Per Serving:
calories: 422 | fat: 27g | protein: 0g | carbs: 40g | fiber: 4g | sodium: 474mg

Roasted Plums with Nut Crumble

Prep time: 5 minutes | Cook time: 25 minutes | Serves 4

- ¼ cup honey
- ¼ cup freshly squeezed orange juice
- 4 large plums, halved and pitted
- ¼ cup whole-wheat pastry flour
- 1 tablespoon pure maple
- sugar
- 1 tablespoon nuts, coarsely chopped (your choice; I like almonds, pecans, and walnuts)
- 1½ teaspoons canola oil
- ½ cup plain Greek yogurt

1. Preheat the oven to 400ºF (205ºC). Combine the honey and orange juice in a square baking dish. Place the plums, cut-side down, in the dish. Roast about 15 minutes, and then turn the plums over and roast an additional 10 minutes, or until tender and juicy. 2. In a medium bowl, combine the flour, maple sugar, nuts, and canola oil and mix well. Spread on a small baking sheet and bake alongside the plums, tossing once, until golden brown, about 5 minutes. Set aside until the plums have finished cooking. 3. Serve the plums drizzled with pan juices and topped with the nut crumble and a dollop of yogurt.

Per Serving:
calories: 175 | fat: 3g | protein: 4g | carbs: 36g | fiber: 2g | sodium: 10mg

Ricotta-Lemon Cheesecake

Prep time: 5 minutes | Cook time: 1 hour | Serves 8 to 10

- 2 (8-ounce / 227-g) packages full-fat cream cheese
- 1 (16-ounce / 454-g) container full-fat ricotta
- cheese
- 1½ cups granulated sugar
- 1 tablespoon lemon zest
- 5 large eggs
- Nonstick cooking spray

1. Preheat the oven to 350°F (180°C) . 2. Using a mixer, blend together the cream cheese and ricotta cheese. 3. Blend in the sugar and lemon zest. 4. Blend in the eggs; drop in 1 egg at a time, blend for 10 seconds, and repeat. 5. Line a 9-inch springform pan with parchment paper and nonstick spray. Wrap the bottom of the pan with foil. Pour the cheesecake batter into the pan. 6. To make a water bath, get a baking or roasting pan larger than the cheesecake pan. Fill the roasting pan about ⅓ of the way up with warm water. Put the cheesecake pan into the water bath. Put the whole thing in the oven and let the cheesecake bake for 1 hour. 7. After baking is complete, remove the cheesecake pan from the water bath and remove the foil. Let the cheesecake cool for 1 hour on the countertop. Then put it in the fridge to cool for at least 3 hours before serving.

Per Serving:
calories: 489 | fat: 31g | protein: 15g | carbs: 42g | fiber: 0g | sodium: 264mg

Lemon Berry Cream Pops

Prep time: 10 minutes | Cook time: 5 minutes | Makes 8 ice pops

Cream Pops:
- 2 cups coconut cream
- 1 tablespoon unsweetened vanilla extract

Coating:
- 1⅓ cups coconut butter
- ¼ cup virgin coconut oil

- Optional: low-carb sweetener, to taste
- 2 cups raspberries, fresh or frozen and defrosted

- Zest from 2 lemons, about 2 tablespoons
- 1 teaspoon unsweetened vanilla extract

1. To make the cream pops: In a bowl, whisk the coconut cream with the vanilla and optional sweetener until smooth and creamy. In another bowl, crush the raspberries using a fork, then add them to the bowl with the coconut cream and mix to combine. 2. Divide the mixture among eight ⅓-cup ice pop molds. Freeze until solid for 3 hours, or until set. 3. To easily remove the ice pops from the molds, fill a pot as tall as the ice pops with warm (not hot) water and dip the ice pop molds in for 15 to 20 seconds. Remove the ice pops from the molds and then freeze again. 4. Meanwhile, prepare the coating: Place the coconut butter and coconut oil in a small saucepan over low heat. Stir until smooth, remove from the heat, and add the lemon zest and vanilla. Let cool to room temperature. 5. Remove the ice pops from the freezer, two at a time, and, holding the ice pops over the saucepan, use a spoon to drizzle the coating all over. Return to the freezer until fully set, about 10 minutes. Store in the freezer in a resealable bag for up to 3 months.

Per Serving:
calories: 549 | fat: 8g | protein: 3g | carbs: 58g | fiber: 3g | sodium: 7mg

Poached Apricots and Pistachios with Greek Yogurt

Prep time: 2 minutes | Cook time: 18 minutes | Serves 4

- ½ cup orange juice
- 2 tablespoons brandy
- 2 tablespoons honey
- ¾ cup water
- 1 cinnamon stick

- 12 dried apricots
- ⅓ cup 2% Greek yogurt
- 2 tablespoons mascarpone cheese
- 2 tablespoons shelled pistachios

1. Place a saucepan over medium heat and add the orange juice, brandy, honey, and water. Stir to combine, then add the cinnamon stick. 2. Once the honey has dissolved, add the apricots. Bring the mixture to a boil, then cover, reduce the heat to low, and simmer for 15 minutes. 3. While the apricots are simmering, combine the Greek yogurt and mascarpone cheese in a small serving bowl. Stir until smooth, then set aside. 4. When the cooking time for the apricots is complete, uncover, add the pistachios, and continue simmering for 3 more minutes. Remove the pan from the heat. 5. To serve, divide the Greek yogurt–mascarpone cheese mixture into 4 serving bowls and top each serving with 3 apricots, a few pistachios, and 1 teaspoon of the syrup. The apricots and syrup can be stored in a jar at room temperature for up to 1 month.

Per Serving:
calories: 146 | fat: 3g | protein: 4g | carbs: 28g | fiber: 4g | sodium: 62mg

Chapter
12

Pizzas, Wraps, and Sandwiches

Chapter 12 Pizzas, Wraps, and Sandwiches

Classic Margherita Pizza

Prep time: 10 minutes | Cook time: 10 minutes | Serves 4

- All-purpose flour, for dusting
- 1 pound (454 g) premade pizza dough
- 1 (15-ounce / 425-g) can crushed San Marzano tomatoes, with their juices
- 2 garlic cloves
- 1 teaspoon Italian seasoning
- Pinch sea salt, plus more as needed
- 1½ teaspoons olive oil, for drizzling
- 10 slices mozzarella cheese
- 12 to 15 fresh basil leaves

1. Preheat the oven to 475°F (245°C). 2. On a floured surface, roll out the dough to a 12-inch round and place it on a lightly floured pizza pan or baking sheet. 3. In a food processor, combine the tomatoes with their juices, garlic, Italian seasoning, and salt and process until smooth. Taste and adjust the seasoning. 4. Drizzle the olive oil over the pizza dough, then spoon the pizza sauce over the dough and spread it out evenly with the back of the spoon, leaving a 1-inch border. Evenly distribute the mozzarella over the pizza. 5. Bake until the crust is cooked through and golden, 8 to 10 minutes. Remove from the oven and let sit for 1 to 2 minutes. Top with the basil right before serving.

Per Serving:
calories: 570 | fat: 21g | protein: 28g | carbs: 66g | fiber: 4g | sodium: 570mg

Grilled Eggplant and Chopped Greek Salad Wraps

Prep time: 10 minutes | Cook time: 20 minutes | Serves 4

- 15 small tomatoes, such as cherry or grape tomatoes, halved
- 10 pitted Kalamata olives, chopped
- 1 medium red onion, halved and thinly sliced
- ¾ cup crumbled feta cheese (about 4 ounces / 113 g)
- 2 tablespoons balsamic vinegar
- 1 tablespoon chopped fresh parsley
- 1 clove garlic, minced
- 2 tablespoons olive oil, plus 2 teaspoons, divided
- ¾ teaspoon salt, divided
- 1 medium cucumber, peeled, halved lengthwise, seeded, and diced
- 1 large eggplant, sliced ½-inch thick
- ½ teaspoon freshly ground black pepper
- 4 whole-wheat sandwich wraps or whole-wheat flour tortillas

1. In a medium bowl, toss together the tomatoes, olives, onion, cheese, vinegar, parsley, garlic, 2 teaspoons olive oil, and ¼ teaspoon of salt. Let sit at room temperature for 20 minutes. Add the cucumber, toss to combine, and let sit another 10 minutes. 2. While the salad is resting, grill the eggplant. Heat a grill or grill pan to high heat. Brush the remaining 2 tablespoons olive oil onto both sides of the eggplant slices. Grill for about 8 to 10 minutes per side, until grill marks appear and the eggplant is tender and cooked through. Transfer to a plate and season with the remaining ½ teaspoon of salt and the pepper. 3. Heat the wraps in a large, dry skillet over medium heat just until warm and soft, about 1 minute on each side. Place 2 or 3 eggplant slices down the center of each wrap. Spoon some of the salad mixture on top of the eggplant, using a slotted spoon so that any excess liquid is drained off. Fold in the sides of the wrap and roll up like a burrito. Serve immediately.

Per Serving:
calories: 233 | fat: 10g | protein: 8g | carbs: 29g | fiber: 7g | sodium: 707mg

Mediterranean-Pita Wraps

Prep time: 5 minutes | Cook time: 14 minutes | Serves 4

- 1 pound (454 g) mackerel fish fillets
- 2 tablespoons olive oil
- 1 tablespoon Mediterranean seasoning mix
- ½ teaspoon chili powder
- Sea salt and freshly ground black pepper, to taste
- 2 ounces (57 g) feta cheese, crumbled
- 4 tortillas

1. Toss the fish fillets with the olive oil; place them in the lightly oiled air fryer basket. 2. Air fry the fish fillets at 400°F (204°C) for about 14 minutes, turning them over halfway through the cooking time. 3. Assemble your pitas with the chopped fish and remaining ingredients and serve warm.

Per Serving:
calories: 275 | fat: 13g | protein: 27g | carbs: 13g | fiber: 2g | sodium: 322mg

Cucumber Basil Sandwiches

Prep time: 10 minutes | Cook time: 0 minutes | Serves 2

- Cucumber Basil Sandwiches
- 4 slices whole-grain bread
- ¼ cup hummus
- 1 large cucumber, thinly sliced
- 4 whole basil leaves

1. Spread the hummus on 2 slices of bread, and layer the cucumbers onto it. Top with the basil leaves and close the sandwiches. 2. Press down lightly and serve immediately.

Per Serving:
calories: 209 | fat: 5g | protein: 9g | carbs: 32g | fiber: 6g | sodium: 275mg

Turkey Burgers with Feta and Dill

Prep time: 5 minutes | Cook time: 15 minutes | Serves 4

- 1 pound (454 g) ground turkey breast
- 1 small red onion, ½ finely chopped, ½ sliced
- ½ cup crumbled feta cheese
- ¼ cup chopped fresh dill
- 1 clove garlic, minced
- ½ teaspoon kosher salt
- ¼ teaspoon ground black pepper
- 4 whole grain hamburger rolls
- 4 thick slices tomato
- 4 leaves lettuce

1. Coat a grill rack or grill pan with olive oil and prepare to medium-high heat. 2. In a large bowl, use your hands to combine the turkey, chopped onion, cheese, dill, garlic, salt, and pepper. Do not overmix. Divide into 4 patties, 4' in diameter. 3. Grill the patties, covered, until a thermometer inserted in the center registers 165°F(74°C), 5 to 6 minutes per side. 4. Serve each patty on a roll with the sliced onion, 1 slice of the tomato, and 1 leaf of the lettuce.
Per Serving:
calories: 305 | fat: 7g | protein: 35g | carbs: 26g | fiber: 3g | sodium: 708mg

Za' atar Pizza

Prep time: 10 minutes | Cook time: 15 minutes | Serves 4 to 6

- 1 sheet puff pastry
- ¼ cup extra-virgin olive oil
- ⅓ cup za'atar seasoning

1. Preheat the oven to 350°F(180°C). 2. Put the puff pastry on a parchment-lined baking sheet. Cut the pastry into desired slices. 3. Brush the pastry with olive oil. Sprinkle with the za'atar. 4. Put the pastry in the oven and bake for 10 to 12 minutes or until edges are lightly browned and puffed up. Serve warm or at room temperature.
Per Serving:
calories: 374 | fat: 30g | protein: 3g | carbs: 20g | fiber: 1g | sodium: 166mg

Sauté ed Mushroom, Onion, and Pecorino Romano Panini

Prep time: 10 minutes | Cook time: 20 minutes | Serves 4

- 3 tablespoons olive oil, divided
- 1 small onion, diced
- 10 ounces (283 g) button or cremini mushrooms, sliced
- ½ teaspoon salt
- ¼ teaspoon freshly ground black pepper
- 4 crusty Italian sandwich rolls
- 4 ounces (113 g) freshly grated Pecorino Romano

1. Heat 1 tablespoon of the olive oil in a skillet over medium-high heat. Add the onion and cook, stirring, until it begins to soften, about 3 minutes. Add the mushrooms, season with salt and pepper, and cook, stirring, until they soften and the liquid they release evaporates, about 7 minutes. 2. To make the panini, heat a skillet or grill pan over high heat and brush with 1 tablespoon olive oil. Brush the inside of the rolls with the remaining 1 tablespoon olive oil. Divide the mushroom mixture evenly among the rolls and top each with ¼ of the grated cheese. 3. Place the sandwiches in the hot pan and place another heavy pan, such as a cast-iron skillet, on top to weigh them down. Cook for about 3 to 4 minutes, until crisp and golden on the bottom, and then flip over and repeat on the second side, cooking for an additional 3 to 4 minutes until golden and crisp. Slice each sandwich in half and serve hot.
Per Serving:
calories: 348 | fat: 20g | protein: 14g | carbs: 30g | fiber: 2g | sodium: 506mg

Jerk Chicken Wraps

Prep time: 30 minutes | Cook time: 15 minutes | Serves 4

- 1 pound (454 g) boneless, skinless chicken tenderloins
- 1 cup jerk marinade
- Olive oil
- 4 large low-carb tortillas
- 1 cup julienned carrots
- 1 cup peeled cucumber ribbons
- 1 cup shredded lettuce
- 1 cup mango or pineapple chunks

1. In a medium bowl, coat the chicken with the jerk marinade, cover, and refrigerate for 1 hour. 2. Spray the air fryer basket lightly with olive oil. 3. Place the chicken in the air fryer basket in a single layer and spray lightly with olive oil. You may need to cook the chicken in batches. Reserve any leftover marinade. 4. Air fry at 375°F (191°C) for 8 minutes. Turn the chicken over and brush with some of the remaining marinade. Cook until the chicken reaches an internal temperature of at least 165°F (74°C), an additional 5 to 7 minutes. 5. To assemble the wraps, fill each tortilla with ¼ cup carrots, ¼ cup cucumber, ¼ cup lettuce, and ¼ cup mango. Place one quarter of the chicken tenderloins on top and roll up the tortilla. These are great served warm or cold.
Per Serving:
calories: 241 | fat: 4g | protein: 28g | carbs: 23g | fiber: 4g | sodium: 85mg

Dill Salmon Salad Wraps

Prep time: 10 minutes |Cook time: 10 minutes| Serves:6

- 1 pound (454 g) salmon filet, cooked and flaked, or 3 (5-ounce / 142-g) cans salmon
- ½ cup diced carrots (about 1 carrot)
- ½ cup diced celery (about 1 celery stalk)
- 3 tablespoons chopped fresh dill
- 3 tablespoons diced red onion (a little less than ⅛ onion)
- 2 tablespoons capers
- 1½ tablespoons extra-virgin olive oil
- 1 tablespoon aged balsamic vinegar
- ½ teaspoon freshly ground black pepper
- ¼ teaspoon kosher or sea salt
- 4 whole-wheat flatbread wraps or soft whole-wheat tortillas

1. In a large bowl, mix together the salmon, carrots, celery, dill, red onion, capers, oil, vinegar, pepper, and salt. 2. Divide the salmon salad among the flatbreads. Fold up the bottom of the flatbread, then roll up the wrap and serve.
Per Serving:
calories: 185 | fat: 8g | protein: 17g | carbs: 12g | fiber: 2g | sodium: 237mg

Greek Salad Pita

Prep time: 15 minutes | Cook time: 0 minutes | Serves 4

- 1 cup chopped romaine lettuce
- 1 tomato, chopped and seeded
- ½ cup baby spinach leaves
- ½ small red onion, thinly sliced
- ½ small cucumber, chopped and deseeded
- 2 tablespoons olive oil
- 1 tablespoon crumbled feta cheese
- ½ tablespoon red wine vinegar
- 1 teaspoon Dijon mustard
- Sea salt and freshly ground pepper, to taste
- 1 whole-wheat pita

1. Combine everything except the sea salt, freshly ground pepper, and pita bread in a medium bowl. 2. Toss until the salad is well combined. 3. Season with sea salt and freshly ground pepper to taste. Fill the pita with the salad mixture, serve, and enjoy!

Per Serving:
calories: 123 | fat: 8g | protein: 3g | carbs: 12g | fiber: 2g | sodium: 125mg

Pesto Chicken Mini Pizzas

Prep time: 5 minutes | Cook time: 10 minutes | Serves 4

- 2 cups shredded cooked chicken
- ¾ cup pesto
- 4 English muffins, split
- 2 cups shredded Mozzarella cheese

1. In a medium bowl, toss the chicken with the pesto. Place one-eighth of the chicken on each English muffin half. Top each English muffin with ¼ cup of the Mozzarella cheese. 2. Put four pizzas at a time in the air fryer and air fry at 350ºF (177ºC) for 5 minutes. Repeat this process with the other four pizzas.

Per Serving:
calories: 617 | fat: 36g | protein: 45g | carbs: 29g | fiber: 3g | sodium: 544mg

Roasted Vegetable Bocadillo with Romesco Sauce

Prep time: 10 minutes | Cook time: 20 minutes | Serves 4

- 2 small yellow squash, sliced lengthwise
- 2 small zucchini, sliced lengthwise
- 1 medium red onion, thinly sliced
- 4 large button mushrooms, sliced
- 2 tablespoons olive oil
- 1 teaspoon salt, divided
- ½ teaspoon freshly ground black pepper, divided
- 2 roasted red peppers from a jar, drained
- 2 tablespoons blanched almonds
- 1 tablespoon sherry vinegar
- 1 small clove garlic
- 4 crusty multigrain rolls
- 4 ounces (113 g) goat cheese, at room temperature
- 1 tablespoon chopped fresh basil

1. Preheat the oven to 400ºF(205ºC). 2. In a medium bowl, toss the yellow squash, zucchini, onion, and mushrooms with the olive oil, ½ teaspoon salt, and ¼ teaspoon pepper. Spread on a large baking sheet. Roast the vegetables in the oven for about 20 minutes, until softened. 3. Meanwhile, in a food processor, combine the roasted peppers, almonds, vinegar, garlic, the remaining ½ teaspoon salt, and the remaining ¼ teaspoon pepper and process until smooth. 4. Split the rolls and spread ¼ of the goat cheese on the bottom of each. Place the roasted vegetables on top of the cheese, dividing equally. Top with chopped basil. Spread the top halves of the rolls with the roasted red pepper sauce and serve immediately.

Per Serving:
calories: 379 | fat: 21g | protein: 17g | carbs: 32g | fiber: 4g | sodium: 592mg

Vegetable Pita Sandwiches

Prep time: 15 minutes | Cook time: 9 to 12 minutes | Serves 4

- 1 baby eggplant, peeled and chopped
- 1 red bell pepper, sliced
- ½ cup diced red onion
- ½ cup shredded carrot
- 1 teaspoon olive oil
- ⅓ cup low-fat Greek yogurt
- ½ teaspoon dried tarragon
- 2 low-sodium whole-wheat pita breads, halved crosswise

1. In a baking pan, stir together the eggplant, red bell pepper, red onion, carrot, and olive oil. Put the vegetable mixture into the air fryer basket and roast at 390ºF (199ºC) for 7 to 9 minutes, stirring once, until the vegetables are tender. Drain if necessary. 2. In a small bowl, thoroughly mix the yogurt and tarragon until well combined. 3. Stir the yogurt mixture into the vegetables. Stuff one-fourth of this mixture into each pita pocket. 4. Place the sandwiches in the air fryer and cook for 2 to 3 minutes, or until the bread is toasted. Serve immediately.

Per Serving:
calories: 115 | fat: 2g | protein: 4g | carbs: 22g | fiber: 6g | sodium: 90mg

Greek Salad Wraps

Prep time: 15 minutes |Cook time: 0 minutes| Serves: 4

- 1½ cups seedless cucumber, peeled and chopped (about 1 large cucumber)
- 1 cup chopped tomato (about 1 large tomato)
- ½ cup finely chopped fresh mint
- 1 (2¼ ounces / 64 g) can sliced black olives (about ½ cup), drained
- ¼ cup diced red onion (about ¼ onion)
- 2 tablespoons extra-virgin
- olive oil
- 1 tablespoon red wine vinegar
- ¼ teaspoon freshly ground black pepper
- ¼ teaspoon kosher or sea salt
- ½ cup crumbled goat cheese (about 2 ounces / 57 g)
- 4 whole-wheat flatbread wraps or soft whole-wheat tortillas

1. In a large bowl, mix together the cucumber, tomato, mint, olives, and onion until well combined. 2. In a small bowl, whisk together the oil, vinegar, pepper, and salt. Drizzle the dressing over the salad, and mix gently. 3. With a knife, spread the goat cheese evenly over the four wraps. Spoon a quarter of the salad filling down the middle of each wrap. 4. Fold up each wrap: Start by folding up the bottom, then fold one side over and fold the other side over the top. Repeat with the remaining wraps and serve.

Per Serving:
calories: 217 | fat: 14g | protein: 7g | carbs: 17g | fiber: 3g | sodium: 329mg

Chapter

13

Pasta

Chapter 13 Pasta

Couscous with Tomatoes and Olives

Prep time: 5 minutes | Cook time: 3 minutes | Serves 4

- 1 tablespoon tomato paste
- 2 cups vegetable broth
- 1 cup couscous
- 1 cup halved cherry tomatoes
- ½ cup halved mixed olives
- ¼ cup minced fresh flat-leaf parsley
- 2 tablespoons minced fresh

- oregano
- 2 tablespoons minced fresh chives
- 1 tablespoon extra-virgin olive oil
- 1 tablespoon red wine vinegar
- ½ teaspoon ground black pepper

1. Pour tomato paste and broth into the Instant Pot® and stir until completely dissolved. Stir in couscous. Close lid, set steam release to Sealing, press the Manual button, and set time to 3 minutes. When the timer beeps, let pressure release naturally for 10 minutes, then quick-release the remaining pressure and open lid. 2. Fluff couscous with a fork. Add tomatoes, olives, parsley, oregano, chives, oil, vinegar, and pepper, and stir until combined. Serve warm or at room temperature.

Per Serving:
calories: 232 | fat: 5g | protein: 7g | carbs: 37g | fiber: 2g | sodium: 513mg

Spaghetti with Fresh Mint Pesto and Ricotta Salata

Prep time: 5 minutes | Cook time: 15 minutes | Serves 4

- 1 pound (454 g) spaghetti
- ¼ cup slivered almonds
- 2 cups packed fresh mint leaves, plus more for garnish
- 3 medium garlic cloves
- 1 tablespoon lemon juice

- and ½ teaspoon lemon zest from 1 lemon
- ⅓ cup olive oil
- ¼ teaspoon freshly ground black pepper
- ½ cup freshly grated ricotta salata, plus more for garnish

1. Set a large pot of salted water over high heat to boil for the pasta. 2. In a food processor, combine the almonds, mint leaves, garlic, lemon juice and zest, olive oil, and pepper and pulse to a smooth paste. Add the cheese and pulse to combine. 3. When the water is boiling, add the pasta and cook according to the package instructions. Drain the pasta and return it to the pot. Add the pesto to the pasta and toss until the pasta is well coated. Serve hot, garnished with additional mint leaves and cheese, if desired.

Per Serving:
calories: 619 | fat: 31g | protein: 21g | carbs: 70g | fiber: 4g | sodium: 113mg

Rotini with Red Wine Marinara

Prep time: 10 minutes | Cook time: 25 minutes | Serves 6

- 1 pound (454 g) rotini
- 4 cups water
- 1 tablespoon olive oil
- ½ medium yellow onion, peeled and diced
- 3 cloves garlic, peeled and minced
- 1 (15-ounce / 425-g) can

- crushed tomatoes
- ½ cup red wine
- 1 teaspoon sugar
- 2 tablespoons chopped fresh basil
- ½ teaspoon salt
- ¼ teaspoon ground black pepper

1. Add pasta and water to the Instant Pot®. Close lid, set steam release to Sealing, press the Manual button, and set time to 4 minutes. When the timer beeps, quick-release the pressure until the float valve drops and open the lid. Press the Cancel button. Drain pasta and set aside. 2. Clean pot and return to machine. Press the Sauté button and heat oil. Add onion and cook until it begins to caramelize, about 10 minutes. Add garlic and cook 30 seconds. Add tomatoes, red wine, and sugar, and simmer for 10 minutes. Add basil, salt, pepper, and pasta. Serve immediately.

Per Serving:
calories: 320 | fat: 4g | protein: 10g | carbs: 59g | fiber: 4g | sodium: 215mg

Israeli Pasta Salad

Prep time: 15 minutes | Cook time: 4 minutes | Serves 6

- ½ pound (227 g) whole-wheat penne pasta
- 4 cups water
- 1 tablespoon plus ¼ cup extra-virgin olive oil, divided
- 1 cup quartered cherry tomatoes
- ½ English cucumber, chopped
- ½ medium orange bell

- pepper, seeded and chopped
- ½ medium red onion, peeled and chopped
- ½ cup crumbled feta cheese
- 1 teaspoon fresh thyme leaves
- 1 teaspoon chopped fresh oregano
- ½ teaspoon ground black pepper
- ¼ cup lemon juice

1. Add pasta, water, and 1 tablespoon oil to the Instant Pot®. Close lid, set steam release to Sealing, press the Manual button, and set time to 4 minutes. 2. When the timer beeps, quick-release the pressure until the float valve drops and open lid. Drain and set aside to cool for 30 minutes. Stir in tomatoes, cucumber, bell pepper, onion, feta, thyme, oregano, black pepper, lemon juice, and remaining ¼ cup oil. Refrigerate for 2 hours.

Per Serving:
calories: 243 | fat: 16g | protein: 7g | carbs: 20g | fiber: 3g | sodium: 180mg

Rigatoni with Lamb Meatballs

Prep time: 15 minutes | Cook time: 3 to 5 hours | Serves 4

- 8 ounces (227 g) dried rigatoni pasta
- 2 (28-ounce / 794-g) cans no-salt-added crushed tomatoes or no-salt-added diced tomatoes
- 1 small onion, diced
- 1 bell pepper, any color, seeded and diced
- 3 garlic cloves, minced, divided
- 1 pound (454 g) raw ground lamb
- 1 large egg
- 2 tablespoons bread crumbs
- 1 tablespoon dried parsley
- 1 teaspoon dried oregano
- 1 teaspoon sea salt
- ½ teaspoon freshly ground black pepper

1. In a slow cooker, combine the pasta, tomatoes, onion, bell pepper, and 1 clove of garlic. Stir to mix well. 2. In a large bowl, mix together the ground lamb, egg, bread crumbs, the remaining 2 garlic cloves, parsley, oregano, salt, and black pepper until all of the ingredients are evenly blended. Shape the meat mixture into 6 to 9 large meatballs. Nestle the meatballs into the pasta and tomato sauce. 3. Cover the cooker and cook for 3 to 5 hours on Low heat, or until the pasta is tender.

Per Serving:
calories: 653 | fat: 29g | protein: 32g | carbs: 69g | fiber: 10g | sodium: 847mg

Orzo with Feta and Marinated Peppers

Prep time:1 hour 25 minutes | Cook time: 37 minutes | Serves 2

- 2 medium red bell peppers
- ¼ cup extra virgin olive oil
- 1 tablespoon balsamic vinegar plus 1 teaspoon for serving
- ¼ teaspoon ground cumin
- Pinch of ground cinnamon
- Pinch of ground cloves
- ¼ teaspoon fine sea salt plus
- a pinch for the orzo
- 1 cup uncooked orzo
- 3 ounces (85 g) crumbled feta
- 1 tablespoon chopped fresh basil
- ¼ teaspoon freshly ground black pepper

1. Preheat the oven at 350°F (180°C). Place the peppers on a baking pan and roast in the oven for 25 minutes or until they're soft and can be pierced with a fork. Set aside to cool for 10 minutes. 2. While the peppers are roasting, combine the olive oil, 1 tablespoon of the balsamic vinegar, cumin, cinnamon, cloves, and ¼ teaspoon of the sea salt. Stir to combine, then set aside. 3. Peel the cooled peppers, remove the seeds, and then chop into large pieces. Place the peppers in the olive oil and vinegar mixture and then toss to coat, ensuring the peppers are covered in the marinade. Cover and place in the refrigerator to marinate for 20 minutes. 4. While the peppers are marinating, prepare the orzo by bringing 3 cups of water and a pinch of salt to a boil in a large pot over high heat. When the water is boiling, add the orzo, reduce the heat to medium, and cook, stirring occasionally, for 10–12 minutes or until soft, then drain and transfer to a serving bowl. 5. Add the peppers and marinade to the orzo, mixing well, then place in the refrigerator and to cool for at least 1 hour. 6. To serve, top with the feta, basil, black pepper, and 1 teaspoon of the balsamic vinegar. Mix well, and serve promptly. Store covered in the refrigerator for up to 3 days.

Per Serving:
calories: 600 | fat: 37g | protein: 15g | carbs: 51g | fiber: 4g | sodium: 690mg

Quick Shrimp Fettuccine

Prep time: 10 minutes | Cook time: 10 minutes | Serves 4 to 6

- 8 ounces (227 g) fettuccine pasta
- ¼ cup extra-virgin olive oil
- 3 tablespoons garlic, minced
- 1 pound (454 g) large shrimp (21-25), peeled and
- deveined
- ⅓ cup lemon juice
- 1 tablespoon lemon zest
- ½ teaspoon salt
- ½ teaspoon freshly ground black pepper

1. Bring a large pot of salted water to a boil. Add the fettuccine and cook for 8 minutes. 2. In a large saucepan over medium heat, cook the olive oil and garlic for 1 minute. 3. Add the shrimp to the saucepan and cook for 3 minutes on each side. Remove the shrimp from the pan and set aside. 4. Add the lemon juice and lemon zest to the saucepan, along with the salt and pepper. 5. Reserve ½ cup of the pasta water and drain the pasta. 6. Add the pasta water to the saucepan with the lemon juice and zest and stir everything together. Add the pasta and toss together to evenly coat the pasta. Transfer the pasta to a serving dish and top with the cooked shrimp. Serve warm.

Per Serving:
calories: 615 | fat: 17g | protein: 33g | carbs: 89g | fiber: 4g | sodium: 407mg

Mixed Vegetable Couscous

Prep time: 20 minutes | Cook time: 10 minutes | Serves 8

- 1 tablespoon light olive oil
- 1 medium zucchini, trimmed and chopped
- 1 medium yellow squash, chopped
- 1 large red bell pepper, seeded and chopped
- 1 large orange bell pepper, seeded and chopped
- 2 tablespoons chopped fresh
- oregano
- 2 cups Israeli couscous
- 3 cups vegetable broth
- ½ cup crumbled feta cheese
- ¼ cup red wine vinegar
- ¼ cup extra-virgin olive oil
- ½ teaspoon ground black pepper
- ¼ cup chopped fresh basil

1. Press the Sauté button on the Instant Pot® and heat light olive oil. Add zucchini, squash, bell peppers, and oregano, and sauté 8 minutes. Press the Cancel button. Transfer to a serving bowl and set aside to cool. 2. Add couscous and broth to the Instant Pot® and stir well. Close lid, set steam release to Sealing, press the Manual button, and set time to 2 minutes. When the timer beeps, let pressure release naturally for 5 minutes, then quick-release the remaining pressure and open lid. 3. Fluff with a fork and stir in cooked vegetables, cheese, vinegar, extra-virgin olive oil, black pepper, and basil. Serve warm.

Per Serving:
calories: 355 | fat: 9g | protein: 14g | carbs: 61g | fiber: 7g | sodium: 588mg

Neapolitan Pasta and Zucchini

Prep time: 5 minutes | Cook time: 28 minutes | Serves 3

- ⅓ cup extra virgin olive oil
- 1 large onion (any variety), diced
- 1 teaspoon fine sea salt, divided
- 2 large zucchini, quartered lengthwise and cut into ½-inch pieces

- 10 ounces (283 g) uncooked spaghetti, broken into 1-inch pieces
- 2 tablespoons grated Parmesan cheese
- 2 ounces (57 g) grated or shaved Parmesan cheese for serving
- ½ teaspoon freshly ground black pepper

1. Add the olive oil to a medium pot over medium heat. When the oil begins to shimmer, add the onions and ¼ teaspoon of the sea salt. Sauté for 3 minutes, add the zucchini, and continue sautéing for 3 more minutes. 2. Add 2 cups of hot water to the pot or enough to just cover the zucchini (the amount of water may vary depending on the size of the pot). Cover, reduce the heat to low, and simmer for 10 minutes. 3. Add the pasta to the pot, stir, then add 2 more cups of hot water. Continue simmering, stirring occasionally, until the pasta is cooked and the mixture has thickened, about 12 minutes. (If the pasta appears to be dry or undercooked, add small amounts of hot water to the pot to ensure the pasta is covered in the water.). When the pasta is cooked, remove the pot from the heat. Add 2 tablespoons of the grated Parmesan and stir. 4. Divide the pasta into three servings and then top each with 1 ounce (28 g) of the grated or shaved Parmesan. Sprinkle the remaining sea salt and black pepper over the top of each serving. Store covered in the refrigerator for up to 3 days.

Per Serving:
calories: 718 | fat: 33g | protein: 24g | carbs: 83g | fiber: 6g | sodium: 815mg

Zucchini with Bow Ties

Prep time: 5 minutes |Cook time: 25 minutes| Serves: 4

- 3 tablespoons extra-virgin olive oil
- 2 garlic cloves, minced (about 1 teaspoon)
- 3 large or 4 medium zucchini, diced (about 4 cups)
- ½ teaspoon freshly ground black pepper
- ¼ teaspoon kosher or sea salt
- ½ cup 2% milk
- ¼ teaspoon ground nutmeg

- 8 ounces (227 g) uncooked farfalle (bow ties) or other small pasta shape
- ½ cup grated Parmesan or Romano cheese (about 2 ounces / 57 g)
- 1 tablespoon freshly squeezed lemon juice (from ½ medium lemon)

1. In a large skillet over medium heat, heat the oil. Add the garlic and cook for 1 minute, stirring frequently. Add the zucchini, pepper, and salt. Stir well, cover, and cook for 15 minutes, stirring once or twice. 2. In a small, microwave-safe bowl, warm the milk in the microwave on high for 30 seconds. Stir the milk and nutmeg into the skillet and cook uncovered for another 5 minutes, stirring occasionally. 3. While the zucchini is cooking, in a large stockpot, cook the pasta according to the package directions. 4. Drain the pasta in a colander, saving about 2 tablespoons of pasta water. Add the pasta and pasta water to the skillet. Mix everything together and remove from the heat. Stir in the cheese and lemon juice and serve.

Per Serving:
calories: 405 | fat: 16g | protein: 12g | carbs: 57g | fiber: 9g | sodium: 407mg

Chapter

14

Staples, Sauces, Dips, and Dressings

Chapter 14 Staples, Sauces, Dips, and Dressings

Classic Basil Pesto

Prep time: 5 minutes | Cook time: 13 minutes | Makes about 1½ cups

- 6 garlic cloves, unpeeled
- ½ cup pine nuts
- 4 cups fresh basil leaves
- ¼ cup fresh parsley leaves
- 1 cup extra-virgin olive oil
- 1 ounce (28 g) Parmesan cheese, grated fine (½ cup)

1. Toast garlic in 8-inch skillet over medium heat, shaking skillet occasionally, until softened and spotty brown, about 8 minutes. When garlic is cool enough to handle, remove and discard skins and chop coarsely. Meanwhile, toast pine nuts in now-empty skillet over medium heat, stirring often, until golden and fragrant, 4 to 5 minutes. 2. Place basil and parsley in 1-gallon zipper-lock bag. Pound bag with flat side of meat pounder or with rolling pin until all leaves are bruised. 3. Process garlic, pine nuts, and herbs in food processor until finely chopped, about 1 minute, scraping down sides of bowl as needed. With processor running, slowly add oil until incorporated. Transfer pesto to bowl, stir in Parmesan, and season with salt and pepper to taste. (Pesto can be refrigerated for up to 3 days or frozen for up to 3 months. To prevent browning, press plastic wrap flush to surface or top with thin layer of olive oil. Bring to room temperature before using.)

Per Serving:

¼ cup: calories: 423 | fat: 45g | protein: 4g | carbs: 4g | fiber: 1g | sodium: 89mg

Roasted Harissa

Prep time: 5 minutes | Cook time: 15 minutes | Makes ¾ cup

- 1 red bell pepper
- 2 small fresh red chiles, or more to taste
- 4 garlic cloves, unpeeled
- ½ teaspoon ground coriander
- ½ teaspoon ground cumin
- ½ teaspoon ground caraway
- 1 tablespoon fresh lemon juice
- ½ teaspoon salt

1. Preheat the broiler to high. 2. Put the bell pepper, chiles, and garlic on a baking sheet and broil for 6 to 8 minutes. Turn the vegetables over and broil for 5 to 6 minutes more, until the pepper and chiles are softened and blackened. Remove from the broiler and set aside until cool enough to handle. Remove and discard the stems, skin, and seeds from the pepper and chiles. Remove and discard the papery skin from the garlic. 3. Put the flesh of the pepper and chiles with the garlic cloves in a blender or food processor. Add the coriander, cumin, caraway, lemon juice, and salt and blend until smooth. 4. This may be stored refrigerated for up

to 3 days. Store in an airtight container, and cover the sauce with a ¼-inch layer of oil.

Per Serving:

calories: 28 | fat: 0g | protein: 1g | carbs: 6g | fiber: 1g | sodium: 393mg

Chermoula

Prep time: 10 minutes | Cook time: 0 minutes | Makes about 1½ cups

- 2¼ cups fresh cilantro leaves
- 8 garlic cloves, minced
- 1½ teaspoons ground cumin
- 1½ teaspoons paprika
- ½ teaspoon cayenne pepper
- ½ teaspoon table salt
- 6 tablespoons lemon juice (2 lemons)
- ¾ cup extra-virgin olive oil

1. Pulse cilantro, garlic, cumin, paprika, cayenne, and salt in food processor until cilantro is coarsely chopped, about 10 pulses. Add lemon juice and pulse briefly to combine. Transfer mixture to medium bowl and slowly whisk in oil until incorporated and mixture is emulsified. Cover and let sit at room temperature for at least 30 minutes to allow flavors to meld. (Sauce can be refrigerated for up to 2 days; bring to room temperature before serving.)

Per Serving:

¼ cup: calories: 253 | fat: 27g | protein: 1g | carbs: 3g | fiber: 1g | sodium: 199mg

Bagna Cauda

Prep time: 5 minutes | Cook time: 20 minutes | Serves 8 to 10

- ½ cup extra-virgin olive oil
- 4 tablespoons (½ stick) butter
- 8 anchovy fillets, very finely chopped
- 4 large garlic cloves, finely minced
- ½ teaspoon salt
- ½ teaspoon freshly ground black pepper

1. In a small saucepan, heat the olive oil and butter over medium-low heat until the butter is melted. 2. Add the anchovies and garlic and stir to combine. Add the salt and pepper and reduce the heat to low. Cook, stirring occasionally, until the anchovies are very soft and the mixture is very fragrant, about 20 minutes. 3. Serve warm, drizzled over steamed vegetables, as a dipping sauce for raw veggies or cooked artichokes, or use as a salad dressing. Store leftovers in an airtight container in the refrigerator for up to 2 weeks.

Per Serving:

calories: 145 | fat: 16g | protein: 1g | carbs: 0g | fiber: 0g | sodium: 235mg

Salsa Verde

Prep time: 5 minutes | Cook time: 0 minutes | Makes about 1½ cups

- 4 cups fresh parsley leaves
- 8 garlic cloves, minced
- ¼ teaspoon table salt
- ¼ cup sherry vinegar
- 1 cup extra-virgin olive oil

1. Pulse parsley, garlic, and salt in food processor until parsley is coarsely chopped, about 10 pulses. Add vinegar and pulse briefly to combine. Transfer mixture to medium bowl and slowly whisk in oil until incorporated. Cover and let sit at room temperature for at least 30 minutes to allow flavors to meld. (Sauce can be refrigerated for up to 2 days; bring to room temperature before serving.)

Per Serving:
¼ cup: calories: 341 | fat: 36g | protein: 1g | carbs: 4g | fiber: 1g | sodium: 121mg

Arugula and Walnut Pesto

Prep time: 5 minutes | Cook time: 0 minutes | Serves 8 to 10

- 6 cups packed arugula
- 1 cup chopped walnuts
- ½ cup shredded Parmesan cheese
- 2 garlic cloves, peeled
- ½ teaspoon salt
- 1 cup extra-virgin olive oil

1. In a food processor, combine the arugula, walnuts, cheese, and garlic and process until very finely chopped. Add the salt. With the processor running, stream in the olive oil until well blended. 2. If the mixture seems too thick, add warm water, 1 tablespoon at a time, until smooth and creamy. Store in a sealed container in the refrigerator.

Per Serving:
calories: 292 | fat: 31g | protein: 4g | carbs: 3g | fiber: 1g | sodium: 210mg

Red Pepper Hummus

Prep time: 5 minutes | Cook time: 30 minutes | Makes 2 cups

- 1 cup dried chickpeas
- 4 cups water
- 1 tablespoon plus ¼ cup extra-virgin olive oil, divided
- ½ cup chopped roasted red pepper, divided
- ⅓ cup tahini
- 1 teaspoon ground cumin
- ¾ teaspoon salt
- ½ teaspoon ground black pepper
- ¼ teaspoon smoked paprika
- ⅓ cup lemon juice
- ½ teaspoon minced garlic

1. Place chickpeas, water, and 1 tablespoon oil in the Instant Pot®. Close the lid, set steam release to Sealing, press the Manual button, and set time to 30 minutes. 2. When the timer beeps, quick-release the pressure until the float valve drops. Press the Cancel button and open lid. Drain, reserving the cooking liquid. 3. Place chickpeas, ⅓ cup roasted red pepper, remaining ¼ cup oil, tahini, cumin, salt, black pepper, paprika, lemon juice, and garlic in a food processor and process until creamy. If hummus is too thick, add reserved cooking liquid 1 tablespoon at a time until it reaches desired consistency. Serve at room temperature, garnished with reserved roasted red pepper on top.

Per Serving:
2 tablespoons: calories: 96 | fat: 8g | protein: 2g | carbs: 10g | fiber: 4g | sodium: 122mg

Piri Piri Sauce

Prep time: 5 minutes | Cook time: 0 minutes | Makes about 1 cup

- 4 to 8 fresh hot, red chiles, stemmed and coarsely chopped
- 2 cloves garlic, minced
- Juice of 1 lemon
- Pinch of salt
- ½ to 1 cup olive oil

1. In a food processor, combine the chiles (with their seeds), garlic, lemon juice, salt, and ½ cup of olive oil. Process to a smooth purée. Add additional oil as needed to reach the desired consistency. 2. Pour the mixture into a glass jar or non-reactive bowl, cover, and refrigerate for at least 3 days before using. Store in the refrigerator for up to a month.

Per Serving:
calories:84 | fat: 10g | protein: 0g | carbs: 0g | fiber: 0g | sodium: 13mg

Vinaigrette

Prep time: 5 minutes | Cook time: 0 minutes | Serves 4

- 2 tablespoons balsamic vinegar
- 2 large garlic cloves, minced
- 1 teaspoon dried rosemary, crushed
- ¼ teaspoon freshly ground black pepper
- ¼ cup olive oil

1. In a small bowl, whisk together the vinegar, garlic, rosemary, and pepper. While whisking, slowly stream in the olive oil and whisk until emulsified. Store in an airtight container in the refrigerator for up to 3 days.

Per Serving:
1 cup: calories: 129 | fat: 1g | protein: 3g | carbs: 0g | fiber: 0g | sodium: 2mg

Pickled Onions

Prep time: 5 minutes | Cook time: 0 minutes | Serves 8 to 10

- 3 red onions, finely chopped
- ½ cup warm water
- ¼ cup granulated sugar
- ¼ cup red wine vinegar
- 1 teaspoon dried oregano

1. In a jar, combine the onions, water, sugar, vinegar, and oregano, then shake well and put it in the refrigerator. The onions will be pickled after 1 hour.

Per Serving:
calories: 40 | fat: 0g | protein: 1g | carbs: 10g | fiber: 1g | sodium: 1mg

Skinny Cider Dressing

Prep time: 5 minutes | Cook time: 0 minutes | Serves 2

- 2 tablespoons apple cider vinegar
- ⅓ lemon, juiced
- ⅓ lemon, zested
- Salt
- Freshly ground black pepper

1. In a jar, combine the vinegar, lemon juice, and zest. Season with salt and pepper, cover, and shake well.
Per Serving:
calories: 2 | fat: 0g | protein: 0g | carbs: 1g | fiber: 0g | sodium: 0mg

Lemon-Dill Vinaigrette

Prep time: 2 minutes | Cook time: 0 minutes | Serves 6 to 8

- 4 large cloves of garlic
- ½ cup fresh dill
- ½ cup parsley
- 1 tablespoon sherry vinegar or red wine vinegar
- 1 tablespoon lemon juice
- ½ teaspoon salt
- ½ cup extra-virgin olive oil

1. Put the garlic, dill, parsley, lemon juice, vinegar, and salt into a blender. Add olive oil and process until smooth. Refrigerate covered up to a day. (I put it into a Ball jar with a tight-fitting top so I can shake it to use later but it stays emulsified.)
Per Serving:
calories: 165 | fat: 18g | protein: 0g | carbs: 1g | fiber: 0g | sodium: 198mg

Zucchini Noodles

Prep time: 5 minutes | Cook time: 0 minutes | Serves 4

- 2 medium to large zucchini

1. Cut off and discard the ends of each zucchini and, using a spiralizer set to the smallest setting, spiralize the zucchini to create zoodles.
2. To serve, simply place a ½ cup or so of spiralized zucchini into the bottom of each bowl and spoon a hot sauce over top to "cook" the zoodles to al dente consistency. Use with any of your favorite sauces, or just toss with warmed pesto for a simple and quick meal.
Per Serving:
calories: 27 | fat: 1g | protein: 2g | carbs: 5g | fiber: 2g | sodium: 13mg

Pickled Turnips

Prep time: 5 minutes | Cook time: 0 minutes | Serves 2

- 1 pound (454 g) turnips, washed well, peeled, and cut into 1-inch batons
- 1 small beet, roasted, peeled, and cut into 1-inch batons
- 2 garlic cloves, smashed
- 1 teaspoon dried Turkish oregano
- 3 cups warm water
- ½ cup red wine vinegar
- ½ cup white vinegar

1. In a jar, combine the turnips, beet, garlic, and oregano. Pour the water and vinegars over the vegetables, cover, then shake well and put it in the refrigerator. The turnips will be pickled after 1 hour.
Per Serving:
calories: 3 | fat: 0g | protein: 1g | carbs: 0g | fiber: 0g | sodium: 6mg

Appendix 1: Measurement Conversion Chart

VOLUME EQUIVALENTS(DRY)

US STANDARD	METRIC (APPROXIMATE)
1/8 teaspoon	0.5 mL
1/4 teaspoon	1 mL
1/2 teaspoon	2 mL
3/4 teaspoon	4 mL
1 teaspoon	5 mL
1 tablespoon	15 mL
1/4 cup	59 mL
1/2 cup	118 mL
3/4 cup	177 mL
1 cup	235 mL
2 cups	475 mL
3 cups	700 mL
4 cups	1 L

VOLUME EQUIVALENTS(LIQUID)

US STANDARD	US STANDARD (OUNCES)	METRIC (APPROXIMATE)
2 tablespoons	1 fl.oz.	30 mL
1/4 cup	2 fl.oz.	60 mL
1/2 cup	4 fl.oz.	120 mL
1 cup	8 fl.oz.	240 mL
1 1/2 cup	12 fl.oz.	355 mL
2 cups or 1 pint	16 fl.oz.	475 mL
4 cups or 1 quart	32 fl.oz.	1 L
1 gallon	128 fl.oz.	4 L

TEMPERATURES EQUIVALENTS

FAHRENHEIT(F)	CELSIUS(C) (APPROXIMATE)
225 °F	107 °C
250 °F	120 °C
275 °F	135 °C
300 °F	150 °C
325 °F	160 °C
350 °F	180 °C
375 °F	190 °C
400 °F	205 °C
425 °F	220 °C
450 °F	235 °C
475 °F	245 °C
500 °F	260 °C

WEIGHT EQUIVALENTS

US STANDARD	METRIC (APPROXIMATE)
1 ounce	28 g
2 ounces	57 g
5 ounces	142 g
10 ounces	284 g
15 ounces	425 g
16 ounces (1 pound)	455 g
1.5 pounds	680 g
2 pounds	907 g

Appendix 2: The Dirty Dozen and Clean Fifteen

The Environmental Working Group (EWG) is a nonprofit, nonpartisan organization dedicated to protecting human health and the environment Its mission is to empower people to live healthier lives in a healthier environment. This organization publishes an annual list of the twelve kinds of produce, in sequence, that have the highest amount of pesticide residue-the Dirty Dozen-as well as a list of the fifteen kinds ofproduce that have the least amount of pesticide residue-the Clean Fifteen.

THE DIRTY DOZEN

- The 2016 Dirty Dozen includes the following produce. These are considered among the year's most important produce to buy organic:

Strawberries	Spinach
Apples	Tomatoes
Nectarines	Bell peppers
Peaches	Cherry tomatoes
Celery	Cucumbers
Grapes	Kale/collard greens
Cherries	Hot peppers

- *The Dirty Dozen list contains two additional itemskale/collard greens and hot peppers-because they tend to contain trace levels of highly hazardous pesticides.*

THE CLEAN FIFTEEN

- The least critical to buy organically are the Clean Fifteen list. The following are on the 2016 list:

Avocados	Papayas
Corn	Kiw
Pineapples	Eggplant
Cabbage	Honeydew
Sweet peas	Grapefruit
Onions	Cantaloupe
Asparagus	Cauliflower
Mangos	

- *Some of the sweet corn sold in the United States are made from genetically engineered (GE) seedstock. Buy organic varieties of these crops to avoid GE produce.*

Appendix 3: Recipes Index

S

T

V

W

Z

Made in the USA
Las Vegas, NV
16 August 2024

93961156R00059